Pillsbury Annual Recipes 2012

Our recipes have been tested in the Pillsbury Kitchens and meet our standards of easy preparation, reliability and great taste.

For more great recipes, visit pillsbury.com

PUBLISHED BY
Taste of Home Books
Reiman Media Group, LLC
5400 S. 60th St., Greendale WI 53129
www.tasteofhome.com

Printed in U.S.A.

Taste of Home® is a registered trademark of Reiman Media Group, LLC.

Bake-Off® is a registered trademark of General Mills.

All recipes were previously published in a slightly different form.

International Standard Book Number (10):
0-89821-974-4
International Standard Book Number (13):
978-0-89821-974-6
International Standard Serial Number:
1930-7349

General Mills, Inc.
EDITORIAL DIRECTOR: JEFF NOWAK
PUBLISHING MANAGER: CHRISTINE GRAY
COOKBOOK EDITOR: GRACE WELLS
EDITORIAL ASSISTANT: KELLY GROSS
DIGITAL ASSETS MANAGER: CARRIE JACOBSON
RECIPE DEVELOPMENT AND TESTING: PILLSBURY TEST KITCHENS
PHOTOGRAPHY: GENERAL MILLS PHOTOGRAPHY STUDIO

Reiman Media Group, LLC
EDITOR-IN-CHIEF: CATHERINE CASSIDY
VICE PRESIDENT, EXECUTIVE EDITOR/BOOKS: HEIDI REUTER LLOYD
CREATIVE DIRECTOR: HOWARD GREENBERG
SENIOR EDITOR/BOOKS: MARK HAGEN
EDITOR: KRISTA LANPHIER
ASSOCIATE CREATIVE DIRECTOR: EDWIN ROBLES JR.
ART DIRECTOR: GRETCHEN TRAUTMAN
CONTENT PRODUCTION MANAGER: JULIE WAGNER
GRAPHIC DESIGN ASSOCIATE: JULI SCHNUCK
COPY CHIEF: DEB WARLAUMONT MULVEY
PROJECT COPY EDITOR: BARBARA SCHUETZ
ADMINISTRATIVE ASSISTANT: BARB CZYSZ
COVER PHOTOGRAPHY: TASTE OF HOME PHOTO STUDIO
  PHOTOGRAPHER: ROB HAGEN
  FOOD STYLIST: KATHRYN CONRAD
  SET STYLIST: STEPHANIE MARCHESE

NORTH AMERICAN CHIEF MARKETING OFFICER: LISA KARPINSKI
VICE PRESIDENT, BOOK MARKETING: DAN FINK
CREATIVE DIRECTOR, CREATIVE MARKETING: JAMES PALMEN

Reader's Digest Association, Inc.
PRESIDENT AND CHIEF EXECUTIVE OFFICER: ROBERT E. GUTH
EXECUTIVE VICE PRESIDENT, RDA, & PRESIDENT,
NORTH AMERICA: DAN LAGANI

FRONT COVER PHOTOGRAPHS:
Mexican Manicotti, Pg. 262; Crumbleberry Pear Pie, Pg. 310; Sweet Potatoes with Caramel Sauce, Pg. 285; Cranberry-Orange Chocolate Meringues, Pg. 309; Country-Style Pork Ribs, Pg. 217.

PAGE 5 PHOTOGRAPHS:
Gingered Rice and Beef, Pg. 169; Caramel Apple Pie, Pg. 334; Roasted Harvest Vegetables, Pg. 301; Tuna Melt, Pg. 127.

BACK COVER PHOTOGRAPHS:
Cranberry Layer Bars, Pg. 315; Barbecue Chili with Corn, Pg. 99; Buffalo Chicken Burgers, Pg. 112; Lickety-Split Alfredo-Style Mac 'n Cheese, Pg. 253.

contents

"Wonderful Recipes to Keep Your Family Happy All Year Long!"

introduction

Here's your one-stop shopping for family-pleasing recipes, because everything you need to create a super supper is right here in *Pillsbury Annual Recipes 2012*. With hundreds of delicious dishes to choose from, this collection makes meal preparation as easy as 1-2-3!

This compilation of recipes and tips—over 400 in all—comes from the 2011 Pillsbury Classic® Cookbooks. Most dishes rely on everyday ingredients and kitchen staples already in your cupboard. And better yet, each recipe comes with a beautiful color photo and easy-to-understand instructions so that even novice cooks can feel comfortable in the kitchen.

From beginning to end, this seventh edition of our popular cookbook series is packed with winning recipes. And every one is sure to turn out right because they've been tested and approved by the food and cooking experts at the Pillsbury Test Kitchen.

The book starts out with the Breakfast & Brunch chapter, full of yummy egg casseroles, pancakes, waffles and more. Whether you are planning a brunch or a quick breakfast, dishes such as Ham and Cheese Omelet Bake (p. 17) and Blueberry-Oat Pancakes (p. 33) will always satisfy.

The Sensational Salads chapter has delicious dishes, such as Creamy Black and Blue Pasta Salad (p. 61), made with blue cheese and steak. For a warm bowl of comfort, turn to Heartwarming Soups & Chilies, full of hearty casual fare, such as Barbecue Chili with Corn (p. 99). And the Sandwiches, Wraps & Burgers chapter is perfect for lunch or a light meal, with tasty choices, such as Buffalo Chicken Burgers (p. 112).

If you're short on time and need to put dinner on the table fast, browse through the 30-Minute Meals, Fresh Pasta Dishes and Reliable Slow Cooker Recipes chapters. Many of the recipes, such as Greek Chicken Pizza (p. 160), Thai Peanut Ramen (p. 187) and Carnitas Soft Tacos (p. 219), take only 15 minutes to prepare!

The recipes in the Hearty Casseroles or Comforting Classics chapters are ideal from fall through summer. Whether you need a robust hot dish for a potluck gathering or a seasonal feast when fall weather comes around, you'll be able to find exactly what you need here with dishes such as Bacon-Alfredo Casserole (p. 256), Citrus Turkey Breast (p. 283) and Sweet Potatoes with Caramel Sauce (p. 285).

And last but not least, the Sweet Temptations chapter is full of scrumptious bars, cookies and pies, plus other treats that will have everyone clamoring for more. Take your pick from irresistible goodies, such as Chewy Chocolate-Peanut Butter Bars (p. 321) or Tiramisu Bites (p. 329).

AT-A-GLANCE ICONS

We've highlighted the easy recipes in this book with an icon that looks like the one at left...so you can quickly find them for yourself. These dishes call for 6 ingredients or less OR are ready to cook in 20 minutes or less OR are ready to eat in 30 minutes or less.

At the top of each recipe, we've also included "Prep" and "Ready in..." times. That way, you'll know exactly how long it takes to prepare each and every dish.

If you are watching what you eat, then you'll appreciate the low-fat icon, located next to recipes that contain 10 grams of fat or less (main dishes) OR 3 grams of fat or less (all other recipes). We've also included Nutrition Facts with every recipe.

Plus, you'll spot a number of Pillsbury Bake-Off® Contest Winners—the recipes judged to be the very best in our popular contests over the years. Simply look for the Bake-Off® icon next to the recipe title.

You'll also notice something new in this year's annual—recipes from contributors who have their own online food blogs, as well as winners from various other contests. These special recipes are tagged, so you can tell which ones they are!

HELPFUL INDEXES

This cookbook is indexed in two helpful ways. The alphabetical index starts on page 344, where you can easily locate recipes by their title. The general index starts on page 346, where you can look up any major ingredient or category, such as "Chicken," "Chocolate" or "Nuts & Peanut Butter" and find a list of the recipes in which it is included.

Or, you may want to simply browse the gorgeous pages of this book, look at the color photographs of the recipes and decide what recipe looks delicious to you. Whatever Pillsbury dishes you choose to serve, they'll surely turn out wonderful! Even better, they just might become family favorites and some of your most-cherished recipes ever!

Breakfast & Brunch

Early-morning menus have never been more fun
(or easy) than with these tasty a.m. treats!

PINEAPPLE-COCONUT STRATA
PG. 13

TOMATO-BASIL EGGS ALFREDO
PG. 9

MEAT 'N PEPPER BREAKFAST KABOBS
PG. 14

CHOCOLATE CHIP-
CINNAMON ROLL RING
PG. 26

Muffuletta Egg Bake

PREP TIME: 15 MINUTES (READY IN 1 HOUR 5 MINUTES)
SERVINGS: 8

 EASY

1 ⅓ cups chopped cooked ham

⅓ cup coarsely chopped pimiento-stuffed green olives

½ cup roasted red bell peppers (from 7-oz jar), drained, chopped

½ loaf (1-lb size) unsliced Italian bread, cut into 1-inch cubes (about 5 ¼ cups)

8 eggs

2 ½ cups milk

6 slices (about ¾ oz each) provolone cheese

1 tablespoon freshly shredded Parmesan cheese

1) Heat oven to 350°F. Grease 11x7-inch (2-quart) glass baking dish with butter or cooking spray. In small bowl, combine ham, olives and roasted peppers. In baking dish, combine bread cubes and half of ham mixture.

2) In large bowl, beat eggs and milk with wire whisk until well combined. Pour over ingredients in baking dish. Top evenly with provolone cheese; sprinkle with remaining half of ham mixture.

3) Bake uncovered 40 to 45 minutes or until set and edges are golden brown. Sprinkle with Parmesan cheese. Let stand 5 minutes. Cut into 8 squares.

1 SERVING: Calories 290; Total Fat 15g; Sodium 830mg; Dietary Fiber 1g; Protein 21g. EXCHANGES: 1/2 Starch, 1/2 Low-Fat Milk, 1/2 Lean Meat, 1 Medium-Fat Meat, 1/2 High-Fat Meat, 1/2 Fat. CARBOHYDRATE CHOICES: 1.

tip

Cooked eggs should not sit out for more than two hours. Refrigerated cooked egg dishes should be used within three to four days.

Tomato-Basil Eggs Alfredo

NIKI PLOURDE | GARDNER, MA

Pillsbury Bake-Off®

BAKE-OFF® CONTEST 44, 2010

PREP TIME:	25 MINUTES (READY IN 25 MINUTES)
SERVINGS:	6

e EASY

1 medium tomato

1 can (11 oz) Pillsbury® refrigerated original breadsticks (12 breadsticks)

¼ cup basil pesto

¼ teaspoon salt

⅛ teaspoon freshly ground pepper

6 eggs

2 tablespoons half-and-half or milk

⅛ teaspoon salt

4 ½ teaspoons chopped fresh basil leaves

2 tablespoons unsalted or salted butter

⅓ cup Alfredo pasta sauce (from 16-oz jar)

1) Heat oven to 375°F. Cut 6 thin slices from tomato; finely dice remaining tomato for garnish. Set aside.

2) Separate dough into 12 breadsticks. Shape 6 breadsticks into coils; place 2 inches apart on large greased cookie sheet. Starting at center, press each coil into 3 ½-inch round. Twist remaining breadsticks; wrap around edge of each round to make ½-inch rim; seal edges. Spread 2 teaspoons pesto on bottom of each round; top with 1 tomato slice. Sprinkle with ¼ teaspoon salt and the pepper. Bake 10 to 15 minutes or until edges are golden brown.

3) In medium bowl, beat eggs and half-and-half. Add ⅛ teaspoon salt and 3 teaspoons of the basil. In 12-inch nonstick skillet, melt butter over medium heat. Add egg mixture. Cook 4 minutes, gently lifting cooked portions with spatula so thin, uncooked portion can flow to bottom, until eggs are thickened but still moist. Stir in Alfredo sauce. Divide mixture evenly among bread baskets. Garnish with diced tomato and remaining 1 ½ teaspoons basil.

1 SERVING: Calories 350; Total Fat 21g; Sodium 710mg; Dietary Fiber 0g; Protein 12g. EXCHANGES: 2 Starch, 1 Lean Meat, 3 Fat. CARBOHYDRATE CHOICES: 2.

Breakfast Egg Scramble with Brie

PREP TIME: 20 MINUTES (READY IN 20 MINUTES)
SERVINGS: 4

 EASY

10 eggs

2 tablespoons milk

2 tablespoons butter

5 oz Canadian bacon, finely chopped (about 1 cup)

2 cups loosely packed fresh baby spinach

4 oz Brie cheese, rind removed, cut into ½-inch pieces

4 English muffins, split, toasted

1) In large bowl, beat eggs and milk with fork or wire whisk. Set aside.

2) In 12-inch nonstick skillet, melt butter over medium heat. Add Canadian bacon and spinach; cook and stir 1 minute, just until spinach begins to wilt.

3) Pour egg mixture over spinach mixture; add cheese. Cook 3 to 5 minutes, stirring occasionally, until eggs are set but slightly moist. Spoon ½ cup egg mixture onto each muffin half.

1 SERVING: Calories 540; Total Fat 31g; Sodium 1180mg; Dietary Fiber 2g; Protein 36g. EXCHANGES: 1-1/2 Starch, 1/2 Vegetable, 4-1/2 Lean Meat, 3-1/2 Fat. CARBOHYDRATE CHOICES: 2.

Make-Ahead Alfredo Strata

PREP TIME: 10 MINUTES (READY IN 5 HOURS 5 MINUTES)
SERVINGS: 8

 EASY

1 loaf (1 lb) unsliced rustic Italian bread, cut into 1-inch cubes (8 cups)

1 cup Green Giant® Valley Fresh Steamers™ frozen chopped broccoli (from 12-oz bag), thawed, drained

2 cups shredded Italian cheese blend (8 oz)

5 eggs

2 cups milk

1 container (10 oz) refrigerated Alfredo pasta sauce

1) Spray 13x9-inch (3-quart) glass baking dish with cooking spray. In baking dish, layer half of the bread cubes, the broccoli, 1 cup of the cheese and the remaining bread cubes.

2) In large bowl, beat eggs, milk and Alfredo sauce with wire whisk until well blended. Pour over ingredients in baking dish. Cover; refrigerate at least 4 hours or overnight.

3) Heat oven to 350°F. Uncover baking dish. Sprinkle with remaining 1 cup cheese. Bake 45 to 50 minutes or until a knife inserted in the center comes out clean and the cheese is deep golden brown. Let stand 5 minutes. Cut into 8 squares.

1 SERVING: Calories 450; Total Fat 25g; Sodium 780mg; Dietary Fiber 2g; Protein 21g. EXCHANGES: 2-1/2 Starch, 1 Medium-Fat Meat, 1 High-Fat Meat, 2 Fat. CARBOHYDRATE CHOICES: 2.

Sausage French Toast Paninis

PREP TIME: 25 MINUTES (READY IN 25 MINUTES)
SERVINGS: 6

 EASY

1 package (10 oz) frozen uncooked pork sausage patties (6 patties), thawed

2 eggs

½ cup milk

1 tablespoon Dijon mustard

6 English muffins, split

12 slices provolone cheese

6 slices Canadian bacon (3 oz)

1) Heat panini pan over medium heat or heat contact grill 5 minutes. Press sausage patties into thinner patties, about 3 to 4 inches in diameter. Cook sausage in panini pan 2 to 3 minutes on each side, or cook in contact grill 2 to 3 minutes, or until thoroughly cooked. Wipe surface of pan or grill. Spray weighted top of panini pan with cooking spray.

2) In small bowl, beat eggs, milk and mustard with wire whisk. Dip muffin halves in egg mixture, soaking well. Place 1 cheese slice and 1 sausage patty on each of 6 muffin halves; top with bacon and second slice of cheese. Cover with remaining muffin halves.

3) Place 3 sandwiches on panini pan; place weighted top over muffins. Cook 2 minutes or until browned. Turn; cook 2 minutes longer or until browned and hot in center. Repeat with remaining sandwiches. Or cook sandwiches in contact grill 2 to 3 minutes.

1 SERVING: Calories 370; Total Fat 18g; Sodium 970mg; Dietary Fiber 2g; Protein 23g. EXCHANGES: 2 Starch, 2 Medium-Fat Meat, 1-1/2 Fat. CARBOHYDRATE CHOICES: 2.

Caramel Sticky Buns

PREP TIME: 15 MINUTES (READY IN 35 MINUTES)
SERVINGS: 12

 EASY

¼ cup butter or margarine, melted

¼ cup packed brown sugar

2 tablespoons light corn syrup

¼ cup chopped pecans

1 tablespoon granulated sugar

½ teaspoon ground cinnamon

1 can (12 oz) Pillsbury® Grands!® Jr. Golden Layers® refrigerated biscuits

1) Heat oven to 375°F. Grease 12 regular-size muffin cups with shortening. In small bowl, mix butter, brown sugar, corn syrup and pecans. Spoon scant tablespoon mixture into each muffin cup.

2) In large resealable food-storage plastic bag, mix granulated sugar and cinnamon. Separate dough into 10 biscuits; cut each biscuit into 6 pieces. Place biscuit pieces in bag; seal bag and shake to coat. Place 5 biscuit pieces in each muffin cup.

3) Place muffin pan on foil or cookie sheet. Bake 15 to 20 minutes or until golden brown. Cool 1 minute. Invert pan onto waxed paper; remove pan. Serve warm.

1 SERVING: Calories 170; Total Fat 9g; Sodium 330mg; Dietary Fiber 0g; Protein 2g. EXCHANGES: 1 Starch, 1/2 Other Carbohydrate, 1-1/2 Fat. CARBOHYDRATE CHOICES: 1.

tip

Refrigerated biscuits are the key to these quick and easy, ooey-gooey buns. For a deeper, richer flavor, substitute dark corn syrup for the light version in this recipe.

Pineapple-Coconut Strata

PREP TIME: 20 MINUTES (READY IN 9 HOURS 25 MINUTES)
SERVINGS: 8

 EASY

12 cups cubes (1 inch) soft French bread (about 1 lb)

8 eggs

1 can (13.66 oz) coconut milk (not cream of coconut)

1 cup half-and-half

1 jar (12 oz) pineapple preserves

1 teaspoon rum extract or vanilla

¼ teaspoon salt

½ cup flaked coconut

⅓ cup chopped macadamia nuts (2 oz)

1) Spray 13x9-inch (3-quart) glass baking dish with cooking spray. Spread bread cubes evenly in baking dish.

2) In medium bowl, beat eggs, coconut milk, half-and-half, preserves, rum extract and salt with wire whisk. Pour over bread. Cover; refrigerate 8 hours or overnight.

3) Heat oven to 350°F. Uncover baking dish; let stand at room temperature 15 minutes. Sprinkle with coconut and nuts. Bake 40 to 50 minutes or until set and knife inserted in center comes out clean. Cut into 8 squares.

1 SERVING: Calories 580; Total Fat 28g; Sodium 510mg; Dietary Fiber 3g; Protein 15g. EXCHANGES: 2-1/2 Starch, 2 Other Carbohydrate, 1 High-Fat Meat, 3-1/2 Fat. CARBOHYDRATE CHOICES: 4-1/2.

Maple-Bacon Buttermilk Waffles

PREP TIME: 55 MINUTES (READY IN 55 MINUTES)
SERVINGS: 12 (ONE 4-INCH WAFFLE EACH)

 LOW FAT

2 cups all-purpose flour

¼ cup sugar

1 ½ teaspoons baking soda

½ teaspoon salt

1 ¾ cups buttermilk

2 eggs

6 tablespoons butter, melted

1 ½ teaspoons maple flavor

1 package or jar (3 oz) cooked real bacon pieces or bits

1 ½ cups real maple or maple-flavored syrup

1) Heat waffle maker. In large bowl, mix flour, sugar, baking soda and salt. In medium bowl, beat buttermilk, eggs, butter and maple flavor with wire whisk until well blended. Pour over dry ingredients; stir just until moistened.

2) Sprinkle about 2 teaspoons bacon pieces on each waffle grid. Spoon batter over bacon, using amount recommended by manufacturer. Close lid of waffle maker. Bake until steaming stops, 3 to 5 minutes. Repeat with remaining bacon and batter. Serve waffles with syrup.

1 SERVING: Calories 250; Total Fat 3g; Sodium 530mg; Dietary Fiber 0g; Protein 7g. EXCHANGES: 1-1/2 Starch, 2 Other Carbohydrate, 1/2 Fat. CARBOHYDRATE CHOICES: 3.

Meat 'n Pepper Breakfast Kabobs

PREP TIME: 55 MINUTES (READY IN 55 MINUTES)
SERVINGS: 6

 EASY

6 pork sausage links, cut into thirds

1 fully cooked ham steak (½ lb), cut into 18 pieces

1 large green, red or yellow bell pepper, cut into 18 pieces

¾ cup barbecue sauce

¼ cup seedless raspberry jam

¼ teaspoon chipotle chile pepper powder

1) Heat oven to 375°F. Line 15x10x1-inch pan with foil. Spray cooling rack with cooking spray; place in pan. On 6 (8-inch) skewers, thread sausage, ham and bell pepper pieces. Place on rack in pan.

2) In small microwavable bowl, microwave remaining ingredients. Microwave on High 30 seconds or until jam is melted and sauce is warm. Brush over kabobs, turning to coat all sides.

3) Bake 30 to 35 minutes or until sausage is thoroughly cooked and bell pepper is tender, turning and brushing with sauce every 10 minutes. Serve immediately.

1 SERVING: Calories 200; Total Fat 7g; Sodium 920mg; Dietary Fiber 0g; Protein 10g. EXCHANGES: 1/2 Starch, 1 Other Carbohydrate, 1 High-Fat Meat. CARBOHYDRATE CHOICES: 1-1/2.

Smoked Salmon and Herb Frittata

PREP TIME: 30 MINUTES (READY IN 30 MINUTES)
SERVINGS: 4

 EASY

6 eggs

2 tablespoons half-and-half or milk

2 tablespoons chopped fresh chives (½-inch pieces)

1 tablespoon coarsely chopped fresh dill weed

¼ teaspoon freshly ground pepper

1 package (3 oz) sliced smoked salmon, cut into 1 ½-inch pieces

2 teaspoons olive oil

1 package (3 oz) cream cheese, softened

Lemon wedges, if desired

1) In medium bowl, beat eggs, half-and-half, chives, dill and pepper. Gently fold in salmon.

2) In 9- or 10-inch nonstick skillet with sloping sides, heat oil over low heat. Pour egg mixture into skillet. Using 2 teaspoons, drop cream cheese over egg mixture.

3) Cover; cook 12 to 15 minutes or until lightly browned and bottom is set, lifting edges occasionally to allow uncooked egg mixture to flow to bottom of skillet. Cut into 8 wedges. Garnish with lemon.

1 SERVING: Calories 240; Total Fat 19g; Sodium 330mg; Dietary Fiber 0g; Protein 15g. EXCHANGES: 1/2 Lean Meat, 1-1/2 Medium-Fat Meat, 2 Fat. CARBOHYDRATE CHOICES: 0.

Peanut Butter Puddles

| PREP TIME: | 20 MINUTES (READY IN 20 MINUTES) |
| SERVINGS: | 8 |

 EASY

1 can (12.4 oz) Pillsbury® refrigerated cinnamon rolls with icing

¼ cup creamy peanut butter

⅓ cup semisweet chocolate chips

1) Heat oven to 400°F. Spray cookie sheet with cooking spray. Set icing from cinnamon rolls aside. Separate dough into 8 rolls; place rolls, cinnamon topping up, 2 inches apart on cookie sheet.

2) Bake 8 to 10 minutes or until golden brown.

3) Meanwhile, place reserved icing in small microwavable bowl. Microwave uncovered on Medium (50%) 5 to 10 seconds or until thin enough to drizzle. Stir in peanut butter; mixture will stiffen. Shape mixture into 8 (1-inch) balls.

4) In small microwavable bowl, microwave chocolate chips, uncovered, on High 30 seconds; stir. Microwave in 15-second increments until chips are melted and can be stirred smooth.

5) Remove rolls from oven; immediately press and flatten 1 peanut butter ball into center of each roll. Drizzle with melted chocolate. Serve warm.

1 SERVING: Calories 230; Total Fat 11g; Sodium 380mg; Dietary Fiber 1g; Protein 4g. EXCHANGES: 1 Starch, 1 Other Carbohydrate, 2 Fat. CARBOHYDRATE CHOICES: 2

tip

After drizzling with chocolate, sprinkle tops of rolls with finely chopped roasted peanuts, if desired.

Ham and Cheese Omelet Bake

JULIE AMBERSON | BROWNS POINT, WA

BAKE-OFF® CONTEST 41, 2004

PREP TIME: 15 MINUTES (READY IN 1 HOUR 15 MINUTES)
SERVINGS: 8

⊖ EASY

- 1 box (10 oz) Green Giant® frozen broccoli & cheese sauce
- 1 can (10.2 oz) Pillsbury® Grands!® flaky layers refrigerated original biscuits (5 biscuits)
- 10 eggs
- 1 ½ cups milk
- 1 teaspoon ground mustard
  Salt and pepper, if desired
- 2 cups diced cooked ham
- 1 small onion, chopped (⅓ cup)
- 1 cup shredded Cheddar cheese (4 oz)
- 1 cup shredded Swiss cheese (4 oz)
- 1 jar (4.5 oz) Green Giant® sliced mushrooms, drained

1) Heat oven to 350°F. Cut small slit in center of broccoli pouch. Microwave on High 3 to 4 minutes, rotating pouch ¼ turn once halfway through microwaving. Cool slightly.

2) Spray bottom only of 13x9-inch (3-quart) glass baking dish with cooking spray. Separate dough into 5 biscuits. Cut each biscuit into 8 pieces; arrange evenly in baking dish.

3) In large bowl, beat eggs, milk, mustard, salt and pepper with wire whisk until well blended. Stir in ham, onion, cheeses, mushrooms and cooked broccoli. Pour over biscuit pieces. Press down with back of spoon, making sure biscuit pieces are covered. Bake uncovered 40 to 50 minutes or until edges are deep golden brown and center is set. Let stand 10 minutes. Cut into 8 squares.

1 SERVING: Calories 420; Total Fat 24g; Sodium 1180mg; Dietary Fiber 1g; Protein 27g. EXCHANGES: 1 Starch, 1/2 Other Carbohydrate, 3 Medium-Fat Meat, 1/2 High-Fat Meat, 1 Fat. CARBOHYDRATE CHOICES: 1-1/2.

Apple-Cinnamon Monkey Bread

PREP TIME: 25 MINUTES (READY IN 1 HOUR 30 MINUTES)
SERVINGS: 12

 EASY

2 cans (17.5 oz each) Pillsbury® Grands!® flaky supreme refrigerated cinnamon rolls with icing

1 medium tart apple, peeled, chopped

½ cup sugar

1 ½ teaspoons ground cinnamon

¼ cup butter, melted

1) Heat oven to 350°F. Grease 12-cup fluted tube cake pan with shortening or cooking spray.

2) Set aside icing tubs from cinnamon rolls. Separate each can of dough into 5 rolls; cut into quarters. Place apple in small bowl. In another small bowl, mix sugar and cinnamon. Add ¼ cup sugar mixture to apple; toss to coat. Sprinkle half of apple pieces in pan. Roll half of dough pieces in sugar mixture; place on apples in pan. Sprinkle with remaining apple pieces. Roll remaining dough pieces in sugar mixture; place on apples. Pour melted butter over top.

3) Bake 40 to 45 minutes or until golden brown across top. Cool 10 minutes; run knife around edge of pan to loosen. Place heatproof serving plate over pan and turn over; remove pan. Cool 10 minutes longer.

4) Drizzle reserved icing over top of bread, allowing some to drizzle down sides. Pull apart to serve; serve warm.

1 SERVING: Calories 390; Total Fat 20g; Sodium 570mg; Dietary Fiber 1g; Protein 3g. EXCHANGES: 1-1/2 Starch, 2 Other Carbohydrate, 3-1/2 Fat. CARBOHYDRATE CHOICES: 3.

Cinnamon Breakfast Bread Pudding

PREP TIME: 10 MINUTES (READY IN 5 HOURS)
SERVINGS: 8 (1 SQUARE WITH 1/4 CUP SYRUP EACH)

 EASY LOW FAT

6 cups cubes (½ inch) raisin cinnamon swirl bread

8 eggs

2 ½ cups milk

½ teaspoon ground cinnamon

¼ teaspoon ground nutmeg

2 cups maple-flavored syrup

1) Grease 13x9-inch (3-quart) glass baking dish with butter or cooking spray. Spread bread cubes evenly in baking dish. In large bowl, beat eggs, milk, cinnamon and nutmeg until well combined. Pour over bread. Cover; refrigerate at least 4 hours or overnight.

2) Heat oven to 350°F. Uncover baking dish. Bake 45 to 50 minutes or until set and top is golden brown. Cut into 8 squares. Serve with syrup.

1 SERVING: Calories 410; Total Fat 8g; Sodium 220mg; Dietary Fiber 1g; Protein 11g. EXCHANGES: 1/2 Starch, 4 Other Carbohydrate, 1/2 Low-Fat Milk, 1 Medium-Fat Meat. CARBOHYDRATE CHOICES: 5.

Italian Egg Bake

PREP TIME: 15 MINUTES (READY IN 1 HOUR 35 MINUTES)
SERVINGS: 6

 EASY

1 lb bulk Italian pork sausage

4 cups frozen diced or shredded hash brown potatoes (from 30- or 32-oz bag), thawed

1 cup shredded Cheddar cheese (4 oz)

1 cup frozen cut leaf spinach, thawed, drained

¼ cup julienne-cut sun-dried tomatoes in oil and herbs (from 8-oz jar)

1 cup shredded mozzarella cheese (4 oz)

4 eggs

¾ cup milk

¼ teaspoon salt

⅛ teaspoon pepper

2 tablespoons shredded Parmesan cheese

1) Heat oven to 350°F. Spray 8-inch square (2-quart) glass baking dish with cooking spray. In 10-inch nonstick skillet, cook sausage over medium-high heat, stirring occasionally, until no longer pink; drain.

2) In medium bowl, mix potatoes and Cheddar cheese. In baking dish, layer half of the potato mixture, the sausage, spinach and tomatoes, remaining potato mixture and mozzarella cheese. In medium bowl, beat eggs slightly with wire whisk. Add milk, salt and pepper; beat well. Pour evenly over potato mixture.

3) Cover with foil; bake 1 hour. Uncover; sprinkle with Parmesan cheese. Bake 15 minutes longer or until knife inserted in center comes out clean. Let stand 5 minutes. Cut into 6 squares.

1 SERVING: Calories 560; Total Fat 37g; Sodium 1080mg; Dietary Fiber 3g; Protein 25g. EXCHANGES: 1-1/2 Starch, 1-1/2 Vegetable, 1 Medium-Fat Meat, 1-1/2 High-Fat Meat, 4 Fat. CARBOHYDRATE CHOICES: 2.

Cheesy Cajun Hash Browns

PREP TIME: 15 MINUTES (READY IN 1 HOUR 5 MINUTES)
SERVINGS: 8

 EASY

2 tablespoons butter

1 small onion, chopped (¼ cup)

1 tablespoon all-purpose flour

1 ¼ teaspoons Cajun seasoning

1 ¼ cups milk

1 ½ cups shredded sharp Cheddar cheese (6 oz)

¾ cup freshly shredded Parmesan cheese (3 oz)

1 bag (20 oz) refrigerated shredded hash brown potatoes

Chopped green onion, if desired

1) Heat oven to 350°F. Spray 1 ½-quart casserole with cooking spray.

2) In 12-inch nonstick skillet, melt butter over medium heat. Cook onion in butter 3 to 4 minutes, stirring frequently, until crisp-tender. Stir in flour and Cajun seasoning until combined. Slowly pour milk into onion mixture, stirring constantly until mixture is well combined and slightly thickened.

3) Reduce heat to medium-low. Stir in Cheddar cheese and ½ cup of the Parmesan cheese until melted. Fold in potatoes until evenly coated with cheese sauce. Spoon mixture into casserole.

4) Bake uncovered 30 minutes. Sprinkle with remaining ¼ cup Parmesan cheese. Bake 14 to 17 minutes longer or until the potatoes are tender and the cheese is melted. Garnish with green onion.

1 SERVING: Calories 270; Total Fat 14g; Sodium 790mg; Dietary Fiber 2g; Protein 12g. EXCHANGES: 1 Starch, 1/2 Milk, 1 Vegetable, 2 Fat. CARBOHYDRATE CHOICES: 1-1/2.

Chocolate Chunk-Cherry Scones

PREP TIME: 15 MINUTES (READY IN 45 MINUTES)
SERVINGS: 8

 EASY

2 ½ cups all-purpose flour

2 teaspoons baking powder

⅓ cup sugar

½ teaspoon salt

5 tablespoons cold butter

2 eggs

1 cup whipping cream

1 teaspoon vanilla

½ cup semisweet chocolate chunks

½ cup dried cherries

1 teaspoon water

1) Heat oven to 400°F. Grease cookie sheet with shortening or cooking spray.

2) In large bowl, mix flour, baking powder, sugar and salt. Cut in butter, using pastry blender or fork, until mixture forms coarse crumbs. In medium bowl, beat 1 of the eggs with fork. Stir in whipping cream and vanilla. Stir in chocolate chunks and cherries until combined. Pour over crumb mixture; stir just until moistened (do not overmix).

3) Place dough on lightly floured surface. Knead lightly 4 times; pat into 7-inch circle, about 1 inch thick. Transfer to cookie sheet. In small bowl, beat remaining egg; stir in water. Brush mixture lightly over top of dough; discard any remaining mixture. Cut into 8 wedges; separate slightly so wedges aren't touching.

4) Bake 15 to 20 minutes or until toothpick comes out clean. Remove to cooling rack; cool 10 minutes. Serve warm.

1 SERVING: Calories 440; Total Fat 21g; Sodium 350mg; Dietary Fiber 2g; Protein 7g. EXCHANGES: 2 Starch, 1-1/2 Other Carbohydrate, 4 Fat. CARBOHYDRATE CHOICES: 3-1/2.

Raspberry-Rhubarb Puff Pancake

PREP TIME: 25 MINUTES (READY IN 25 MINUTES)
SERVINGS: 4

 EASY

¾ cup all-purpose flour

¾ cup milk

3 eggs

½ teaspoon vanilla

2 tablespoons butter

¾ cup ricotta cheese

2 tablespoons powdered sugar

1 cup chopped fresh or frozen rhubarb

¼ cup granulated sugar

¼ cup water

2 teaspoons cornstarch

1 cup fresh or frozen (thawed) raspberries

1) Heat oven to 425°F. In medium bowl, beat flour, milk, eggs and vanilla with wire whisk until combined.

2) Place butter in 9 ½-inch glass deep-dish pie plate. Place in hot oven until butter is melted, about 5 minutes. Using oven mitts, carefully tilt pie plate to coat bottom with melted butter. Slowly pour batter into hot plate. Bake 18 to 20 minutes or until puffed and deep golden brown (do not underbake).

3) In small bowl, mix cheese and powdered sugar; set aside. In 1-quart saucepan, cook and stir rhubarb, granulated sugar, water and cornstarch over medium-low heat until rhubarb is tender, about 4 minutes. Cool slightly. Stir in raspberries.

4) Remove pancake from oven. Carefully spread cheese filling over bottom of pancake. Cut into quarters. If necessary, run spatula under pancake to loosen. Top with fruit filling.

1 SERVING: Calories 370; Total Fat 15g; Sodium 170mg; Dietary Fiber 3g; Protein 14g. EXCHANGES: 1-1/2 Starch, 1 Fruit, 1/2 Other Carbohydrate, 1-1/2 Lean Meat, 2 Fat. CARBOHYDRATE CHOICES: 3.

Stuffed Blueberry French Toast

PREP TIME: 20 MINUTES (READY IN 8 HOURS 55 MINUTES)
SERVINGS: 6 (2 FRENCH TOAST SANDWICHES AND 1/3 CUP TOPPING EACH)

 EASY

1 loaf (18 inch) soft French bread (1 lb), cut into 24 (¾-inch) slices

½ cup cream cheese spread

½ cup blueberry preserves

4 eggs

¾ cup milk

2 tablespoons sugar

¼ teaspoon salt

2 tablespoons butter or margarine, melted

½ cup water

2 tablespoons sugar

2 teaspoons cornstarch

3 cups fresh blueberries

1) Spray 13x9-inch (3-quart) glass baking dish with cooking spray. Spread each of 12 slices with 2 teaspoons cream cheese and 2 teaspoons preserves. Top with remaining bread to make 12 sandwiches. Arrange in baking dish, pressing together if necessary to fit.

2) In medium bowl, beat eggs, milk, 2 tablespoons sugar and the salt with wire whisk until well blended. Pour over bread. Let stand 5 minutes. Cover with foil; refrigerate 8 hours or overnight.

3) Heat oven to 400°F. Uncover baking dish; drizzle French toast with butter. Cover again with foil; bake 10 minutes. Uncover; bake 15 to 20 minutes longer or until golden brown.

4) Meanwhile, in 2-quart saucepan, mix water, 2 tablespoons sugar and the cornstarch. Stir in 1 cup of the blueberries. Heat to boiling over medium-high heat. Reduce heat to medium; cook and stir 1 to 2 minutes until slightly thickened. Remove from heat. Stir in remaining 2 cups blueberries. Serve with French toast.

1 SERVING: Calories 550; Total Fat 16g; Sodium 750mg; Dietary Fiber 4g; Protein 15g. EXCHANGES: 2 Starch, 1 Fruit, 3 Other Carbohydrate, 1 Lean Meat, 2-1/2 Fat. CARBOHYDRATE CHOICES: 6.

tip

Frozen berries can be substituted for the fresh. When the remaining 2 cups frozen berries are stirred into the sauce, let the mixture stand 3 to 5 minutes to allow the berries thaw before serving.

Crowd-Size Coffee Cake

PREP TIME: 15 MINUTES (READY IN 50 MINUTES)   EASY
SERVINGS: 20

- ½ cup butter or margarine, melted
- ¾ cup packed brown sugar
- 2 teaspoons grated orange peel
- ¾ cup chopped pecans
- ⅓ cup granulated sugar
- 1 teaspoon ground cinnamon
- 2 cans (17.5 oz each) Pillsbury® Grands!® refrigerated cinnamon rolls with cream cheese icing

1) Heat oven to 375°F. Spray 13x9-inch pan with cooking spray.

2) In small bowl, mix butter, brown sugar and orange peel; pour into pan. Sprinkle evenly with ½ cup of the pecans.

3) In medium bowl, mix granulated sugar and cinnamon. Set icing from cinnamon rolls aside. Separate dough into 10 rolls; cut each roll into quarters. Add dough pieces to sugar mixture; toss to coat. Arrange in single layer in pan.

4) Bake 20 to 25 minutes or until golden brown and no longer doughy in center. Drop reserved icing by teaspoonfuls over top of coffee cake; sprinkle with remaining ¼ cup pecans. Cool 10 minutes. Cut into 20 squares; serve warm.

1 SERVING: Calories 270; Total Fat 12g; Sodium 360mg; Dietary Fiber 1g; Protein 2g. EXCHANGES: 1 Starch, 1-1/2 Other Carbohydrate, 2-1/2 Fat. CARBOHYDRATE CHOICES: 2-1/2.

If you want to freeze part of this coffee cake, wrap in foil and seal in a plastic freezer bag. When ready to serve, remove from bag, thaw and reheat in foil in the oven.

Strawberry Cheesecake Pancakes

PREP TIME: 25 MINUTES (READY IN 25 MINUTES)
SERVINGS: 4

4 oz (half of 8-oz package) ⅓-less-fat cream cheese (Neufchâtel), softened

1 box (4-serving size) cheesecake instant pudding and pie filling mix

1 cup milk

2 cups sliced fresh strawberries

½ cup strawberry syrup

1 ¼ cups Fiber One® original complete pancake mix

⅔ cup graham cracker crumbs

1 cup water

1) In medium bowl, beat cream cheese with electric mixer on medium speed until creamy; add pudding mix and milk. Beat until thick and creamy, scraping sides of bowl as necessary. In small bowl, mix strawberries and syrup; set aside.

2) In large bowl, mix remaining ingredients just until blended.

3) Heat griddle or skillet over medium heat or to 375°F. Grease griddle with butter or vegetable oil if necessary (or spray with cooking spray before heating). For each pancake, pour ¼ cup batter onto hot griddle and spread slightly to 4½-inch diameter. Cook pancakes until bubbles form on top and edges are dry. Turn and cook other sides until golden brown.

4) Place 1 pancake on each of 4 serving plates. Top each with ⅓ cup of the cream cheese filling and ¼ cup of the berry topping. Top with a second pancake and another ¼ cup topping.

1 SERVING: Calories 470; Total Fat 11g; Sodium 760mg; Dietary Fiber 4g; Protein 9g. EXCHANGES: 1 Starch, 1 Fruit, 3-1/2 Other Carbohydrate, 1 High-Fat Meat, 1/2 Fat. CARBOHYDRATE CHOICES: 5-1/2.

Chocolate Chip-Cinnamon Roll Ring

PREP TIME: 10 MINUTES (READY IN 55 MINUTES)
SERVINGS: 16

 EASY

½ cup butter, softened (do not use margarine)

2 cans (12.4 oz each) Pillsbury® refrigerated cinnamon rolls with icing

1 box (4-serving size) vanilla pudding and pie filling mix (not instant)

½ cup packed brown sugar

¼ cup miniature semisweet chocolate chips

1) Heat oven to 375°F. Using 1 tablespoon of the butter, generously butter 12-cup fluted tube cake pan. In small microwavable bowl, microwave remaining butter on High 1 minute or until melted.

2) Set icing from cinnamon rolls aside. Separate each can of dough into 8 rolls. Cut each roll in half crosswise; place half of roll pieces in pan. Sprinkle with half of the dry pudding mix and half of the brown sugar. Drizzle with half of the melted butter. Repeat with remaining roll pieces, pudding mix, brown sugar and melted butter. Sprinkle with chocolate chips.

3) Bake 24 to 28 minutes or until rolls are deep golden brown and dough appears done when slightly pulled apart. Cool 2 minutes. Place heatproof serving platter upside down over pan; turn platter and pan over. Remove pan. Cool 15 minutes. Microwave reserved icing on High 10 seconds to soften. Drizzle icing over ring. Cut into 16 wedges; serve warm.

1 SERVING: Calories 260; Total Fat 12g; Sodium 420mg; Dietary Fiber 0g; Protein 2g. EXCHANGES: 1 Starch, 1-1/2 Other Carbohydrate, 2 Fat. CARBOHYDRATE CHOICES: 2-1/2.

Horseradish Potatoes and Asparagus

PREP TIME: 40 MINUTES (READY IN 2 HOURS 40 MINUTES)
SERVINGS: 12 (2/3 CUP EACH)

2 lb small red potatoes, cut into ¾-inch pieces (about 6 cups)

1 ½ lb fresh asparagus, trimmed, cut into 1-inch pieces

½ cup sour cream

¼ cup creamy horseradish sauce

⅔ cup half-and-half

2 teaspoons salt

⅛ to ¼ teaspoon freshly ground black pepper

¼ cup fresh dill weed sprigs

1) In 4-quart saucepan, place potatoes and enough water to cover by 1 inch. Heat to boiling; reduce heat to medium. Cook uncovered 10 to 12 minutes. Add asparagus. Cover; cook 2 to 3 minutes longer or until potatoes are tender when pierced with fork and asparagus is crisp-tender. Drain; rinse with cold water.

2) In large bowl, mix sour cream, horseradish sauce, half-and-half, salt and pepper with whisk until smooth. Add potatoes and asparagus; gently toss to coat. Fold in dill. Cover; refrigerate at least 2 hours or until serving time.

1 SERVING: Calories 110; Total Fat 3.5g; Sodium 430mg; Dietary Fiber 3g; Protein 3g. EXCHANGES: 1 Starch, 1/2 Vegetable, 1/2 Fat. CARBOHYDRATE CHOICES: 1.

Bunny Rabbit Pancakes

PREP TIME: 10 MINUTES (READY IN 10 MINUTES)
SERVINGS: 1

 EASY LOW FAT

3 Pillsbury® frozen homestyle original pancakes (from 16.4-oz box)

8 raisins

1 maraschino cherry

2 pieces red string licorice (1 ½ inches)

¼ cup maple-flavored syrup

1) Stack pancakes on microwavable plate. Microwave on High 30 seconds. Place 1 pancake on cutting board; with table knife, cut pancake into pieces for ears and bow tie. Arrange ears and bow tie around 2 pancakes on plate to look like a bunny.

2) Microwave on High 30 to 45 seconds or until pancakes are thoroughly heated. Place 2 of the raisins on top pancake for eyes; place remaining 6 raisins on bow tie. Add cherry for the nose and licorice for the mouth. Drizzle syrup over pancakes.

1 SERVING: Calories 490; Total Fat 4g; Sodium 430mg; Dietary Fiber 1g; Protein 4g. EXCHANGES: 2 Starch, 5 Other Carbohydrate, 1/2 Fat. CARBOHYDRATE CHOICES: 7.

Breakfast Burgers

| PREP TIME: | 20 MINUTES (READY IN 30 MINUTES) | EASY |
| SERVINGS: | 6 | |

1 package (19.5 oz) refrigerated hot Italian turkey sausage links

1 medium onion, finely chopped (½ cup)

½ cup finely chopped red bell pepper

1 ½ cups frozen shredded hash brown potatoes, thawed

2 teaspoons vegetable oil

6 slices (1 oz each) pepper Jack cheese

6 English muffins, split, toasted

1) Remove casing from sausage; crumble sausage into medium bowl. Add onion, bell pepper and potatoes; mix well. Shape mixture into 6 patties, about 1 inch thick.

2) In 12-inch nonstick skillet, heat oil over medium heat. Cook patties in oil 13 to 16 minutes, turning once or twice, until thermometer inserted in center of patties reads 165°F.

3) Top each patty with 1 slice cheese. Cover; let stand 1 minute until cheese is melted. Serve on toasted muffins.

1 SERVING: Calories 520; Total Fat 28g; Sodium 1270mg; Dietary Fiber 3g; Protein 25g. EXCHANGES: 2 Starch, 1/2 Other Carbohydrate, 2-1/2 High-Fat Meat, 1-1/2 Fat. CARBOHYDRATE CHOICES: 3.

tip

Refrigerate the patties before cooking for easier handling. Mild turkey sausage can be substituted for the hot turkey sausage.

Blueberry-Oat Pancakes

PREP TIME: 30 MINUTES (READY IN 30 MINUTES)
SERVINGS: 6

 EASY   **lf** LOW FAT

1 cup Cheerios® cereal

¾ cup whole wheat flour

½ cup all-purpose flour

2 teaspoons baking powder

½ teaspoon baking soda

1 container (6 oz) Yoplait® original 99% fat free lemon burst or French vanilla yogurt

¾ cup fat-free (skim) milk

2 tablespoons canola oil

1 egg

1 cup fresh or frozen blueberries (do not thaw)

Additional Yoplait® original 99% fat free lemon burst or French vanilla yogurt

Additional fresh blueberries

1) Place cereal in resealable food-storage plastic bag; seal bag and slightly crush with rolling pin. In medium bowl, mix cereal, flours, baking powder and baking soda.

2) In small bowl, beat 1 container yogurt, the milk, oil and egg with wire whisk until well blended. Stir yogurt mixture into flour mixture with wire whisk until blended. Stir in 1 cup blueberries.

3) Brush griddle or 10-inch skillet with oil; heat over medium-high heat (375°F). For each pancake, use slightly less than ¼ cup batter. Cook about 2 minutes or until puffed and dry around the edges. Turn; cook other sides 1 to 2 minutes or until golden brown.

4) Top individual servings with additional yogurt and blueberries, if desired.

1 SERVING: Calories 220; Total Fat 6g; Sodium 340mg; Dietary Fiber 3g; Protein 6g. EXCHANGES: 2 Starch, 1 Fat. CARBOHYDRATE CHOICES: 2.

Orange-Spice Carrot Muffins

PREP TIME: 20 MINUTES (READY IN 55 MINUTES)
SERVINGS: 12

 EASY

1 box (15.2 oz) cinnamon streusel muffin mix

½ teaspoon ground ginger

¼ teaspoon ground nutmeg

2 eggs

¼ cup frozen (thawed) orange juice concentrate

¼ cup milk

¼ cup vegetable or canola oil

1 ½ cups packed shredded carrots

1 cup chopped walnuts

1) Heat oven to 400°F (375°F for dark or nonstick pan). Spray bottoms only of 12 regular-size muffin cups with cooking spray or place paper baking cup in each muffin cup.

2) Set aside streusel packet from muffin mix. In large bowl, stir muffin mix, ginger and nutmeg. In medium bowl, beat eggs with fork. Stir in orange juice concentrate, milk and oil. Stir in carrots and ½ cup of the walnuts. Using rubber spatula, fold wet ingredients into dry ingredients just until moistened (batter may be slightly lumpy; do not overmix).

3) Divide batter evenly among muffin cups, using ¼ cup for each. (If any carrots are sticking out of batter, push in with finger.) Sprinkle reserved streusel over batter; top with remaining ½ cup walnuts. Bake 17 to 22 minutes or until golden brown and toothpick comes out almost clean. Cool 10 minutes; remove from pan to cooling rack.

1 SERVING: Calories 280; Total Fat 15g; Sodium 210mg; Dietary Fiber 1g; Protein 4g. EXCHANGES: 1/2 Starch, 1-1/2 Other Carbohydrate, 3 Fat. CARBOHYDRATE CHOICES: 2.

Overnight Brunch Egg Bake

PREP TIME: 30 MINUTES (READY IN 9 HOURS 45 MINUTES)
SERVINGS: 12

6 cups shredded Colby-Monterey Jack cheese blend (24 oz)

2 tablespoons butter or margarine

5 medium green onions, sliced (⅓ cup)

1 small red bell pepper, chopped (½ cup)

1 jar (4.5 oz) Green Giant® sliced mushrooms, drained

8 oz cooked ham, cut into thin bite-size strips

8 eggs

½ cup all-purpose flour

2 tablespoons chopped fresh parsley

1¾ cups milk

Additional chopped red bell pepper and fresh parsley, if desired

Chopped fresh strawberries and green onions, if desired

1) Sprinkle 3 cups of the cheese into greased 13x9-inch (3-quart) glass baking dish. In 10-inch skillet, melt butter over medium heat. Cook onions, bell pepper and mushrooms in butter, stirring occasionally, until tender. Spoon vegetables over cheese. Top with ham and remaining 3 cups cheese.

2) In large bowl, beat the eggs with a wire whisk. Add the flour, parsley and milk; beat well. Pour over mixture in baking dish. Cover with foil; refrigerate 8 hours or overnight.

3) Heat oven to 350°F. Bake uncovered 55 to 65 minutes or until set and top is lightly browned. Let stand 10 minutes. Cut into 12 squares. Garnish with bell pepper, parsley, strawberries and green onions.

1 SERVING: Calories 350; Total Fat 25g; Sodium 650mg; Dietary Fiber 0g; Protein 24g. EXCHANGES: 1/2 Starch, 1-1/2 Medium-Fat Meat, 1-1/2 High-Fat Meat, 1 Fat. CARBOHYDRATE CHOICES: 1/2.

Lemon Bread with Apricots

PREP TIME: 20 MINUTES (READY IN 3 HOURS 30 MINUTES)
SERVINGS: 16

 EASY

BREAD

- 2 ½ cups all-purpose flour
- 2 teaspoons baking powder
- ½ teaspoon salt
- 2 eggs
- ¾ cup granulated sugar
- 1 cup milk
- ⅓ cup butter, melted
- 2 teaspoons grated lemon peel (from 1 medium lemon)
- 1 bag (6 oz) dried apricots, chopped (about 1 cup)

GLAZE

- ½ cup powdered sugar
- 2 to 3 teaspoons lemon juice

GARNISH, IF DESIRED

Grated lemon peel strips

1) Heat oven to 350°F. Grease bottom only of 9x5-inch (1 ½ -quart) glass baking dish with shortening or cooking spray.

2) In large bowl, mix flour, baking powder and salt. In medium bowl, beat eggs and granulated sugar with wire whisk. Stir in milk, butter, 2 teaspoons lemon peel and the apricots. Using rubber spatula, fold wet ingredients into dry ingredients just until moistened (batter may be slightly lumpy; do not overmix). Pour into pan.

3) Bake 1 hour or until golden brown and toothpick inserted in center comes out clean. Cool 10 minutes; remove from pan to cooling rack. Cool completely, about 2 hours.

4) In small bowl, stir glaze ingredients until smooth and thin enough to drizzle. Drizzle glaze over bread. Garnish with lemon peel strips. Cut with serrated knife.

1 SERVING: Calories 240; Total Fat 8g; Sodium 210mg; Dietary Fiber 1g; Protein 6g. EXCHANGES: 1 Starch, 1-1/2 Other Carbohydrate, 1-1/2 Fat. CARBOHYDRATE CHOICES: 2-1/2.

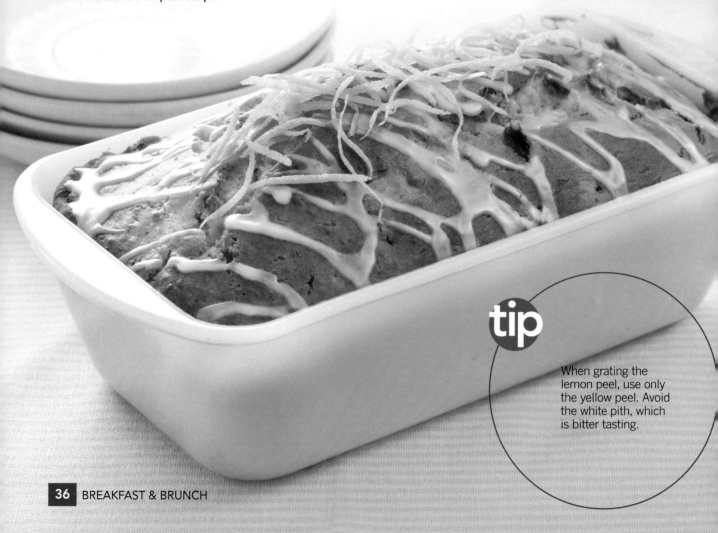

tip

When grating the lemon peel, use only the yellow peel. Avoid the white pith, which is bitter tasting.

Pecan Pancakes with Fudge Syrup

PREP TIME: 25 MINUTES (READY IN 25 MINUTES)
SERVINGS: 4 (3 PANCAKES AND 3 TABLESPOONS SYRUP EACH)

 EASY

1 cup maple-flavored or real maple syrup

¼ cup hot fudge topping

1 ½ cups all-purpose flour

2 tablespoons packed brown sugar

1 teaspoon baking powder

¼ teaspoon baking soda

¼ teaspoon salt

½ cup chopped pecans

1 ½ cups buttermilk

2 eggs, beaten

2 tablespoons butter, melted

1) In 1-quart nonstick saucepan, heat syrup and fudge topping over medium heat until warm, stirring until smooth. Keep warm.

2) In medium bowl, mix flour, brown sugar, baking powder, baking soda, salt and pecans. Beat in buttermilk, eggs and butter with spoon or wire whisk just until blended.

3) Heat griddle or skillet over medium heat or to 375°F. Grease griddle with butter or vegetable oil if necessary (or spray with cooking spray before heating). For each pancake, pour about ¼ cup batter onto hot griddle. Cook pancakes until bubbles form on top and edges are dry. Turn and cook other sides until golden brown. Serve with warm syrup.

1 SERVING: Calories 710; Total Fat 21g; Sodium 610mg; Dietary Fiber 3g; Protein 13g. EXCHANGES: 3-1/2 Starch, 4 Other Carbohydrate, 1/2 High-Fat Meat, 3 Fat. CARBOHYDRATE CHOICES: 8.

Apple-Cinnamon French Toast

PREP TIME: 25 MINUTES (READY IN 9 HOURS 50 MINUTES)
SERVINGS: 12 (1 SQUARE WITH 2 TABLESPOONS SYRUP EACH)

10 slices whole-grain bread

4 medium cooking apples, peeled, cubed (4 cups)

8 eggs

2 ½ cups half-and-half

2 ¼ cups sugar

1 tablespoon vanilla

1 cup chopped pecans

3 ¼ teaspoons ground cinnamon

1 ¼ teaspoons ground nutmeg

3 tablespoons all-purpose flour

2 cups apple cider

¼ cup butter or margarine

1) Grease 13x9-inch baking dish with shortening or cooking spray. Arrange 5 bread slices in baking dish, trimming to fit if necessary. Spoon apples evenly over bread; top with remaining 5 bread slices.

2) In large bowl, beat eggs, half-and-half, ¼ cup of the sugar and the vanilla until smooth. Slowly pour mixture over bread. In small bowl, mix 1 cup of the sugar, the pecans, 3 teaspoons of the cinnamon and 1 tablespoon of the nutmeg. Sprinkle over bread. Cover with foil; refrigerate 8 hours or overnight.

3) Heat oven to 350°F. Bake French toast covered 30 minutes. Remove foil; bake 35 to 45 minutes longer or until knife inserted halfway between center and edge comes out clean and top is golden brown. Let stand 10 minutes. Cut into 12 squares. In 2-quart saucepan, mix remaining 1 cup sugar, flour, cider, and remaining ¼ teaspoon cinnamon and nutmeg. Heat to boiling; reduce heat to low. Add butter; cook and stir until melted. Serve with French toast.

1 SERVING: Calories 520; Total Fat 21g; Sodium 250mg; Dietary Fiber 4g; Protein 11g. EXCHANGES: 1-1/2 Starch, 1/2 Fruit, 2-1/2 Other Carbohydrate, 1 Medium-Fat Meat, 3 Fat. CARBOHYDRATE CHOICES: 4-1/2.

Apple Pancakes with Sausage

PREP TIME: 20 MINUTES (READY IN 20 MINUTES)
SERVINGS: 2

⋺ EASY

6 oz bulk pork sausage	¼ teaspoon ground cinnamon
⅓ cup maple-flavored syrup	1 medium Gala apple, sliced
2 tablespoons butter or margarine, softened	6 Pillsbury® frozen buttermilk pancakes (from 16.4-oz box)

1) Heat contact grill 5 minutes. Meanwhile, shape sausage into 2 patties. In 2-cup glass measuring cup, mix syrup, butter and cinnamon.

2) When grill is heated, place sausage patties on lower part of grill surface and apple slices on upper part of grill; close grill. Cook 4 to 5 minutes or until sausage is no longer pink in center.

3) Meanwhile, microwave syrup mixture on High 45 to 60 seconds or until heated; set aside. Microwave pancakes as directed on box.

4) Place sausage patties on serving plates. Stir apple slices into syrup mixture. Arrange 3 pancakes on each plate with sausage. Spoon apples with syrup over pancakes.

1 SERVING: Calories 680; Total Fat 27g; Sodium 800mg; Dietary Fiber 3g; Protein 12g. EXCHANGES: 2 Starch, 1/2 Fruit, 4 Other Carbohydrate, 1 High-Fat Meat, 3-1/2 Fat. CARBOHYDRATE CHOICES: 6-1/2.

Pineapple-Cherry Quick Bread

PREP TIME: 30 MINUTES (READY IN 2 HOURS 35 MINUTES)
SERVINGS: 24

4 cups all-purpose flour	4 eggs
1 ½ cups granulated sugar	1 can (8 oz) crushed pineapple in juice, undrained
1 teaspoon baking soda	1 jar (10 oz) maraschino cherries, quartered, well drained
1 teaspoon salt	
¾ cup vegetable oil	
1 tablespoon vanilla	2 teaspoons powdered sugar

1) Heat oven to 325°F. Grease bottoms only of 2 (8x4-inch) loaf pans with shortening or cooking spray; lightly flour.

2) In large bowl, mix flour, granulated sugar, baking soda and salt. Add oil, vanilla, eggs and pineapple with liquid; beat with electric mixer on low speed until combined. Fold in cherries. Divide evenly between pans.

3) Bake 45 to 55 minutes or until toothpick inserted in center comes out clean. Cool 10 minutes. Remove from pans to cooling racks. Cool completely, about 1 hour. Sprinkle with powdered sugar.

1 SERVING: Calories 230; Total Fat 8g; Sodium 160mg; Dietary Fiber 1g; Protein 3g. EXCHANGES: 1 Starch, 1-1/2 Other Carbohydrate, 1-1/2 Fat. CARBOHYDRATE CHOICES: 2.

Huevos Rancheros Casserole

PREP TIME:	20 MINUTES (READY IN 9 HOURS 15 MINUTES)
SERVINGS:	6

 EASY

5 soft corn tortillas (6 inch)

1 ½ cups finely shredded Colby-Monterey Jack cheese blend (6 oz)

½ lb smoked cooked chorizo sausage, coarsely chopped

1 can (4.5 oz) Old El Paso® chopped green chiles

6 eggs

½ cup milk

½ teaspoon dried oregano leaves

⅛ teaspoon ground red pepper (cayenne)

GARNISHES, IF DESIRED

Old El Paso® salsa

Guacamole

Fresh cilantro leaves

1) Spray 8-inch square (2-quart) glass baking dish with cooking spray. Place 4 of the tortillas in bottom of baking dish and ½ to 1 inch up sides, overlapping as necessary. Cut remaining tortilla in half; cut into ½-inch-wide strips. Sprinkle ½ cup of the cheese over tortillas in baking dish. Top with chorizo, chiles and ½ cup cheese. Arrange tortilla strips over cheese.

2) In medium bowl, beat eggs, milk, oregano and red pepper with wire whisk. Pour over mixture in baking dish. Sprinkle with remaining ½ cup cheese; press lightly into egg mixture. Cover with foil; refrigerate at least 8 hours or overnight.

3) Heat oven to 350°F. Bake casserole, covered, 30 minutes. Uncover; bake 15 to 20 minutes longer or until knife inserted in center comes out clean. Let stand 5 minutes. Cut into 6 squares. Top with garnishes.

1 SERVING: Calories 430; Total Fat 30g; Sodium 1070mg; Dietary Fiber 1g; Protein 24g. EXCHANGES: 1 Starch, 1-1/2 Medium-Fat Meat, 1-1/2 High-Fat Meat, 2 Fat. CARBOHYDRATE CHOICES: 1.

Cheesy Ham Breakfast Casserole

PREP TIME: 15 MINUTES (READY IN 5 HOURS 15 MINUTES)
SERVINGS: 6

 EASY

CASSEROLE

- 5 eggs
- ¾ cup milk
- ½ cup chives-and-onion cream cheese, softened
- ½ teaspoon ground mustard
- ¼ teaspoon salt
- ⅛ teaspoon pepper
- 2 cups refrigerated southwest-style shredded hash brown potatoes (from 20-oz bag)
- 1 cup shredded Cheddar cheese (4 oz)
- ¼ cup diced red bell pepper
- ⅔ cup diced cooked ham (from 8-oz package)

TOPPING

- ½ cup Progresso® panko crispy bread crumbs
- ¼ cup shredded Parmesan cheese (1 oz)
- 1 tablespoon butter, melted

1) Grease 8- or 9-inch square baking dish with butter or cooking spray. In large bowl, beat eggs, milk and cream cheese until well combined. Stir in mustard, salt, pepper, potatoes, Cheddar cheese, bell pepper and ham. Pour mixture into baking dish. Cover with foil; refrigerate at least 4 hours or overnight.

2) Heat oven to 350°F. Uncover baking dish. Bake 40 minutes. In small bowl, combine remaining ingredients. Sprinkle over casserole. Bake 10 to 15 minutes longer or until set and top is golden brown. Cut into 6 squares and cut each square in half diagonally.

1 SERVING: Calories 358; Total Fat 22g; Sodium 786mg; Dietary Fiber 2g; Protein 18g. EXCHANGES: 1 Starch, 2 Medium-Fat Meat, 2 Fat. CARBOHYDRATE CHOICES: 1.

tip

Panko bread crumbs are crispier and fluffier than regular dry bread crumbs. In the grocery store, panko can be found with other styles of bread crumbs in the bread aisle.

Orange Pancakes with Raspberry Topping

PREP TIME: 25 MINUTES (READY IN 25 MINUTES)
SERVINGS: 4 (2 PANCAKES AND 1/4 CUP TOPPING EACH)

 EASY   LOW FAT

TOPPING

- ½ cup orange juice
- 1 tablespoon cornstarch
- 1 package (10 oz) frozen raspberries in syrup, thawed

PANCAKES

- 1 cup all-purpose flour
- 2 tablespoons powdered sugar
- ¼ teaspoon baking soda
- ¼ teaspoon salt
- 2 teaspoons grated orange peel
- ¾ cup milk
- 2 tablespoons butter, melted
- 1 egg
- 2 tablespoons orange juice
- Frozen whipped topping, thawed, if desired
- Fresh raspberries, if desired

1) In 1-quart saucepan, stir ½ cup orange juice and the cornstarch until smooth. Heat to boiling over medium heat; boil 1 minute. Meanwhile, pour raspberries and syrup in strainer over medium bowl to drain. Stir syrup into juice mixture; cool slightly. Stir in raspberries; set aside.

2) In medium bowl, mix flour, powdered sugar, baking soda, salt and orange peel. Beat in milk, butter, egg and 2 tablespoons orange juice with spoon or wire whisk just until blended.

3) Heat griddle or skillet over medium heat or to 375°F. Grease griddle with butter or vegetable oil if necessary. For each pancake, pour about ¼ cup batter onto hot griddle. Cook pancakes until bubbles form on top and edges are dry. Turn and cook other sides until golden brown. Serve with raspberry topping. Garnish with whipped topping and fresh berries, if desired.

1 SERVING: Calories 320; Total Fat 8g; Sodium 300mg; Dietary Fiber 4g; Protein 7g. EXCHANGES: 2 Starch, 1 Fruit, 1/2 Other Carbohydrate, 1-1/2 Fat. CARBOHYDRATE CHOICES: 3-1/2.

Pecan-Chocolate Chip Waffles

PREP TIME: 50 MINUTES (READY IN 50 MINUTES)
SERVINGS: 18

3 cups all-purpose flour

1 tablespoon baking powder

¼ cup sugar

⅔ cup finely chopped pecans

⅔ cup miniature semisweet chocolate chips

4 eggs

1 cup butter, melted

2 ½ cups milk

2 teaspoons vanilla

2 ¼ cups maple-flavored syrup

Additional coarsely chopped pecans and miniature semisweet chocolate chips, if desired

1) Heat waffle maker. In large bowl, mix flour, baking powder, sugar, pecans and chocolate chips. In medium bowl, beat eggs, butter, milk and vanilla with wire whisk. Pour over dry ingredients; stir just until moistened.

2) Spoon batter onto waffle maker, following manufacturer's directions for recommended amount. Close the lid of the waffle maker. Bake until the steaming stops and the waffles are deep golden brown. Serve with syrup. Top with additional pecans and chocolate chips, if desired.

1 SERVING: Calories 380; Total Fat 17g; Sodium 190mg; Dietary Fiber 1g; Protein 5g. EXCHANGES: 1-1/2 Starch, 2 Other Carbohydrate, 3 Fat. CARBOHYDRATE CHOICES: 3-1/2.

Raised Belgian Waffles

PREP TIME: 55 MINUTES (READY IN 1 HOUR 25 MINUTES)
SERVINGS: 8 (ONE 7-1/2 INCH WAFFLE EACH)

2 ¾ cups milk

1 package fast-acting dry yeast

½ cup sugar

3 eggs, separated

¾ cup butter, melted

2 teaspoons vanilla

1 teaspoon salt

4 cups all-purpose flour

TOPPINGS

Blueberry syrup

Whipped cream

Fresh blueberries

1) In 1-cup microwavable measuring cup, microwave ¼ cup of the milk on High 10 to 20 seconds or until 110°F to 115°F. Stir in yeast and ½ teaspoon of the granulated sugar. Let stand 5 minutes or until foamy. In 4-cup microwavable measuring cup, heat remaining 2 ½ cups milk on High 2 to 3 minutes or until 120°F to 130°F.

2) In large bowl, beat warm milk, remaining sugar, the egg yolks, butter, vanilla and salt with wire whisk until well blended. Beat in yeast mixture and flour until smooth.

3) In medium bowl, beat egg whites with electric mixer until stiff peaks form. Fold into batter until small flecks of white are visible. Cover; let stand 30 minutes or until batter starts to rise.

4) Spray Belgian waffle maker with cooking spray; heat waffle maker. Gently stir batter; spoon batter onto waffle maker. Close lid. Bake 4 minutes or until steaming stops and waffles are golden brown. Serve with syrup, whipped cream and blueberries.

1 SERVING: Calories 500; Total Fat 22g; Sodium 480mg; Dietary Fiber 2g; Protein 12g. EXCHANGES: 3-1/2 Starch, 1 Other Carbohydrate, 4 Fat. CARBOHYDRATE CHOICES: 4.

Chocolate Cherry Croissants

PREP TIME: 10 MINUTES (READY IN 20 MINUTES)
SERVINGS: 4

 EASY

4 large croissants, split

½ cup cream cheese spread (from 8-oz container)

8 teaspoons cherry preserves

¼ cup semisweet chocolate chips

1 teaspoon powdered sugar

1) Heat oven to 400°F. Spray 15x10x1-inch pan with cooking spray.

2) On bottom half of each croissant, spread 2 tablespoons cream cheese and 2 teaspoons preserves; sprinkle each with 1 tablespoon chocolate chips. Replace top halves of croissants. Place in pan.

3) Bake uncovered 7 to 9 minutes or until heated through. Sprinkle with powdered sugar. Serve warm.

1 SERVING: Calories 500; Total Fat 31g; Sodium 190mg; Dietary Fiber 2g; Protein 7g. EXCHANGES: 2 Starch, 1 Other Carbohydrate, 6 Fat. CARBOHYDRATE CHOICES: 3.

Orange-Rhubarb Bread

PREP TIME: 20 MINUTES (READY IN 3 HOURS 25 MINUTES)
SERVINGS: 24

 EASY

1 cup sugar

½ cup vegetable oil

2 eggs

½ cup milk

2 teaspoons grated orange peel (from 1 medium orange)

2 ¼ cups all-purpose flour

2 ½ teaspoons baking powder

1 teaspoon salt

1 ½ cups finely chopped fresh rhubarb

½ cup sliced almonds

2 tablespoons sugar

1) Heat oven to 350°F (325°F for dark or nonstick pans). Grease bottoms only of 2 (8x4-inch) loaf pans with shortening or cooking spray.

2) In large bowl, beat 1 cup sugar, the oil, eggs, milk and orange peel with wire whisk. Stir in flour, baking powder and salt all at once just until flour is moistened. Stir in rhubarb.

3) Divide batter evenly between pans. Sprinkle each pan with 1/4 cup almonds; lightly press almonds into batter. Sprinkle each with 1 tablespoon sugar.

4) Bake 45 to 55 minutes or until toothpick inserted in center comes out clean. Cool 10 minutes; remove from pans to cooling rack. Cool completely, about 2 hours. Cut with serrated knife.

1 SERVING: Calories 140; Total Fat 6g; Sodium 160mg; Dietary Fiber 0g; Protein 2g. EXCHANGES: 1/2 Starch, 1 Other Carbohydrate, 1 Fat. CARBOHYDRATE CHOICES: 1.

LAYERED CARIBBEAN CHICKEN SALAD
PG. 78

Sensational Salads

For fun yet light fare, try any of these palate-pleasing pasta, side or entree salads!

CHINESE CHICKEN SALAD
PG. 59

EDAMAME-BLACK BEAN SALAD
PG. 57

CALIFORNIA "SUSHI" RICE SALAD
PG. 54

Spinach Salad with Cranberry Vinaigrette

PREP TIME: 25 MINUTES (READY IN 25 MINUTES)
SERVINGS: 8

 EASY

VINAIGRETTE

½ cup whole berry cranberry sauce

¼ cup vegetable oil

2 tablespoons orange juice

2 tablespoons honey

2 tablespoons balsamic vinegar

¼ teaspoon salt

SALAD

1 bag (10 oz) fresh baby spinach leaves

2 avocados, pitted, peeled and sliced

1 tablespoon orange juice

½ cup pomegranate seeds

Pomegranates are available from late September to November. Select those with fresh leather-like skin free from cracks and splits. Skin color varies from bright to deep red.

1) In jar with tight-fitting lid, place all vinaigrette ingredients; shake until well blended. Refrigerate until serving time.

2) Divide spinach leaves evenly among salad plates. Coat avocado slices with 1 tablespoon orange juice; arrange over spinach. Sprinkle with pomegranate seeds. Drizzle salads with vinaigrette.

1 SERVING: Calories 190; Total Fat 12g; Sodium 110mg; Dietary Fiber 3g; Protein 2g. EXCHANGES: 1 Fruit, 1 Vegetable, 2-1/2 Fat. CARBOHYDRATE CHOICES: 1.

Turkey-Cranberry Bacon Ranch Pasta Salad

PREP TIME: 25 MINUTES (READY IN 25 MINUTES)
SERVINGS: 7 (1 CUP EACH)

 EASY

1 box (7.5 oz) Betty Crocker® Suddenly Salad® ranch and bacon salad mix

½ cup mayonnaise or salad dressing

1 ½ cups cubed (½ inch) cooked turkey breast

1 cup sliced celery

½ cup sweetened dried cranberries

4 oz provolone cheese, cut into ½-inch cubes (1 cup)

½ cup sliced almonds, toasted

1) Fill 3-quart saucepan ⅔ full of water; heat to boiling. Add pasta. Gently boil, uncovered, 12 minutes, stirring occasionally; drain. Rinse with cold water to cool; drain well.

2) In large bowl, combine seasoning mix from packet and mayonnaise. Stir in turkey, celery, cranberries and cheese until well mixed. Stir in cooked pasta. Transfer to serving dish. Top with almonds.

1 SERVING: Calories 400; Total Fat 22g; Sodium 510mg; Dietary Fiber 2g; Protein 18g. EXCHANGES: 1-1/2 Starch, 1/2 Other Carbohydrate, 2 Lean Meat, 3 Fat. CARBOHYDRATE CHOICES: 2.

Crunchy Fruit Salads

| PREP TIME: | 15 MINUTES (READY IN 15 MINUTES) |
| SERVINGS: | 4 |

 EASY   LOW FAT

1 large apple or pear, cut into bite-size pieces

1 large stalk celery, sliced

¼ cup raisins or peanuts, if desired

¼ cup reduced-fat ranch salad dressing or mayonnaise

Lettuce leaves

1 cup Cheerios® or MultiGrain Cheerios® cereal, slightly crushed

1) In medium bowl, mix apple, celery, raisins and dressing until blended. Refrigerate until serving time.

2) Just before serving, arrange lettuce leaves in 4 salad bowls or on plates. Spoon apple mixture over lettuce. Top each serving with ¼ cup cereal. Serve immediately.

1 SERVING: Calories 100; Total Fat 2.5g; Sodium 200mg; Dietary Fiber 2g; Protein 1g. EXCHANGES: 1/2 Starch, 1/2 Other Carbohydrate, 1/2 Vegetable, 1/2 Fat. CARBOHYDRATE CHOICES: 1.

Tailgate Pasta Salad

| PREP TIME: | 25 MINUTES (READY IN 2 HOURS 25 MINUTES) |
| SERVINGS: | 6 (1-1/3 CUPS EACH) |

SALAD

8 oz uncooked gemelli or rotini pasta

1 medium zucchini, cut in half lengthwise, thinly sliced (2 cups)

1 can (14 oz) artichoke hearts, drained, chopped

1 cup cherry tomatoes, cut in half

4 oz fresh baby spinach leaves

½ cup chopped fresh basil leaves

DRESSING

¼ cup olive oil or vegetable oil

3 tablespoons red wine vinegar

1 teaspoon coarse-grained mustard

1 teaspoon salt

½ teaspoon pepper

1 garlic clove, crushed

1) Cook and drain pasta as directed on package. Rinse with cold water to cool; drain well.

2) Meanwhile, in small bowl, mix all dressing ingredients until well blended.

3) In large bowl, mix cooked pasta with remaining salad ingredients and ¼ cup of the basil. Pour dressing over salad; toss until coated. Cover; refrigerate 2 to 3 hours to blend flavors.

4) Just before serving, sprinkle the remaining ¼ cup chopped basil over the top of the salad.

1 SERVING: Calories 290; Total Fat 10g; Sodium 550mg; Dietary Fiber 7g; Protein 9g. EXCHANGES: 2 Starch, 2 Vegetable, 2 Fat. CARBOHYDRATE CHOICES: 3.

Raspberry-Lemon Salad

PREP TIME: 25 MINUTES (READY IN 25 MINUTES)
SERVINGS: 6

 EASY

DRESSING

- 3 tablespoons olive oil
- 3 tablespoons honey
- 2 teaspoons grated lemon peel
- 2 tablespoons fresh lemon juice
- ¼ teaspoon salt

SALAD

- ¼ cup sliced almonds
- 6 cups loosely packed torn Boston lettuce (about 1 large head)
- 2 cups loosely packed torn romaine lettuce (about ½ bunch)
- ¼ cup chopped fresh chives
- 1 container (6 oz) fresh raspberries (about 1 cup)

1) In small bowl, mix all dressing ingredients with a wire whisk.

2) Sprinkle almonds in ungreased heavy skillet. Cook over medium heat 5 to 7 minutes, stirring frequently until the nuts begin to brown, then stirring constantly until the nuts are light brown. Cool.

3) In large bowl, toss lettuces and chives. Drizzle with dressing and toss to coat. Add raspberries and toasted almonds; toss gently. Serve immediately.

1 SERVING: Calories 150; Total Fat 9g; Sodium 105mg; Dietary Fiber 3g; Protein 2g. EXCHANGES: 1/2 Starch, 1/2 Other Carbohydrate, 1-1/2 Fat. CARBOHYDRATE CHOICES: 1.

California "Sushi" Rice Salad

PREP TIME: 30 MINUTES (READY IN 1 HOUR 25 MINUTES)
SERVINGS: 8 (1-1/4 CUPS EACH)

 LOW FAT

2 cups uncooked regular long-grain white rice

⅓ cup rice vinegar (not seasoned)

¼ cup sugar

1 teaspoon salt

2 teaspoons grated gingerroot

2 large cucumbers, seeded, chopped

2 medium carrots, finely shredded (1 cup)

8 medium green onions, sliced (½ cup)

2 packages (8 oz each) imitation crabmeat sticks, sliced

1 small avocado, pitted, peeled and thinly sliced

1) In 3-quart saucepan, cook rice in water as directed on package. Spread rice in 13x9-inch baking dish, cover with plastic wrap and refrigerate for 1 hour or until completely cool.

2) Meanwhile, in small microwavable bowl, mix vinegar, sugar and salt. Microwave 20 to 30 seconds; whisk until sugar is dissolved. Stir in gingerroot.

3) In large bowl, toss cooled rice with vinegar mixture. Stir in cucumbers, carrots, green onions and crabmeat; mix well. Top with avocado.

1 SERVING: Calories 310; Total Fat 3.5g; Sodium 800mg; Dietary Fiber 3g; Protein 13g. EXCHANGES: 2 Starch, 1 Other Carbohydrate, 1-1/2 Vegetable, 1/2 Lean Meat, 1/2 Fat. CARBOHYDRATE CHOICES: 4.

Asiago Cheese-Chick Pea Pasta Salad

PREP TIME: 25 MINUTES (READY IN 1 HOUR 25 MINUTES)
SERVINGS: 10 (1/2 CUP EACH)

1 box (7.75 oz) Betty Crocker®
  Suddenly Salad® classic salad mix

2 tablespoons finely chopped
  sun-dried tomatoes in oil
  (from 7-oz jar)

3 tablespoons oil from sun-dried
  tomatoes

¼ cup water

¼ teaspoon cracked black pepper

¼ teaspoon crushed red pepper flakes

2 oz Asiago cheese, cut into ¼-inch
  cubes (½ cup)

3 tablespoons chopped fresh parsley

2 tablespoons finely chopped red
  onion

1 plum (Roma) tomato, seeded, diced

6 fresh basil leaves, thinly sliced

1 can (15 oz) Progresso® chick peas
  (garbanzo beans), drained, rinsed

1) Fill 3-quart saucepan ⅔ full of water; heat to boiling. Add pasta. Gently boil, uncovered, 12 minutes, stirring occasionally; drain. Rinse with cold water to cool; drain well.

2) Meanwhile, in large bowl, combine seasoning mix from packet, sun-dried tomatoes and oil, water, black pepper and red pepper flakes. Add the remaining ingredients; stir in cooked pasta. Refrigerate salad at least 1 hour to blend the flavors.

1 SERVING: Calories 200; Total Fat 8g; Sodium 430mg; Dietary Fiber 2g; Protein 7g. EXCHANGES: 1-1/2 Starch, 1/2 Vegetable, 1-1/2 Fat. CARBOHYDRATE CHOICES: 2.

Black and White Bean Salad

PREP TIME: 20 MINUTES (READY IN 20 MINUTES)
SERVINGS: 6

 EASY   LOW FAT

3 large red bell peppers

¼ cup red wine vinegar

1 teaspoon chili powder

¼ teaspoon salt

2 tablespoons oil

1 cup finely chopped jicama

1 can (15-oz) Progresso® great northern beans, drained, rinsed

1 can (15 oz) Progresso® black beans, drained, rinsed

1 (7 oz) can Green Giant® Niblets® whole kernel sweet corn, drained

1 (4.5-oz.) can Old El Paso® chopped green chiles

Lettuce leaves

1) In Dutch oven or large saucepan, bring 6 cups water to a boil. Meanwhile, cut bell peppers in half lengthwise; remove seeds. Place peppers in boiling water for 2 minutes. Drain and rinse with cold water until cool.

2) In large bowl, combine vinegar, chili powder, salt and oil; blend well. Add all remaining ingredients except lettuce and bell peppers; blend well.

3) Spoon bean mixture into pepper halves. Serve immediately on lettuce-lined plates, or refrigerate until serving time.

1 SERVING: Calories 320; Total Fat 6g; Sodium 840mg; Dietary Fiber 16g; Protein 15g. EXCHANGES: 1-1/2 Starch, 1/2 Other Carbohydrate, 4-1/2 Vegetable, 1 Fat. CARBOHYDRATE CHOICES: 3-1/2.

Festive Cranberry-Raspberry Salad

PREP TIME: 15 MINUTES (READY IN 1 HOUR 50 MINUTES)
SERVINGS: 12 (1/2 CUP EACH)

 EASY   LOW FAT

1 envelope unflavored gelatin

½ cup raspberry-cranberry juice

2 boxes (4-serving size each) cranberry- or raspberry-flavored gelatin

½ teaspoon ground ginger

2 cups boiling water

1 can (14 to 16 oz) whole berry cranberry sauce

½ cup cold water

1 bag (12 oz) frozen unsweetened raspberries

1) In small bowl, sprinkle unflavored gelatin over juice. Set aside.

2) In large heatproof bowl, mix flavored gelatin and ginger. Pour boiling water on gelatin; stir until gelatin is dissolved. Stir in cranberry sauce, cold water and unflavored gelatin mixture; mix well. Refrigerate 30 minutes.

3) Stir frozen raspberries into gelatin. Let stand about 5 minutes or until mixture begins to set up. Spoon into serving bowl; refrigerate at least 1 hour or until serving time. Garnish with fresh raspberries or orange slices, if desired.

1 SERVING: Calories 130; Total Fat 0g; Sodium 80mg; Dietary Fiber 2g; Protein 2g. EXCHANGES: 1/2 Fruit, 1-1/2 Other Carbohydrate. CARBOHYDRATE CHOICES: 2.

Edamame-Black Bean Salad

PREP TIME: 20 MINUTES (READY IN 20 MINUTES)
SERVINGS: 5 (1 CUP EACH)

 EASY

1 bag (12 oz) frozen shelled edamame

1 can (15 oz) Progresso® black beans, drained, rinsed

2 medium plum (Roma) tomatoes, chopped

1 medium bell pepper, chopped (1 cup)

4 medium green onions, sliced (¼ cup)

¼ cup chopped fresh cilantro or flat-leaf parsley

½ cup balsamic vinaigrette dressing

¼ teaspoon salt

¼ teaspoon cracked black pepper

1) In 2-quart saucepan, cook edamame according to package directions; drain and rinse with cold water.

2) In large bowl, toss edamame with remaining ingredients. Serve immediately or refrigerate until serving.

1 SERVING: Calories 290; Total Fat 15g; Sodium 300mg; Dietary Fiber 11g; Protein 13g. EXCHANGES: 1 Starch, 2-1/2 Vegetable, 1/2 Lean Meat, 2-1/2 Fat. CARBOHYDRATE CHOICES: 2.

Fruity, Stir-Crazy and Nuts over Suddenly Salad

PREP TIME: 25 MINUTES (READY IN 25 MINUTES)
SERVINGS: 6 (1-1/3 CUPS EACH)

 EASY

1 box (7.5 oz) Betty Crocker® Suddenly Salad® ranch and bacon salad mix

6 slices bacon, cut into ½ inch slices

¾ cup cranberry-pomegranate juice

¼ cup olive oil or vegetable oil

3 cups chopped romaine lettuce (6 leaves)

1 cup sweetened dried cranberries

1 cup coarsely chopped pecans, toasted

1 medium stalk celery, sliced (½ cup)

⅓ cup thinly sliced red onion

1 cup Roquefort or other blue cheese, crumbled (4 oz)

1) Fill 3-quart saucepan ⅔ full of water; heat to boiling. Add pasta. Gently boil, uncovered, 12 minutes, stirring occasionally; drain. Rinse with cold water to cool; drain well.

2) Meanwhile, in 10-inch nonstick skillet, cook bacon over medium heat 6 to 8 minutes or until crisp. Drain on paper towels.

3) In small bowl, combine seasoning mix from packet, juice and oil. In large bowl, stir together cooked pasta and remaining ingredients except cheese.

4) Just before serving, toss salad with dressing and sprinkle with cheese.

1 SERVING: Calories 560; Total Fat 33g; Sodium 830mg; Dietary Fiber 4g; Protein 14g. EXCHANGES: 1-1/2 Starch, 1/2 Fruit, 1 Other Carbohydrate, 1 Vegetable, 1 High-Fat Meat, 5 Fat. CARBOHYDRATE CHOICES: 3-1/2.

Chinese Chicken Salad

PREP TIME:	25 MINUTES (READY IN 25 MINUTES)			
SERVINGS:	6 (1-2/3 CUPS EACH)			

e EASY

Shreya Sasaki
San Diego, CA
www.recipematcher.com

¼ cup rice vinegar

2 tablespoons sugar

½ teaspoon salt

¼ cup peanut oil

2 ½ cups chopped cooked chicken

1 head iceberg lettuce, torn into bite-size pieces (about 8 cups)

4 medium stalks celery, thinly sliced (2 cups)

1 medium carrot, shredded (½ cup)

½ cup walnuts, coarsely chopped

4 medium green onions, sliced (¼ cup)

2 tablespoons sesame seed, toasted

½ cup chow mein noodles

1) In small bowl, stir together vinegar, sugar and salt until sugar is dissolved. Whisk in oil.

2) In large salad bowl, stir together chicken, lettuce, celery, carrot, walnuts, green onions and sesame seed until well mixed. Just before serving, pour dressing over salad; toss until coated. Top with chow mein noodles.

1 SERVING: Calories 330; Total Fat 22g; Sodium 540mg; Dietary Fiber 3g; Protein 19g. EXCHANGES: 2-1/2 Vegetable, 2 Lean Meat, 3-1/2 Fat. CARBOHYDRATE CHOICES: 1.

Mixed Green Salad with Dijon Vinaigrette

PREP TIME:	20 MINUTES (READY IN 20 MINUTES)
SERVINGS:	6 (ABOUT 1 CUP EACH)

 EASY

VINAIGRETTE

- 1 tablespoon Dijon mustard
- 1 tablespoon red wine vinegar
- ½ teaspoon sugar
- 3 tablespoons olive oil
- Dash salt and pepper

SALAD

- 1 bag (5 oz) spring lettuce mix
- 1 cup grape tomatoes, cut in half lengthwise
- 1 cup sliced (⅛ inch) seeded peeled cucumber
- 1 cup sliced (⅛ inch) halved red onion

1) In small bowl, mix mustard, vinegar and sugar with wire whisk. Gradually add oil, beating constantly until well blended. Season to taste with salt and pepper.

2) In large salad bowl, place salad ingredients. Pour vinaigrette over salad; toss gently to mix.

1 SERVING: Calories 90; Total Fat 7g; Sodium 95mg; Dietary Fiber 1g; Protein 1g. EXCHANGES: 1 Vegetable, 1-1/2 Fat. CARBOHYDRATE CHOICES: 1/2.

Creamy Black and Blue Pasta Salad

PREP TIME: 25 MINUTES (READY IN 1 HOUR 25 MINUTES)
SERVINGS: 4

1 box (7.5 oz) Betty Crocker® Suddenly Salad® ranch and bacon salad mix

⅓ cup mayonnaise or salad dressing

¼ cup sour cream

2 oz blue cheese, crumbled (½ cup)

1 tablespoon fresh lemon juice

1 cup grape tomatoes, cut in half

1 red bell pepper, chopped

¼ cup finely chopped red onion

1 package (6 oz) refrigerated seasoned steak strips, chopped

1 bag (6 oz) fresh baby spinach leaves

1) Fill 3-quart saucepan ⅔ full of water; heat to boiling. Add pasta. Gently boil, uncovered, 12 minutes, stirring occasionally; drain. Rinse with cold water to cool; drain well.

2) Meanwhile, in large bowl, combine seasoning mix from packet, mayonnaise, sour cream, blue cheese and lemon juice. Stir in remaining ingredients except spinach. Refrigerate at least 1 hour.

3) Just before serving, place 2 cups of the spinach on each of 4 plates; divide the pasta salad evenly over the spinach.

1 SERVING: Calories 540; Total Fat 27g; Sodium 950mg; Dietary Fiber 3g; Protein 28g. EXCHANGES: 1-1/2 Starch, 1/2 Other Carbohydrate, 3 Vegetable, 2-1/2 Medium-Fat Meat, 3 Fat. CARBOHYDRATE CHOICES: 3.

Strawberry-Grapefruit Spinach Toss

PREP TIME: 25 MINUTES (READY IN 25 MINUTES)   EASY
SERVINGS: 12

⅓ cup vegetable oil

½ cup sliced almonds

3 tablespoons honey

   Dash ground cinnamon

½ teaspoon grated lime peel

3 tablespoons fresh lime juice

1 teaspoon Dijon mustard

¼ teaspoon salt

1 package (10 oz) fresh spinach, stems removed, torn

2 cups fresh strawberries, sliced

1 grapefruit, peeled, sectioned

1) Line cookie sheet with foil; spray foil with cooking spray. In 7-inch skillet, heat 2 teaspoons of the oil over medium heat. Cook and stir almonds in oil until lightly browned. Add 1 tablespoon of the honey and the cinnamon; cook and stir 1 to 2 minutes longer or until almonds are glazed and golden brown. Transfer to cookie sheet; cool.

2) Meanwhile, in jar with tight-fitting lid, place remaining oil and honey, the lime peel, lime juice, mustard and salt; shake until well blended.

3) In large serving bowl, combine spinach, strawberries and grapefruit. Just before serving, drizzle dressing over salad; toss lightly to coat. Sprinkle with toasted almonds.

1 SERVING: Calories 130; Total Fat 8g; Sodium 80mg; Dietary Fiber 2g; Protein 2g. EXCHANGES: 1/2 Fruit, 1 Vegetable, 1-1/2 Fat. CARBOHYDRATE CHOICES: 1.

Three-Bean Pasta Salad

PREP TIME: 20 MINUTES (READY IN 20 MINUTES)   EASY
SERVINGS: 3 (1-1/3 CUPS EACH)

1 ¼ cups uncooked rotini pasta (4 oz)

1 can (15 oz) Green Giant® three-bean salad, undrained, chilled

4 oz provolone cheese, cut into small cubes (1 cup)

1 tablespoon chopped fresh oregano leaves

1) Cook and drain pasta as directed on package. Rinse with cold water to cool; drain well.

2) In serving bowl, stir pasta and remaining ingredients. Serve immediately, or refrigerate 1 hour before serving.

1 SERVING: Calories 390; Total Fat 11g; Sodium 1030mg; Dietary Fiber 5g; Protein 19g. EXCHANGES: 2-1/2 Starch, 1/2 Other Carbohydrate, 1 Vegetable, 1 Very Lean Meat, 1/2 High-Fat Meat, 1 Fat. CARBOHYDRATE CHOICES: 3-1/2.

Smoked Turkey Salad with Strawberries

PREP TIME: 20 MINUTES (READY IN 20 MINUTES)
SERVINGS: 8

 EASY   LOW FAT

CREAMY HONEY DRESSING

- 1 cup Yoplait® fat free plain yogurt (from 2-lb container)
- ¼ cup honey
- 2 tablespoons chopped fresh parsley
- 1 tablespoon lemon juice
- 2 teaspoons ground mustard

SALAD

- 1 lb smoked turkey or chicken, cut into ¼-inch strips (4 cups)
- 4 oz provolone or Swiss cheese, cut into cubes
- 4 medium celery stalks, sliced (2 cups)
- ½ cup honey-roasted cashews
- 1 quart strawberries, cut in half (4 cups)

  Salad greens, if desired

  Strawberries, if desired

1) In large bowl, mix dressing ingredients until well blended.

2) Add turkey, cheese, celery and honey-roasted cashews; toss gently to coat. Add strawberries; carefully toss until evenly coated. If desired, serve on salad greens; garnish with additional strawberries.

1 SERVING: Calories 250; Total Fat 10g; Sodium 860mg; Dietary Fiber 2g; Protein 17g. EXCHANGES: 1 Fruit, 1 Vegetable, 2-1/2 Lean Meat, 1/2 Fat. CARBOHYDRATE CHOICES: 1-1/2.

Suddenly Hot Bacon Salad

| PREP TIME: | 25 MINUTES (READY IN 25 MINUTES) | EASY |
| SERVINGS: | 4 (1-3/4 CUPS EACH) | |

1 box (7.75 oz) Betty Crocker®
Suddenly Salad® classic salad mix

4 slices bacon, cut into 1-inch pieces

¼ cup sliced onion

3 tablespoons balsamic vinegar

1 tablespoon packed brown sugar

1 tablespoon olive oil or vegetable oil

¼ teaspoon Dijon mustard

4 cups baby spinach

1 pear, cut into bite-size pieces

4 oz blue cheese, crumbled (1 cup)

1) Fill 3-quart saucepan ⅔ full of water; heat to boiling. Add pasta. Gently boil, uncovered, 12 minutes, stirring occasionally; drain. Rinse with cold water to cool; drain well.

2) Meanwhile, in 10-inch nonstick skillet, cook bacon and onion, stirring occasionally, until bacon is crisp. Transfer bacon and onion to large bowl with slotted spoon, reserving bacon drippings. Stir seasoning mix from packet, vinegar, brown sugar, oil and mustard into drippings.

3) In large bowl, toss bacon and onion mixture, spinach, pear and dressing until mixed; stir in cooked pasta. Sprinkle cheese over top of salad. Serve warm.

1 SERVING: Calories 430; Total Fat 16g; Sodium 1530mg; Dietary Fiber 3g; Protein 16g. EXCHANGES: 2-1/2 Starch, 1 Other Carbohydrate, 1/2 Vegetable, 1 High-Fat Meat, 1-1/2 Fat. CARBOHYDRATE CHOICES: 4.

Thai Shrimp and Mango Pasta Salad

PREP TIME: 25 MINUTES (READY IN 25 MINUTES)
SERVINGS: 4 (1-1/4 CUPS EACH)

 EASY

1 box (7.75 oz) Betty Crocker® Suddenly Salad® classic salad mix

3 tablespoons fresh lime juice

2 tablespoons vegetable oil

1 tablespoon sesame oil

1 tablespoon water

2 teaspoons sugar

1 teaspoon soy sauce

¼ teaspoon crushed red pepper flakes

½ lb cooked medium (31 to 35 count) shrimp, peeled, deveined and tail shells removed

½ medium orange or red bell pepper, seeded, cut into bite-size pieces

1 medium mango, seed removed, peeled and cut into bite-size pieces

8 medium green onions, finely chopped (½ cup)

⅓ cup chopped fresh cilantro

¼ cup sesame seed, toasted

1) Fill 3-quart saucepan ⅔ full of water; heat to boiling. Add pasta. Gently boil, uncovered, 12 minutes, stirring occasionally; drain. Rinse with cold water to cool; drain well.

2) In large bowl, combine seasoning mix from packet, lime juice, vegetable oil, sesame oil, water, sugar, soy sauce and red pepper flakes with whisk. Add shrimp, bell pepper, mango, green onions, cilantro and sesame seed. Toss until well combined. Stir in cooked pasta. Cover and refrigerate until ready to serve.

1 SERVING: Calories 450; Total Fat 16g; Sodium 1120mg; Dietary Fiber 4g; Protein 20g. EXCHANGES: 2 Starch, 1/2 Fruit, 1 Other Carbohydrate, 1 Vegetable, 2 Lean Meat, 1-1/2 Fat. CARBOHYDRATE CHOICES: 4.

Bacon 'n Basil Pasta Salad

PREP TIME: 25 MINUTES (READY IN 2 HOURS 25 MINUTES)
SERVINGS: 22 (1/2 CUP EACH)

1 package (16 oz) penne pasta

½ lb sliced bacon

1 pint grape tomatoes, cut in half

2 medium red or green bell peppers
  or 1 of each, chopped (2 cups)

4 medium green onions, sliced (⅓ cup)

⅓ cup red wine vinegar

1 tablespoon Dijon mustard

½ cup olive oil

½ cup chopped fresh basil leaves

1 teaspoon salt

½ teaspoon freshly ground pepper

1) Cook and drain pasta as directed on package. Rinse with cold water to cool; drain.

2) Meanwhile, in 10-inch nonstick skillet, cook bacon over medium heat 5 to 8 minutes until crisp; drain on paper towels. Crumble bacon; refrigerate until serving time.

3) In large bowl, mix pasta, tomatoes, bell peppers and onions. In small bowl, beat vinegar and mustard with whisk. Add oil; beat with whisk until blended. Stir in basil, salt and pepper. Pour over pasta mixture and toss to combine. Cover; refrigerate 2 hours or until chilled.

4) Just before serving, sprinkle bacon over salad and toss to combine.

1 SERVING: Calories 160; Total Fat 7g; Sodium 270mg; Dietary Fiber 1g; Protein 4g. EXCHANGES: 1 Starch, 1/2 Vegetable, 1-1/2 Fat. CARBOHYDRATE CHOICES: 1.

Tomato Basil Pasta Salad

PREP TIME: 25 MINUTES (READY IN 2 HOURS 25 MINUTES)
SERVINGS: 24 (1/2 CUP EACH)

Shreya Sasaki
San Diego, CA
www.recipematcher.com

2 lb plum (Roma) tomatoes, chopped (8 to 10 medium)

4 garlic cloves, finely chopped

1 ½ teaspoons salt

½ teaspoon pepper

½ cup olive or vegetable oil

½ cup chopped fresh basil leaves

8 oz mozzarella cheese, cut into ½-inch cubes (2 cups)

1 package (1 lb) rotini pasta

½ cup grated Parmesan cheese

1) In large bowl, mix tomatoes, garlic, salt, pepper, oil, basil and mozzarella cheese. Cover; refrigerate 2 hours to blend flavors.

2) Meanwhile, cook and drain pasta as directed on package. Rinse with cold water to cool; drain.

3) In large serving bowl, mix cooked pasta and tomato mixture until well combined. Sprinkle Parmesan cheese over top of salad.

1 SERVING: Calories 170; Total Fat 8g; Sodium 240mg; Dietary Fiber 1g; Protein 6g. EXCHANGES: 1 Starch, 1/2 Vegetable, 1/2 High-Fat Meat, 1/2 Fat. CARBOHYDRATE CHOICES: 1.

tip

Before cutting fresh basil, sprinkle a few drops of vegetable oil on the leaves and gently rub to evenly coat. This will prevent them from darkening.

Chinese Chicken Noodle Salad

PREP TIME:	30 MINUTES (READY IN 30 MINUTES)
SERVINGS:	8 (1-1/2 CUPS EACH)

 EASY   LOW FAT

Shreya Sasaki
San Diego, CA
www.recipematcher.com

1 package (16 oz) spaghetti

8 oz fresh snow pea pods (2 cups), sliced diagonally

4 cups shredded cooked chicken

1 cup red bell pepper, cut into bite-size strips

8 medium green onions, sliced (½ cup)

¾ cup teriyaki sauce

2 tablespoons dark sesame oil

1 tablespoon toasted sesame seed

¼ teaspoon salt

¼ teaspoon pepper

½ teaspoon chili oil, if desired

1) In 5-quart Dutch oven, cook spaghetti as directed on package, adding pea pods during last minute of cooking time; drain. Rinse with cold water to cool; drain well.

2) In large bowl, stir together spaghetti with pea pods, chicken, bell pepper and green onions.

3) In small bowl, mix teriyaki sauce, sesame oil, sesame seed, salt, black pepper and chili oil. Pour over spaghetti mixture; toss until coated. Serve at room temperature or refrigerate until chilled.

1 SERVING: Calories 440; Total Fat 10g; Sodium 1450mg; Dietary Fiber 4g; Protein 31g. EXCHANGES: 3-1/2 Starch, 1/2 Vegetable, 2-1/2 Lean Meat. CARBOHYDRATE CHOICES: 4.

tip

For this recipe, we used 4 cups of chicken from a deli rotisserie chicken. If you are roasting your own chicken, a 2-lb chicken yields about 4 cups of shredded, cooked chicken.

Chicken and Black Bean Salad

PREP TIME: 25 MINUTES (READY IN 25 MINUTES)
SERVINGS: 4

 EASY

Jill McKeever
Sulfur Springs, TX
www.simpledailyrecipes.com

1 package (1 lb) boneless skinless chicken breasts

1 teaspoon salt

1 teaspoon pepper

1 tablespoon olive oil or vegetable oil

8 cups torn leaf lettuce (1 medium head)

1 can (15 oz) black beans, drained, rinsed

1 pint grape tomatoes, cut in half (about 2 cups)

1 large carrot, sliced (1 cup)

8 green onions, chopped

1 cup finely shredded Mexican cheese blend (4 oz)

½ cup honey Dijon dressing

1) Sprinkle both sides of the chicken breasts with salt and pepper, then cut into strips.

2) In 12-inch nonstick skillet, heat oil over medium-high heat. Stir in chicken; cook 3 to 5 minutes or until golden brown. Turn chicken strips over; cook 3 to 4 minutes longer until chicken is no longer pink in center. Transfer to paper towel-lined plate.

3) Just before serving, on each of 4 plates, layer one-fourth of lettuce, beans, tomatoes, carrot, green onions, cheese and chicken. Drizzle each salad with 2 tablespoons dressing.

1 SERVING: Calories 480; Total Fat 18g; Sodium 1620mg; Dietary Fiber 13g; Protein 43g. EXCHANGES: 1/2 Starch, 1/2 Other Carbohydrate, 4 Vegetable, 5 Lean Meat, 1/2 Fat. CARBOHYDRATE CHOICES: 2-1/2.

Tuscan Couscous with Lemon Basil Dressing

PREP TIME: 20 MINUTES (READY IN 20 MINUTES)
SERVINGS: 12 (1/2 CUP EACH)

 EASY LOW FAT

COUSCOUS

- 1 cup water
- ¼ teaspoon salt
- ¾ cup uncooked couscous

DRESSING

- ¼ teaspoon finely grated lemon peel
- 2 tablespoons lemon juice
- 2 tablespoons olive oil or vegetable oil
- 1 tablespoon chopped fresh or
  1 teaspoon dried basil leaves
- ¼ teaspoon salt
- 1 garlic clove, finely chopped
- 4 to 5 drops red pepper sauce

SALAD

- 1 can (15 oz) Progresso® cannellini beans, drained, rinsed
- ½ cup chopped unpeeled cucumber
- ¼ cup halved pitted kalamata olives
- 4 medium green onions, sliced (¼ cup)
- 1 cup grape tomatoes, cut in half

1) In 1 quart saucepan, heat water and ¼ teaspoon salt to boiling. Remove from heat; immediately stir in couscous. Cover; let stand 5 minutes. Fluff couscous with fork.

2) Meanwhile, in a small nonmetal bowl, combine all the dressing ingredients; mix well.

3) In large bowl, gently toss the cooked couscous, beans, cucumber, olives and green onions. Pour the dressing over couscous mixture; gently toss until coated.

4) Just before serving, add tomatoes; toss gently. Serve warm.

1 SERVING: Calories 100; Total Fat 3g; Sodium 130mg; Dietary Fiber 2g; Protein 4g. EXCHANGES: 1 Starch, 1/2 Vegetable, 1/2 Fat. CARBOHYDRATE CHOICES: 1.

tip

This salad is also delicious when it is served cold. For larger size couscous with a chewy texture, use Israeli couscous as seen in the photo.

Chicken and Sugar Snap Peas Pasta Salad

PREP TIME: 20 MINUTES (READY IN 20 MINUTES)
SERVINGS: 4

⊖ EASY

3 cups uncooked mini lasagna (mafalda) noodles (6 oz)

2 cups fresh sugar snap peas, trimmed, halved

¾ cup creamy Caesar dressing

2 tablespoons chopped fresh mint

1 tablespoon red wine vinegar

½ teaspoon salt

2 cups chopped deli rotisserie chicken (from 2-lb chicken)

¼ cup chopped red onion

1) In 3-quart saucepan, cook noodles as directed on package, adding peas during last minute of cooking. Rinse with cold water; drain. In large bowl, mix dressing, mint, vinegar and salt. Stir in chicken, onion, noodles and peas. Serve immediately, or cover and refrigerate until ready to serve.

1 SERVING: Calories 560; Total Fat 32g; Sodium 1110mg; Dietary Fiber 3g; Protein 28g. EXCHANGES: 2-1/2 Starch, 1 Vegetable, 2-1/2 Medium-Fat Meat, 3-1/2 Fat. CARBOHYDRATE CHOICES: 3.

Tropical Quinoa Salad

PREP TIME: 25 MINUTES (READY IN 1 HOUR 25 MINUTES)
SERVINGS: 10 (1/2 CUP EACH)

1 cup uncooked quinoa

2 cups water

1 bag (6 oz) dried pineapple, chopped (about 1 cup)

1 bag (5 oz) dried mango, chopped (about 1 cup)

1 bag (2 oz) chopped macadamia nuts (about ½ cup)

½ cup sweetened dried cranberries

2 tablespoons orange marmalade

¼ cup orange juice

¼ cup flaked coconut

10 leaves Bibb lettuce

1) In 2-quart saucepan, heat quinoa and water to boiling; reduce heat to low. Cover; cook 10 to 15 minutes or until water is absorbed. Meanwhile, in large bowl, mix remaining ingredients except coconut and lettuce. Stir in quinoa. Cover; refrigerate at least 1 hour or until serving time.

2) Sprinkle coconut in ungreased heavy skillet. Cook over medium-low heat 6 to 10 minutes, stirring frequently until browning begins, then stirring constantly until light brown. Cool. To serve, spoon ½ cup salad onto each lettuce leaf; sprinkle with toasted coconut.

1 SERVING: Calories 250; Total Fat 7g; Sodium 25mg; Dietary Fiber 3g; Protein 3g. EXCHANGES: 1 Starch, 2 Other Carbohydrate, 1 Fat. CARBOHYDRATE CHOICES: 3.

Melon Salad with Grapefruit Syrup

PREP TIME:	20 MINUTES (READY IN 50 MINUTES)
SERVINGS:	10 (1/2 CUP EACH)

 EASY   LOW FAT

½ cup sugar

½ cup fresh or bottled grapefruit juice

2 teaspoons cornstarch

1 tablespoon thinly sliced fresh mint leaves

½ small honeydew melon, cut into ½-inch pieces (about 2 ¼ cups)

½ small cantaloupe, cut into ½-inch pieces (about 2 ¼ cups)

2 medium bananas, cut in half lengthwise, sliced

Fresh mint sprigs

1) In 1-quart saucepan, mix sugar, grapefruit juice and cornstarch. Heat to boiling over medium heat, stirring constantly, until thickened. Stir in sliced mint. Cover; refrigerate at least 30 minutes.

2) Divide honeydew, cantaloupe and bananas among 10 individual serving dishes; spoon syrup over fruit. Garnish with mint sprigs.

1 SERVING: Calories 100; Total Fat 0g; Sodium 15mg; Dietary Fiber 1g; Protein 0g. EXCHANGES: 1/2 Starch, 1 Other Carbohydrate. CARBOHYDRATE CHOICES: 1-1/2.

Mimosa Fruit Cups

PREP TIME: 15 MINUTES (READY IN 1 HOUR 15 MINUTES)
SERVINGS: 8 (3/4 CUP EACH)

 EASY LOW FAT

¼ cup sugar

1 teaspoon grated orange peel

1 cup fresh orange juice

1 large orange, peeled, cut into bite-size pieces

1 large red apple, cut into bite-size pieces

1 large pear, cut into bite-size pieces

1 cup seedless green grapes

1 large banana, sliced

1 ½ cups champagne or sparkling white grape juice

Fresh mint sprigs

1) In large bowl, stir sugar, orange peel and orange juice until sugar is dissolved. Gently stir in orange, apple, pear and grapes until coated. Cover; refrigerate at least 1 hour or overnight.

2) Just before serving, stir in banana and champagne. Spoon about ¾ cup fruit with juice into each of 8 footed dessert cups. Garnish with mint.

1 SERVING: Calories 130; Total Fat 0g; Sodium 0mg; Dietary Fiber 3g; Protein 1g. EXCHANGES: 1/2 Starch, 1/2 Fruit, 1 Other Carbohydrate. CARBOHYDRATE CHOICES: 2.

Gazpacho Pasta Salad

PREP TIME: 25 MINUTES (READY IN 2 HOURS 25 MINUTES)
SERVINGS: 22 (1/2 CUP EACH)

1 package (16 oz) rotini pasta

4 large tomatoes, seeded, chopped (about 4 cups)

1 large unpeeled cucumber, seeded, chopped (about 2 cups)

½ medium red onion, chopped (about 1 cup)

1 cup spicy hot vegetable juice

⅓ cup red wine vinegar

2 cloves garlic, finely chopped

2 teaspoons salt or to taste

1 teaspoon red pepper sauce

⅔ cup olive oil

1 cup chopped fresh cilantro

1) Cook and drain pasta as directed on package. Rinse with cold water to cool; drain. In large bowl, mix pasta, tomatoes, cucumber and onion.

2) In small bowl, mix vegetable juice, vinegar, garlic, salt and red pepper sauce. Add oil; beat with whisk until blended. Stir in cilantro. Pour over pasta mixture and toss to combine. Cover; refrigerate 2 hours or until chilled. Stir before serving.

1 SERVING: Calories 160; Total Fat 7g; Sodium 330mg; Dietary Fiber 1g; Protein 3g. EXCHANGES: 1 Starch, 1/2 Vegetable, 1-1/2 Fat. CARBOHYDRATE CHOICES: 1.

Grilled Vegetable Salad

PREP TIME: 30 MINUTES (READY IN 30 MINUTES)
SERVINGS: 6 (1-1/2 CUPS EACH)

 EASY

4 cups uncooked radiatore (nuggets) pasta (8 oz)

4 medium tomatoes, chopped

3 tablespoons chopped fresh oregano leaves

2 cloves garlic, finely chopped

¼ cup extra-virgin olive oil

¼ cup white wine vinegar

1 teaspoon sugar

½ teaspoon salt

¼ teaspoon coarse ground black pepper

1 yellow bell pepper, quartered

1 red bell pepper, quartered

1 medium zucchini, halved

1 large onion, cut into ¼-inch slices

Olive oil cooking spray

¼ cup crumbled feta cheese (1 oz)

1) Heat gas or charcoal grill. In 5-quart Dutch oven, cook pasta as directed on package. Drain and return to Dutch oven; cover to keep warm. In large bowl, toss tomatoes, oregano and garlic. In small bowl, mix oil, vinegar, sugar, salt and pepper. Add to tomato mixture; mix well. Set aside.

2) Place bell peppers, zucchini and onion on ungreased cookie sheet. Spray vegetables with cooking spray. Lightly sprinkle with salt, if desired. Place vegetables directly on grill over medium heat. Cook uncovered 8 to 14 minutes, turning frequently. Remove vegetables from grill as they become crisp-tender. Coarsely chop vegetables. Add to tomato mixture; mix well. Add mixture to pasta in Dutch oven; toss gently. Spoon into serving bowl; sprinkle with cheese.

1 SERVING: Calories 310; Total Fat 12g; Sodium 410mg; Dietary Fiber 5g; Protein 8g. EXCHANGES: 2 Starch, 1/2 Other Carbohydrate, 1 Vegetable, 2 Fat. CARBOHYDRATE CHOICES: 3.

Gelatin Pretzel Salad Dressed Up for Thanksgiving

PREP TIME: 20 MINUTES (READY IN 10 HOURS 20 MINUTES)
SERVINGS: 16

 EASY

Alvin Singer
Cleveland, OH
Celebrate the Season—Thanksgiving Cooking Contest

2 ½ cups pretzel sticks

3 tablespoons packed brown sugar

½ teaspoon pumpkin pie spice

⅔ cup unsalted butter, melted

2 cups boiling water

2 packages (4-serving size each) cranberry-flavored gelatin

1 ¼ to 1 ½ cups cold water

1 can (11 oz) mandarin orange segments, drained, juice reserved

1 package (8 oz) cream cheese, softened

1 cup granulated sugar

1 container (8 oz) frozen whipped topping, thawed

1) Heat oven to 350°F. Spray 13x9-inch (3-quart) glass baking dish with cooking spray.

2) Place pretzels in resealable food-storage plastic bag; smash with rolling pin or flat side of meat mallet until crushed. In medium bowl, mix crushed pretzels, brown sugar and pumpkin pie spice. Stir in butter. Press mixture onto bottom of baking dish. Bake 9 to 11 minutes or until set. Cool on cooling rack.

3) Meanwhile, in large heatproof bowl, pour boiling water on gelatin; stir until gelatin is dissolved. Add enough cold water to the reserved juice to equal 2 cups, then stir into the gelatin. Refrigerate until partially set, about 1 hour 45 minutes.

4) In medium bowl, beat cream cheese and granulated sugar with electric mixer on medium speed until light and fluffy. Fold in whipped topping. Spread the mixture evenly over pretzel crust.

5) Finely chop mandarin orange segments; gently stir into partially set gelatin. Carefully pour over cream cheese layer. Refrigerate 8 hours or overnight. Cut into squares.

1 SERVING: Calories 300; Total Fat 15g; Sodium 230mg; Dietary Fiber 0g; Protein 3g. EXCHANGES: 2 Other Carbohydrate, 1/2 Low-Fat Milk, 2-1/2 Fat. CARBOHYDRATE CHOICES: 2-1/2.

On-the-Go Taco Salad

PREP TIME: 25 MINUTES (READY IN 25 MINUTES)
SERVINGS: 12

 EASY

CHILI

- 1 ½ lb lean (at least 80%) ground beef
- 1 large onion, coarsely chopped (1 cup)
- 1 package (1 oz) chili seasoning mix
- 1 can (15.5 oz) red beans, drained
- 1 can (8 oz) tomato sauce
- 12 bags (1 ¼ oz each) corn chips

TOPPINGS

- 1 ½ cups shredded cheese (6 oz)
- 1 ½ cups shredded lettuce
- ¾ cup sour cream, if desired

1) In 4-quart nonstick Dutch oven, cook beef and onion over medium-high heat 5 to 7 minutes, stirring occasionally, until beef is thoroughly cooked; drain. Stir in chili seasoning mix, beans and tomato sauce. Reduce heat to low. Cover; cook 10 minutes, stirring occasionally, until thoroughly heated.

2) Let each guest serve themselves by opening 1 bag of corn chips and topping with generous ⅓ cup beef mixture, some cheese, shredded lettuce and sour cream.

1 SERVING: Calories 400; Total Fat 23g; Sodium 560mg; Dietary Fiber 4g; Protein 18g. EXCHANGES: 2 Starch, 1-1/2 Medium-Fat Meat, 3 Fat. CARBOHYDRATE CHOICES: 2.

Honey-Dijon Chef's Salad

PREP TIME: 25 MINUTES (READY IN 25 MINUTES)
SERVINGS: 6 (1-3/4 CUPS EACH)

 EASY

- 1 bag (5 oz) mixed spring greens
- ¾ cup honey Dijon dressing
- 1 package (8 oz) diced cooked ham (about 1 ½ cups)
- 6 oz Swiss cheese, cut into ¼-inch cubes (about 1 cup)
- ¾ cup canned garbanzo beans, drained
- 1 small cucumber, cut in half lengthwise, then sliced (about 1 cup)
- 1 cup halved grape tomatoes
- ¼ cup roasted salted sunflower nuts
- 4 medium green onions, chopped (¼ cup)

1) Place greens on large platter; drizzle with dressing. Arrange ham, cheese, beans, cucumber and tomatoes in stripe pattern over greens. Sprinkle with sunflower nuts and onions.

1 SERVING: Calories 360; Total Fat 25g; Sodium 870mg; Dietary Fiber 3g; Protein 20g. EXCHANGES: 1/2 Starch, 2 Vegetable, 2 Lean Meat, 3-1/2 Fat. CARBOHYDRATE CHOICES: 1.

Layered Caribbean Chicken Salad

PREP TIME:	30 MINUTES (READY IN 30 MINUTES)	EASY
SERVINGS:	10 (1-1/4 CUPS EACH)	

SALAD

- 4 cups torn romaine lettuce
- 3 cups cut-up cooked chicken
- 1 can (15 oz) Progresso® black beans, drained, rinsed
- 1 ½ cups chopped tomatoes
- 2 ripe medium mangoes, seed removed, peeled and chopped

DRESSING

- ⅓ cup vegetable oil
- ⅓ cup lime juice
- ¼ cup chopped fresh cilantro
- 2 tablespoons sugar
- ¾ teaspoon salt
- ¼ teaspoon ground cinnamon, if desired
- 2 cloves garlic, finely chopped
- Red pepper sauce, if desired

1) In 3-quart glass trifle bowl, layer lettuce, chicken, black beans, tomatoes and mangoes.

2) In jar with tight-fitting lid, shake dressing ingredients. Drizzle over salad; serve immediately. Or, cover and refrigerate salad and dressing separately up to 4 hours; drizzle salad with dressing just before serving.

1 SERVING: Calories 250; Total Fat 12g; Sodium 350mg; Dietary Fiber 5g; Protein 15g. EXCHANGES: 1 Starch, 1 Vegetable, 1-1/2 Lean Meat, 1-1/2 Fat. CARBOHYDRATE CHOICES: 1.

Mix up the flavor of this salad by substituting fresh mint for the cilantro and pineapple or papaya for the mangoes.

Caesar Tuna "Noodle" Salad

PREP TIME: 25 MINUTES (READY IN 1 HOUR 25 MINUTES)
SERVINGS: 4 (1-1/2 CUPS EACH)

1 box (7.25 oz) Betty Crocker® Suddenly Salad® Caesar salad mix

1 package (9 oz) Green Giant® frozen baby sweet peas

¼ cup olive oil

¼ cup mayonnaise or salad dressing

2 tablespoons milk

1 medium stalk celery, sliced (½ cup)

4 medium green onions, thinly sliced (¼ cup)

1 can (12 oz) albacore tuna, drained

¼ cup shredded Parmesan cheese (1 oz)

12 leaves romaine lettuce

1 lemon, cut into 8 wedges

1) Fill 3-quart saucepan ⅔ full of water; heat to boiling. Add pasta. Gently boil, uncovered, 12 minutes, stirring occasionally and adding peas during last 2 minutes of cooking. Drain. Rinse with cold water to cool; drain well.

2) Meanwhile, in large bowl, combine the seasoning and crouton blend, oil, mayonnaise and milk. Stir in the celery and green onions. Add the tuna and cheese; mix well. Stir in the cooked pasta.

3) Cover; refrigerate for about 1 hour or until chilled. Place 3 leaves of lettuce on each of 4 plates. Divide salad evenly over lettuce; top each with 2 lemon wedges.

1 SERVING: Calories 590; Total Fat 29g; Sodium 1160mg; Dietary Fiber 5g; Protein 34g. EXCHANGES: 2 Starch, 1/2 Other Carbohydrate, 3 Vegetable, 3 Lean Meat, 4 Fat. CARBOHYDRATE CHOICES: 3.

Texas-Style Pasta Salad

PREP TIME: 30 MINUTES (READY IN 30 MINUTES)
SERVINGS: 20 (1/2 CUP EACH)

 EASY

1 package (16 oz) penne pasta

1 can (4 oz) Old El Paso® whole green chiles, drained, diced

1 medium red bell pepper, chopped (1 cup)

8 oz Cheddar cheese, cut into ½-inch cubes (1 ¾ cups)

3 medium green onions, chopped (3 tablespoons)

½ cup chopped fresh cilantro

1 cup Old El Paso® medium taco sauce

¼ cup vegetable oil

2 tablespoons lime juice

½ to 1 teaspoon ground cumin

1 cup nacho-flavored tortilla chips, coarsely crushed

1) Cook and drain pasta as directed on package. Rinse with cold water to cool; drain.

2) In large bowl, mix pasta, chiles, bell pepper, cheese, onions and cilantro.

3) In small bowl, mix taco sauce, oil, lime juice and cumin. Pour over pasta mixture and toss gently to combine. Top with crushed tortilla chips. Serve immediately.

1 SERVING: Calories 200; Total Fat 8g; Sodium 280mg; Dietary Fiber 1g; Protein 7g. EXCHANGES: 1-1/2 Starch, 1/2 High-Fat Meat, 1/2 Fat. CARBOHYDRATE CHOICES: 1-1/2.

Tuscan Pasta Salad

PREP TIME: 25 MINUTES (READY IN 2 HOURS 25 MINUTES)
SERVINGS: 8 (1-1/2 CUPS EACH)

3 cups uncooked bow-tie (farfalle) pasta (8 oz)

4 oz hard salami, cut into thin strips about 1x¼ inch

1 medium red bell pepper, chopped (1 cup)

½ medium red onion, chopped (about 1 cup)

⅓ cup red wine vinegar

2 cloves garlic, finely chopped

¼ teaspoon pepper

½ cup olive oil

1 package (9 oz) romaine salad mix or 6 cups torn romaine

½ cup shredded Parmesan cheese (2 oz)

1) Cook and drain pasta as directed on package. Rinse with cold water to cool; drain. In large bowl, mix pasta, salami, bell pepper and onion.

2) In small bowl, mix vinegar, garlic and pepper. Add oil; beat with whisk until blended. Pour over pasta mixture and toss to combine. Cover; refrigerate 2 hours or until chilled.

3) Just before serving, add the romaine and toss to combine. Sprinkle with the cheese.

1 SERVING: Calories 340; Total Fat 20g; Sodium 510mg; Dietary Fiber 2g; Protein 11g. EXCHANGES: 1 Starch, 1/2 Other Carbohydrate, 1/2 Vegetable, 1/2 Lean Meat, 1/2 High-Fat Meat, 3 Fat. CARBOHYDRATE CHOICES: 2.

Gorgonzola Chicken Salad

| PREP TIME: | 30 MINUTES (READY IN 30 MINUTES) |
| SERVINGS: | 8 (1-1/2 CUPS EACH) |

e EASY   **lf** LOW FAT

---

3 cups uncooked bow-tie (farfalle) pasta (8 oz)

²⁄₃ cup buttermilk

¹⁄₃ cup light mayonnaise

1 large clove garlic, finely chopped

2 tablespoons white wine vinegar

½ teaspoon Worcestershire sauce

¼ teaspoon salt

1 deli rotisserie chicken (2 lb), shredded (about 4 cups)

2 cups lightly packed fresh baby spinach leaves (about 3 oz)

1 lb fresh strawberries, cut in half

¾ cup crumbled Gorgonzola cheese (3 oz)

1) Cook and drain pasta as directed on package. Rinse with cold water to cool; drain.

2) In small bowl, slowly beat buttermilk, mayonnaise, garlic, vinegar, Worcestershire sauce and salt with whisk until smooth.

3) In large bowl, toss pasta and chicken. Just before serving, pour buttermilk dressing over pasta mixture and toss to combine. Add spinach and toss gently. Spoon the salad onto a serving platter or in bowls; top with strawberries and cheese.

1 SERVING: Calories 320; Total Fat 10g; Sodium 640mg; Dietary Fiber 2g; Protein 26g. EXCHANGES: 2 Starch, 1-1/2 Lean Meat, 1 Medium-Fat Meat. CARBOHYDRATE CHOICES: 2.

Southwestern Chicken Pasta Salad

PREP TIME: 30 MINUTES (READY IN 30 MINUTES)
SERVINGS: 7 (1 CUP EACH)

 EASY

1 cup uncooked small pasta shells (4 oz)

½ cup Green Giant® Valley Fresh Steamers™ frozen sweet peas

1 ½ cups cubed cooked chicken

1 cup chopped red bell pepper

1 cup chopped yellow summer squash

½ cup sliced carrot

½ cup sliced green onions

½ cup fresh whole kernel corn

1 can (15 oz) Progresso® black beans, drained, rinsed

¼ cup rice vinegar

3 tablespoons olive oil

2 teaspoons Dijon mustard

½ teaspoon ground cumin

¼ teaspoon salt

¼ teaspoon red pepper sauce

1) Cook and drain pasta as directed on package, adding peas during last 4 minutes of cooking time. Rinse with cold water to cool; drain.

2) In large bowl, mix pasta, peas, chicken, bell pepper, squash, carrot, onions, corn and beans. In small bowl, beat remaining ingredients with whisk until blended.

3) Pour dressing over pasta mixture, toss gently to coat. Serve immediately, or cover and refrigerate until chilled.

1 SERVING: Calories 173; Total Fat 7g; Sodium 280mg; Dietary Fiber 4g. EXCHANGES: 1 Starch, 1/2 Vegetable, 1 Fat, 1/2 Lean Meat. CARBOHYDRATE CHOICES: 1.

Heartwarming Soups & Chilies

Ladle up a hearty, warm bowl of comfort for a satisfying lunch or dinner any day of the week!

SPICY ASIAN CARROT SOUP
PG. 88

BARBECUE CHILI WITH CORN
PG. 99

SOUTHWESTERN CHICKEN SOUP
PG. 105

CURRIED PUMPKIN-VEGETABLE SOUP
PG. 96

Chicken and Barley Soup

PREP TIME: 15 MINUTES (READY IN 35 MINUTES)
SERVINGS: 6 (1-1/3 CUPS EACH)

 EASY   LOW FAT

- 1 carton (32 oz) Progresso® chicken broth (4 cups)
- 1 can (14.5 oz) diced tomatoes, undrained
- 2 medium carrots, sliced (1 cup)
- 2 medium stalks celery, sliced (1 cup)
- 1 cup sliced fresh mushrooms (about 3 oz)
- ⅓ cup uncooked quick-cooking barley
- 1 teaspoon dried minced onion
- 2 cups chopped deli rotisserie chicken (from 2- to 2 ½ -lb chicken)

tip

Be sure to use quick-cooking barley for this dish, because regular barley needs to cook longer than this recipe allows.

1) In 3-quart saucepan, mix all ingredients except chicken. Heat to boiling over medium-high heat. Reduce heat to medium. Cover; simmer 15 to 20 minutes or until barley is tender.

2) Add chicken. Cover; cook about 3 minutes or until chicken is hot.

1 SERVING: Calories 180; Total Fat 4.5g; Sodium 1000mg; Dietary Fiber 4g; Protein 19g. EXCHANGES: 1 Starch, 2 Lean Meat. CARBOHYDRATE CHOICES: 1.

Fish Chowder

PREP TIME: 30 MINUTES (READY IN 30 MINUTES)
SERVINGS: 5 (1-1/2 CUPS EACH)

e EASY **lf** LOW FAT

2 teaspoons canola oil

1 small onion, chopped (¼ cup)

1 medium stalk celery, chopped (½ cup)

2 cups frozen potatoes O'Brien with onions and peppers

1 can (14.75 oz) Green Giant® cream style sweet corn

1 ¾ cups Progresso® reduced-sodium chicken broth (from 32-oz carton)

1 ¼ lb firm white fish fillets (such as cod or pollock), skin removed

1 cup fat-free (skim) milk

2 teaspoons cornstarch

1) In 3-quart saucepan, heat oil over medium heat. Add onion and celery; cook 2 to 3 minutes, stirring occasionally, until tender.

2) Stir in potatoes, corn and broth. Heat to boiling. Reduce heat; simmer, uncovered, about 5 minutes or until potatoes are tender.

3) Add whole fish fillets. Cover; cook 5 to 7 minutes or until fish flakes easily with fork. In measuring cup, mix milk and cornstarch; stir into chowder. Cook, stirring constantly, until mixture boils and thickens.

1 SERVING: Calories 260; Total Fat 4g; Sodium 580mg; Dietary Fiber 2g; Protein 27g. EXCHANGES: 1-1/2 Starch, 1/2 Other Carbohydrate, 3 Very Lean Meat. CARBOHYDRATE CHOICES: 2.

Spicy Asian Carrot Soup

PREP TIME: 25 MINUTES (READY IN 8 HOURS 40 MINUTES)
SERVINGS: 7 (1 CUP EACH)

 LOW FAT

4 cups sliced carrots (¾ to 1 inch thick; about 6 large)

1 medium yellow onion, chopped (½ cup)

3 cloves garlic, cut in half

1 piece (1 inch) gingerroot, peeled, sliced

2 tablespoons rice vinegar

2 tablespoons soy sauce

2 teaspoons honey

¼ to ½ teaspoon crushed red pepper flakes

½ teaspoon salt

¼ teaspoon pepper

1 carton (32 oz) vegetable broth

1 cup half-and-half

Chopped fresh cilantro leaves

1) Spray 3 ½- to 4-quart slow cooker with cooking spray. In slow cooker, place all ingredients except half-and-half and cilantro; stir well. Cover; cook on Low heat setting 8 to 9 hours or until carrots are very tender.

2) Carefully ladle 4 ½ cups soup mixture into blender. Cover; blend on low speed until smooth. Transfer to large bowl. Repeat with remaining soup mixture. Return soup to slow cooker. Stir in ½ cup of the half-and-half. Increase heat setting to High. Cover; cook 15 to 20 minutes or until the soup is hot.

3) Ladle soup into serving bowls. To garnish, drizzle about 1 tablespoon of the remaining half-and-half over top of each bowl; swirl gently with tip of knife. Sprinkle with cilantro.

1 SERVING: Calories 100; Total Fat 4g; Sodium 1000mg; Dietary Fiber 2g; Protein 2g. EXCHANGES: 1/2 Other Carbohydrate, 1/2 Vegetable, 1 Fat. CARBOHYDRATE CHOICES: 1.

Two-Bean Minestrone

PREP TIME: 10 MINUTES (READY IN 8 HOURS 25 MINUTES)
SERVINGS: 6 (1-1/2 CUPS EACH)

 EASY   LOW FAT

1 can (15 oz) Progresso® dark red kidney beans, drained

1 can (15 oz) Progresso® chick peas (garbanzo beans), drained

1 bag (12 oz) Green Giant® Valley Fresh Steamers™ frozen mixed vegetables

1 can (14.5 oz) diced tomatoes with basil, garlic and oregano, undrained

1 can (11.5 oz) vegetable juice

1 cup Progresso® chicken broth (from 32-oz carton)

½ cup uncooked elbow macaroni

6 teaspoons refrigerated basil pesto (from 7-oz container)

1) Spray 3- to 4-quart slow cooker with cooking spray. Mix all ingredients except macaroni and pesto in cooker. Cover and cook on Low heat setting 8 to 10 hours.

2) Stir in macaroni. Cover; cook on Low heat setting about 15 minutes longer or until macaroni is tender. Top each serving with 1 teaspoon of pesto.

1 SERVING: Calories 350; Total Fat 5g; Sodium 720mg; Dietary Fiber 13g; Protein 17g. EXCHANGES: 3 Starch, 1/2 Other Carbohydrate, 1 Vegetable, 1 Lean Meat. CARBOHYDRATE CHOICES: 4.

Vegetable and Bean Chili

PREP TIME: 1 HOUR (READY IN 1 HOUR)
SERVINGS: 6

 LOW FAT

1 tablespoon olive or vegetable oil

1 large onion, coarsely chopped (1 cup)

2 teaspoons finely chopped garlic

1 bag (1 lb) frozen broccoli, cauliflower and carrots

1 can (15 to 16 oz) red beans, drained, rinsed

1 can (15 oz) Progresso® chick peas (garbanzo beans), drained, rinsed

2 cans (14.5 oz each) diced tomatoes with green chiles, undrained

1 can (8 oz) tomato sauce

2 cups Green Giant® Valley Fresh Steamers™ Niblets® frozen corn

2 tablespoons chili powder

1 tablespoon ground cumin

¾ teaspoon salt

⅛ teaspoon ground red pepper (cayenne)

1) In 4 ½- to 5-quart Dutch oven, heat oil over medium-high heat. Add onion and garlic; cook 4 to 5 minutes, stirring frequently, until onions are softened.

2) Stir in remaining ingredients. Heat to boiling. Reduce heat to medium-low; cover and cook 15 to 20 minutes, stirring occasionally, until chili is hot and vegetables are crisp-tender.

1 SERVING: Calories 360; Total Fat 5g; Sodium 950mg; Dietary Fiber 15g; Protein 16g. EXCHANGES: 2-1/2 Starch, 1 Other Carbohydrate, 2 Vegetable, 1/2 Very Lean Meat, 1/2 Fat. CARBOHYDRATE CHOICES: 4.

tip

Break out of the box by trying this chili with any combo of your favorite vegetables. Other varieties of canned beans work well in this recipe, too.

German Sausage and Cabbage Soup

PREP TIME: 30 MINUTES (READY IN 30 MINUTES)
SERVINGS: 5 (1-1/2 CUPS EACH)

 EASY

1 tablespoon butter or margarine

3 cups coleslaw mix (from 16-oz bag)

1 medium onion, coarsely chopped (½ cup)

1 stalk celery, sliced (½ cup)

½ teaspoon caraway seed

¾ lb cooked kielbasa, quartered lengthwise, then cut into ½-inch slices

3 cups frozen southern-style diced hash brown potatoes (from 32-oz bag)

3 ½ cups Progresso® chicken broth (from 32-oz carton)

¼ teaspoon coarse ground black pepper

1) In large saucepan or Dutch oven, melt butter over medium heat. Cook coleslaw mix, onion, celery and caraway seed in butter 2 to 3 minutes, stirring frequently, until vegetables are crisp-tender.

2) Stir in remaining ingredients. Heat to boiling; reduce heat. Cover; simmer 5 to 10 minutes, stirring occasionally, until potatoes are tender and soup is thoroughly heated.

1 SERVING: Calories 370; Total Fat 21g; Sodium 1600mg; Dietary Fiber 4g; Protein 12g. EXCHANGES: 1 Starch, 1/2 Other Carbohydrate, 2 Vegetable, 1 Medium-Fat Meat, 3 Fat. CARBOHYDRATE CHOICES: 2.

Vegetarian Noodle Soup

PREP TIME: 30 MINUTES (READY IN 30 MINUTES)
SERVINGS: 5 (1-1/2 CUPS EACH)

 EASY LOW FAT

2 cups Green Giant® Valley Fresh Steamers™ frozen mixed vegetables (from 12-oz bag)

1 package (9 oz) Green Giant® Simply Steam® frozen baby lima beans

1 medium stalk celery, sliced (½ cup)

1 small onion, chopped (⅓ cup)

5 ½ cups water

½ teaspoon salt

½ teaspoon dried basil leaves

⅛ teaspoon dried thyme leaves

⅛ teaspoon pepper

2 vegetable bouillon cubes

1 ½ cups uncooked medium egg noodles (3 oz)

1) In 4- to 5-quart saucepan, mix all ingredients except the noodles. Heat to boiling over high heat.

2) Stir in noodles. Return to boiling; reduce heat to medium-low. Cover; simmer 8 to 10 minutes or until vegetables and noodles are tender, stirring occasionally.

1 SERVING: Calories 140; Total Fat 1g; Sodium 890mg; Dietary Fiber 4g; Protein 6g. EXCHANGES: 1-1/2 Starch, 1 Vegetable. CARBOHYDRATE CHOICES: 2.

Cheesy Tuna-Vegetable Chowder

PREP TIME: 20 MINUTES (READY IN 20 MINUTES)
SERVINGS: 4 (1-1/4 CUPS EACH)

 EASY

¼ cup butter or margarine

½ cup chopped onion (1 medium)

¼ cup all-purpose flour

½ teaspoon ground mustard

⅛ teaspoon pepper

2 cups milk

1 cup Progresso® chicken broth
(from 32-oz carton)

2 cups Green Giant® Valley Fresh
Steamers™ frozen mixed vegetables

¼ teaspoon dried marjoram leaves,
crushed

1 cup shredded Cheddar and
American cheese blend (4 oz)

2 cans (5 oz each) Progresso® tuna,
drained, flaked

1) In 3-quart saucepan, melt butter over medium heat. Add onion; cook and stir until tender. Reduce heat to low. Stir in flour, mustard and pepper; cook and stir until mixture is smooth and bubbly.

2) Gradually stir in milk and broth. Stir in frozen vegetables and marjoram. Heat to boiling over medium heat, stirring occasionally. Reduce heat to low; cover and simmer 3 to 5 minutes or until vegetables are crisp-tender.

1 SERVING: Calories 450; Total Fat 27g; Sodium 950mg; Dietary Fiber 4g; Protein 24g. EXCHANGES: 1 Other Carbohydrate, 1/2 Low-Fat Milk, 1 Vegetable, 3 Medium-Fat Meat,2 Fat. CARBOHYDRATE CHOICES: 2.

Italian Vegetable Soup with White Beans

PREP TIME: 5 MINUTES (READY IN 8 HOURS 20 MINUTES)
SERVINGS: 6 (1-1/3 CUPS EACH)

 EASY   LOW FAT

2 cans (19 oz each) Progresso® cannellini beans, drained, rinsed

1 bag (1 lb) frozen mixed vegetables, thawed

1 can (14.5 oz) diced tomatoes with basil, garlic and oregano, undrained

1 bottle (12 oz) vegetable juice

½ teaspoon salt

1 cup water

½ cup uncooked penne or mostaccioli pasta (1 ½ oz)

¼ cup basil pesto

1) Spray 3- to 4-quart slow cooker with cooking spray. In slow cooker, mix all ingredients except pasta and pesto.

2) Cover; cook on Low heat setting 8 to 9 hours.

3) About 20 minutes before serving, stir pasta into soup. Increase heat setting to High. Cover; cook 15 to 20 minutes longer or until pasta is tender. Top each serving with 2 teaspoons pesto.

1 SERVING: Calories 330; Total Fat 6g; Sodium 1020mg; Dietary Fiber 12g; Protein 17g. EXCHANGES: 1-1/2 Starch, 1-1/2 Other Carbohydrate, 1 Vegetable, 1 Lean Meat, 1/2 Medium-Fat Meat. CARBOHYDRATE CHOICES: 3.

Curried Squash Soup

PREP TIME: 30 MINUTES (READY IN 30 MINUTES)
SERVINGS: 5 (1 CUP EACH)

 EASY LOW FAT

1 tablespoon olive oil or butter

1 medium onion, chopped (½ cup)

1 clove garlic, finely chopped

1 ¾ cups Progresso® reduced-sodium chicken broth (from 32-oz carton)

¼ cup apple juice

2 boxes (10 oz each) frozen winter squash, thawed

2 teaspoons curry powder

½ teaspoon coarse (kosher or sea) salt

¼ cup half-and-half

1) In 4-quart saucepan, heat oil over medium heat. Add onion and garlic; cook 3 to 5 minutes, stirring frequently, until tender.

2) Stir in broth, apple juice, squash, curry powder and salt. Heat to boiling, stirring occasionally. Simmer, uncovered, 5 minutes, stirring occasionally.

3) Stir in half-and-half. Cook 3 to 5 minutes, stirring occasionally, until hot (do not boil).

1 SERVING: Calories 110; Total Fat 4g; Sodium 430mg; Dietary Fiber 2g; Protein 3g. EXCHANGES: 1/2 Other Carbohydrate, 1 Vegetable, 1 Fat. CARBOHYDRATE CHOICES: 1.

Chicken and Pastina Soup

PREP TIME: 30 MINUTES (READY IN 45 MINUTES)
SERVINGS: 10 (1-1/2 CUPS EACH)

LOW FAT

2 lb boneless skinless chicken breasts

2 cartons (32 oz each) Progresso® chicken broth (8 cups)

1 tablespoon olive oil

½ cup chopped onion (1 medium)

½ cup diced carrot (1 medium)

½ cup diced celery (1 medium stalk)

1 cup crushed tomatoes (from 28-oz can)

½ teaspoon gray salt or sea salt

¼ teaspoon freshly ground black pepper

1 dried bay leaf

1 cup uncooked acini di pepe pasta or other small round pasta (8 oz)

2 cups chopped, lightly packed mustard greens, spinach, Swiss chard or other greens

⅓ cup shredded Parmesan cheese

1) Place chicken in 12-inch skillet. Add 1 carton of the broth. Heat to boiling. Reduce heat; cover and simmer 20 minutes or until juice of chicken is clear when center of thickest part is cut (170°F).

2) Meanwhile, in 5-quart stockpot, heat oil over medium heat. Add onion, carrot and celery; cook 8 to 10 minutes, stirring occasionally, until vegetables are tender.

3) Drain chicken, reserving broth; set chicken aside. Strain broth; add broth to vegetables. Stir remaining carton of broth, the tomatoes, salt, pepper and bay leaf into stockpot. Heat to boiling. Stir in pasta. Reduce heat; cover and simmer 15 minutes.

4) Shred or cut chicken into bite-size pieces; add to the soup. Stir in greens just until wilted. Remove bay leaf. Serve with a sprinkle of additional freshly ground pepper and the cheese.

1 SERVING: Calories 260; Total Fat 6g; Sodium 950mg; Dietary Fiber 2g; Protein 28g. EXCHANGES: 1 Starch, 1 Vegetable, 3 Very Lean Meat, 1 Fat. CARBOHYDRATE CHOICES: 1-1/2.

tip

Adding chopped fresh herbs, such as basil, parsley or chives, to each serving of this soup will add a touch of lively flavor.

Curried Pumpkin-Vegetable Soup

PREP TIME: 20 MINUTES (READY IN 20 MINUTES)
SERVINGS: 4 (1-1/2 CUPS EACH)

 e EASY **lf** LOW FAT

1 teaspoon olive oil

1 medium onion, chopped (½ cup)

1 clove garlic, finely chopped

2 cups Green Giant® Valley Fresh Steamers™ frozen mixed vegetables (from 12-oz bag)

1 can (15 oz) pumpkin (not pumpkin pie mix)

1 can (14.5 oz) diced tomatoes, undrained

1 can (14 oz) fat-free chicken broth with ⅓ less sodium

½ cup water

½ teaspoon sugar

1 ½ teaspoons curry powder

1 teaspoon paprika

1) In 3-quart saucepan, heat oil over medium-high heat. Cook onion and garlic in oil 1 to 2 minutes, stirring frequently, until onion is crisp-tender.

2) Stir in all remaining ingredients. Heat to boiling; reduce heat to low. Cover; simmer 10 to 12 minutes, stirring occasionally, until vegetables are tender. If desired, season to taste with pepper.

1 SERVING: Calories 130; Total Fat 2g; Sodium 550mg; Dietary Fiber 6g; Protein 5g. EXCHANGES: 1 Starch, 2 Vegetable. CARBOHYDRATE CHOICES: 1-1/2.

Spicy Chili

PREP TIME: 20 MINUTES (READY IN 7 HOURS 20 MINUTES)
SERVINGS: 6 (1-1/2 CUPS EACH)

 EASY

1 lb lean (at least 80%) ground beef

½ lb bulk Italian pork sausage

1 medium onion, chopped (½ cup)

1 can (28 oz) whole tomatoes, undrained, cut up

1 can (15 oz) tomato sauce

2 teaspoons chili powder

1 to 1 ½ teaspoons ground cumin

1 teaspoon sugar

1 teaspoon dried oregano leaves

1 can (15 oz) spicy chili beans, undrained

1 can (15 oz) Progresso® chick peas (garbanzo beans), drained, rinsed

Sour cream, if desired

Sliced green onions, if desired

1) In 10-inch skillet, cook beef, sausage and onion over medium-high heat 5 to 7 minutes, stirring occasionally, until beef and sausage are thoroughly cooked; drain.

2) Spray 3- to 4-quart slow cooker with cooking spray. In cooker, mix beef mixture and remaining ingredients except sour cream and green onions.

3) Cover; cook on Low heat setting 7 to 8 hours. Top individual servings with sour cream and green onions.

1 SERVING: Calories 420; Total Fat 16g; Sodium 1220mg; Dietary Fiber 10g; Protein 28g. EXCHANGES: 1-1/2 Starch, 1 Other Carbohydrate, 1 Vegetable, 3 Medium-Fat Meat. CARBOHYDRATE CHOICES: 3.

Enchilada Soup

PREP TIME: 10 MINUTES (READY IN 7 HOURS 20 MINUTES)
SERVINGS: 6 (1-1/3 CUPS EACH)

 EASY  LOW FAT

2 cups Progresso® chicken broth (from 32-oz carton)

1 can (19 oz) Old El Paso® mild or hot enchilada sauce

1 can (4.5 oz) Old El Paso® chopped mild green chiles

1 package (20 oz) bone-in chicken breasts, skin removed

1 can (15 oz) Progresso® black beans, drained, rinsed

1 bag (12 oz) Green Giant® Valley Fresh Steamers™ Niblets® frozen corn, thawed, drained

Shredded Mexican cheese blend, if desired

Chopped fresh cilantro, if desired

Crushed tortilla chips, if desired

1) Spray 4- to 5-quart slow cooker with cooking spray. In cooker, mix broth, enchilada sauce and chiles. Place chicken into enchilada sauce mixture; spoon sauce over chicken. Cover; cook on Low heat setting 7 to 8 hours.

2) Remove chicken from cooker with slotted spoon. Stir beans and corn into mixture in cooker. Increase heat setting to High. Cover; cook 5 to 10 minutes longer.

3) Meanwhile, shred chicken by pulling apart with 2 forks; return to cooker. Cook until thoroughly heated. Top each serving with cheese, cilantro and tortilla chips.

1 SERVING: Calories 230; Total Fat 3g; Sodium 940mg; Dietary Fiber 7g; Protein 21g. EXCHANGES: 2 Starch, 2 Lean Meat. CARBOHYDRATE CHOICES: 2.

tip

Change the amount of spiciness in this soup by varying the type of enchilada sauce, mild or hot. You can also serve hot red pepper sauce on the side.

Barbecue Chili with Corn

PREP TIME:	30 MINUTES (READY IN 30 MINUTES)
SERVINGS:	6 (1-1/3 CUPS EACH)

 EASY

1 lb lean (at least 80%) ground beef

1 large onion, chopped (1 cup)

1 can (22 oz) southern pit barbecue grilling beans, undrained

1 can (14.5 oz) Muir Glen® organic fire roasted diced tomatoes, undrained

1 can (8 oz) tomato sauce

1 box (9 oz) Green Giant® Simply Steam® Niblets® frozen corn

1 tablespoon chili powder

1 teaspoon ground cumin

½ cup shredded Cheddar cheese (2 oz)

2 cups corn chips

1) In heavy 3-quart saucepan, cook beef and onion over medium-high heat 5 to 7 minutes, stirring occasionally, until beef is thoroughly cooked; drain.

2) Stir in remaining ingredients except cheese and corn chips. Heat to boiling; reduce heat. Simmer uncovered 5 to 10 minutes, stirring occasionally, until corn is tender. Top individual servings with cheese and corn chips.

1 SERVING: Calories 440; Total Fat 18g; Sodium 900mg; Dietary Fiber 7g; Protein 23g. EXCHANGES: 1-1/2 Starch, 1 Other Carbohydrate, 1-1/2 Vegetable, 2 Medium-Fat Meat, 1-1/2 Fat. CARBOHYDRATE CHOICES: 3.

Chicken Tortilla Soup

PREP TIME:	10 MINUTES (READY IN 6 HOURS 25 MINUTES)
SERVINGS:	6 (1-1/2 CUPS EACH)

 EASY   **LOW FAT**

SOUP

- 1 lb boneless skinless chicken breasts, cut into bite-size pieces
- 1 cup chopped onion
- 2 tablespoons ground cumin
- 1 tablespoon chili powder
- 2 teaspoons dried minced garlic
- ¼ teaspoon salt
- ¼ teaspoon ground red pepper (cayenne)
- 1 can (28 oz) diced tomatoes, undrained
- 1 carton (32 oz) Progresso® chicken broth (4 cups)
- 4 corn tortillas (6 inch), cut into 1-inch pieces
- ½ cup chopped fresh cilantro

GARNISHES, IF DESIRED

Shredded Cheddar cheese

Sour cream

1) Spray 3 ½- to 4-quart slow cooker with cooking spray. In cooker, mix all the soup ingredients except chopped cilantro.

2) Cover and cook on Low heat setting 6 to 8 hours.

3) Stir in the cilantro. Increase the heat setting to High. Cover and cook 15 minutes longer. Garnish each serving with shredded cheese and sour cream.

1 SERVING: Calories 190; Total Fat 4g; Sodium 920mg; Dietary Fiber 3g; Protein 22g. EXCHANGES: 1 Starch, 2-1/2 Lean Meat. CARBOHYDRATE CHOICES: 1.

Curried Carrot Soup

PREP TIME: 15 MINUTES (READY IN 7 HOURS 25 MINUTES)
SERVINGS: 6 (1 CUP EACH)

 EASY LOW FAT

SOUP

1 ⅔ cups chopped onion

1 tablespoon dried minced garlic

2 bags (16 oz each) frozen sliced carrots

1 to 2 tablespoons curry powder

⅛ teaspoon crushed red pepper flakes

¼ teaspoon salt

1 carton (32 oz) Progresso® reduced-sodium chicken broth (4 cups)

1 cup half-and-half

GARNISHES, IF DESIRED

Chopped roasted peanuts

Chopped fresh cilantro or parsley

1) Spray 3 ½- to 4-quart slow cooker with cooking spray. In cooker, mix all soup ingredients except half-and-half. Cover; cook on Low heat setting 7 to 9 hours.

2) Strain cooked vegetables from cooking liquid, reserving liquid. In blender or food processor, cover and blend vegetables until smooth. Return vegetable puree to cooker. Stir in 1 ½ cups of the reserved liquid and the half-and-half. Cover; cook on Low heat setting about 10 minutes longer or until warm.

3) Garnish each serving with peanuts and cilantro.

1 SERVING: Calories 150; Total Fat 6g; Sodium 580mg; Dietary Fiber 6g; Protein 4g. EXCHANGES: 1/2 Other Carbohydrate, 2 Vegetable, 1-1/2 Fat. CARBOHYDRATE CHOICES: 1.

Orange-Green Chile Pumpkin Soup
With Toasted Pumpkin Seeds

Cheryl Perry
Hertford, NC
Celebrate the Season—Thanksgiving Cooking Contest

PREP TIME: 40 MINUTES (READY IN 40 MINUTES)
SERVINGS: 10 (1 CUP EACH)

1 tablespoon vegetable oil

½ cup chopped shallots

4 cloves garlic, finely chopped

5 cups vegetable broth

1 can (29 oz) pumpkin (not pumpkin pie mix)

2 cups half-and-half

1 tablespoon cornstarch

1 package (1 oz) green chile dip mix, if desired

1 can (4.5 oz) Old El Paso® chopped green chiles, undrained

2 to 3 teaspoons grated orange peel

3 teaspoons ground cumin

1½ teaspoons kosher (coarse) salt

½ teaspoon pepper

¼ cup toasted and salted shelled pumpkin seeds (pepitas)

1) In 4-quart Dutch oven, heat oil over medium-low heat. Cook shallots in oil 3 minutes, stirring frequently. Add garlic; cook 2 minutes longer or until shallots are tender. Stir in broth and pumpkin. Heat to boiling; reduce heat. Simmer, uncovered, 15 minutes, stirring occasionally.

2) In small bowl, mix half-and-half, cornstarch and dip mix with whisk until smooth. Stir into pumpkin mixture. Stir in chiles, orange peel, cumin, salt and pepper. Simmer 10 minutes longer, stirring occasionally, until thickened. Garnish individual servings with toasted pumpkin seeds.

1 SERVING: Calories 160; Total Fat 10g; Sodium 920mg; Dietary Fiber 3g; Protein 4g. EXCHANGES: 1/2 Other Carbohydrate, 1 Vegetable, 2 Fat. CARBOHYDRATE CHOICES: 1.

tip

If you have fresh cooking pumpkin on hand, you can substitute 3 cups of fresh cooked pumpkin puree for the canned pumpkin in this soup.

Creamy Fresh Tomato Soup

PREP TIME: 30 MINUTES (READY IN 30 MINUTES)
SERVINGS: 4 (1-1/4 CUPS EACH)

 EASY

2 lb fresh tomatoes
   (about 4 to 5 medium)

1 tablespoon olive oil

1 large onion, chopped (1 cup)

1 ½ cups vegetable broth

1 can (6 oz) tomato paste

1 teaspoon salt

¼ teaspoon ground nutmeg

⅛ teaspoon ground red pepper
   (cayenne)

½ cup whipping cream

¼ cup chopped fresh basil

1) In large saucepan, heat 3 quarts water to boiling. With sharp knife, cut shallow X in bottom of each tomato. Add to boiling water, 2 or 3 at a time, for 10 seconds. Using a slotted spoon, remove tomatoes from boiling water; immediately plunge into ice water until cold. Drain. Peel and chop the tomatoes.

2) In heavy 3-quart saucepan, heat oil over medium heat. Cook onion in oil 3 to 5 minutes, stirring frequently, until tender. Stir in chopped tomatoes, broth, tomato paste, salt, nutmeg and red pepper. Heat to boiling; reduce heat. Simmer uncovered 5 minutes or until tomatoes are soft. Stir in whipping cream.

3) In blender or food processor, place 2 ½ cups tomato mixture. Cover; blend on medium speed 30 seconds or until smooth. Pour mixture into large bowl. Repeat with remaining tomato mixture. Return pureed mixture to saucepan. Heat over medium heat, stirring frequently, until hot. Top each serving with basil.

1 SERVING: Calories 230; Total Fat 13g; Sodium 1300mg; Dietary Fiber 5g; Protein 5g. EXCHANGES: 1/2 Other Carbohydrate, 3-1/2 Vegetable, 2-1/2 Fat. CARBOHYDRATE CHOICES: 1-1/2.

Cheesy Broccoli-Potato Soup

PREP TIME:	15 MINUTES (READY IN 15 MINUTES)
SERVINGS:	6

 EASY

2 cups Progresso® chicken broth (from 32-oz carton)

⅓ cup chopped onion

1 bag (12 oz) Green Giant® Valley Fresh Steamers™ frozen chopped broccoli

1 ⅓ cups plain mashed potato mix (dry)

2 cups cut-up cooked chicken

2 cups shredded Swiss cheese (8 oz)

2 cups milk

½ teaspoon salt

1) In 3-quart saucepan, heat broth, onion and frozen broccoli to boiling. Reduce heat; cover and simmer 5 minutes, stirring occasionally.

2) Stir in potatoes until well blended. Stir in remaining ingredients. Heat over low heat about 5 minutes, stirring occasionally, until soup is hot and cheese is melted.

1 SERVING: Calories 460; Total Fat 16g; Sodium 660mg; Dietary Fiber 5g; Protein 32g. EXCHANGES: 2-1/2 Starch, 1/2 Low-Fat Milk, 1 Vegetable, 2-1/2 Lean Meat, 1 Fat. CARBOHYDRATE CHOICES: 3.

Southwestern Chicken Soup

PREP TIME: 10 MINUTES (READY IN 6 HOURS 20 MINUTES)
SERVINGS: 6 (ABOUT 1 CUP EACH)

 EASY    LOW FAT

1 lb boneless skinless chicken breasts

1 medium onion, finely chopped
(½ cup)

1 can (10 oz) diced tomatoes with
green chiles, undrained

1 can (10 oz) Old El Paso® mild
enchilada sauce

1 can (4.5 oz) Old El Paso® chopped
green chiles

1 ¾ cups Progresso® chicken broth
(from 32-oz carton)

1 cup Green Giant® Valley Fresh
Steamers™ Extra Sweet Niblets®
frozen corn (from 12-oz bag),
thawed

3 teaspoons dried minced garlic

2 teaspoons chili powder

1 ½ teaspoons ground cumin

½ teaspoon salt

4 soft corn tortillas (5 to 6 inch), cut
into 1-inch strips

1) Spray 3 ½- to 4-quart slow cooker with cooking spray. Place chicken in
slow cooker. Add all remaining ingredients. Cover; cook on Low heat
setting 6 to 7 hours.

2) Remove the chicken and shred with 2 forks. Return to the slow cooker and
stir well to blend.

1 SERVING: Calories 200; Total Fat 3.5g; Sodium 1000mg; Dietary Fiber 3g; Protein 20g.
EXCHANGES: 1-1/2 Other Carbohydrate, 1/2 Vegetable, 1-1/2 Very Lean Meat, 1 Lean Meat.
CARBOHYDRATE CHOICES: 1-1/2.

Cooking the corn
tortilla strips in the
soup the entire time
it's cooking adds a
traditional Mexican
flavor to the dish.

French Vegetable Soup

PREP TIME: 15 MINUTES (READY IN 7 HOURS 35 MINUTES)
SERVINGS: 6 (1-1/3 CUPS EACH)

 EASY   LOW FAT

2 cups chopped onions

4 unpeeled small red potatoes, cut into about ¾-inch cubes

1 small zucchini, halved lengthwise, then cut crosswise into ½-inch slices

1 can (14.5 oz) diced tomatoes, undrained

1 carton (32 oz) Progresso® reduced-sodium chicken broth (4 cups)

2 teaspoons dried minced garlic

1 tablespoon Italian seasoning

¼ teaspoon salt

¼ teaspoon pepper

1 cup Green Giant® Valley Fresh Steamers™ frozen mixed vegetables, thawed, drained

1 oz uncooked thin spaghetti or vermicelli, broken into 2-inch pieces (about ½ cup)

1 can (15 oz) Progresso® cannellini beans, drained, rinsed

3 tablespoons basil pesto

1) Spray 3 ½- to 4-quart slow cooker with cooking spray. In cooker, mix all ingredients except mixed vegetables, spaghetti, beans and pesto.

2) Cover and cook on Low heat setting 7 to 9 hours.

3) Stir in mixed vegetables, spaghetti and beans. Increase heat setting to High. Cover; cook 20 minutes longer. Garnish each serving with about 1 ½ teaspoons pesto.

1 SERVING: Calories 240; Total Fat 4.5g; Sodium 850mg; Dietary Fiber 8 g; Protein 11g. EXCHANGES: 1 Starch, 1-1/2 Other Carbohydrate, 1 Vegetable, 1 Lean Meat. CARBOHYDRATE CHOICES: 2 1/2.

Italian Meatball Soup

PREP TIME: 10 MINUTES (READY IN 8 HOURS 10 MINUTES)
SERVINGS: 5 (1-1/2 CUPS EACH)

 EASY

1 bag (16 oz) frozen cooked Italian meatballs, thawed

1 ¾ cups Progresso® beef flavored broth (from 32-oz carton)

1 cup water

1 can (14.5 oz) diced tomatoes with basil, garlic and oregano, undrained

1 can (19 oz) Progresso® cannellini beans, drained

⅓ cup shredded Parmesan cheese

1) Spray 3- to 4-quart slow cooker with cooking spray. Mix all ingredients except cheese in cooker.

2) Cover and cook on Low heat setting 8 to 10 hours.

3) Garnish individual servings with shredded Parmesan cheese.

1 SERVING: Calories 410; Total Fat 15g; Sodium 1540mg; Dietary Fiber 6g; Protein 31g. EXCHANGES: 2 Starch, 1/2 Other Carbohydrate, 3-1/2 Lean Meat, 1/2 Fat. CARBOHYDRATE CHOICES: 2-1/2.

Cincinnati Chili

PREP TIME: 15 MINUTES (READY IN 7 HOURS 35 MINUTES)
SERVINGS: 8

 EASY

2 lb lean (at least 80%) ground beef

1 cup chopped yellow onion

1 can (14.5 oz) fire-roasted diced tomatoes, undrained

1 can (6 oz) tomato paste

1 package (1 ⅜ oz) Old El Paso® chili seasoning mix

2 ½ cups Progresso® beef flavored broth (from 32-oz carton)

2 tablespoons cider vinegar

1 teaspoon Worcestershire sauce

½ teaspoon ground cinnamon

½ teaspoon ground allspice

½ teaspoon salt

½ teaspoon pepper

1 box (16 oz) spaghetti, broken into thirds

Shredded Cheddar cheese

1) In 12-inch skillet, cook beef and onion over medium-high heat 8 to 10 minutes, stirring occasionally, until beef is thoroughly cooked; drain.

2) Spray 3 ½- to 4-quart slow cooker with cooking spray. In cooker, mix beef and remaining ingredients except spaghetti.

3) Cover; cook on Low heat setting 7 to 9 hours.

4) About 15 minutes before serving, cook spaghetti as directed on box. Spoon the chili over the spaghetti and serve with shredded Cheddar cheese if desired.

1 SERVING: Calories 500; Total Fat 14g; Sodium 1190mg; Dietary Fiber 5g; Protein 31g. EXCHANGES: 4 Starch, 2-1/2 Medium-Fat Meat. CARBOHYDRATE CHOICES: 4.

tip

For an even heartier chili, stir in 1 can (15 oz) of pinto beans, drained and rinsed, during the last 30 minutes of cooking.

Buffalo Chicken Chili

PREP TIME: 45 MINUTES (READY IN 45 MINUTES)
SERVINGS: 6 (1-1/2 CUPS EACH)

lf LOW FAT

1 tablespoon vegetable oil

1 large onion, chopped (1 cup)

1 medium red or yellow bell pepper, chopped (1 cup)

2 cups cubed deli rotisserie chicken (from 2- to 2 ½-lb chicken)

1 cup Progresso® chicken broth (from 32-oz carton)

1 tablespoon chili powder

5 or 6 drops red pepper sauce

2 cans (15 oz each) pinto beans, drained

1 can (28 oz) crushed tomatoes, undrained

1 can (14.5 oz) diced tomatoes, undrained

½ cup sliced celery

½ cup crumbled blue cheese

1) In 3-quart saucepan, heat oil over medium-high heat. Cook onion and bell pepper in oil about 5 minutes, stirring occasionally, until crisp-tender.

2) Stir in remaining ingredients except celery and blue cheese. Heat to boiling; reduce heat to medium-low. Simmer uncovered 10 to 15 minutes, stirring occasionally. Serve topped with celery and blue cheese.

1 SERVING: Calories 380; Total Fat 10g; Sodium 1060mg; Dietary Fiber 13g; Protein 28g. EXCHANGES: 2-1/2 Starch, 1 Vegetable, 2-1/2 Lean Meat, 1/2 Fat. CARBOHYDRATE CHOICES: 3.

GREEK TUNA SALAD PITA SANDWICHES
WITH FETA CHEESE
PG. 129

Sandwiches, Wraps & Burgers

When you need a fast lunch or dinner, these delicious and quick ideas are here for the taking!

SMOKED TURKEY AND CREAMY ARTICHOKE SANDWICHES
PG. 123

BUFFALO CHICKEN BURGERS
PG. 112

VEGGIE WRAPS
PG. 125

Buffalo Chicken Burgers

MIKE WAIDHOFER | LEAGUE CITY, TX

Bake-Off — BAKE-OFF® CONTEST 44, 2010

PREP TIME: 40 MINUTES (READY IN 40 MINUTES)
SERVINGS: 8 SANDWICHES

1 can (16.3 oz) Pillsbury® Grands!® Flaky Layers Butter Tastin'® refrigerated biscuits (8 biscuits)

3 tablespoons Land O Lakes® unsalted or salted butter

2 lb boneless skinless chicken breasts, cut into ¾-inch pieces

1 tablespoon Cajun seasoning

1 teaspoon ground red pepper (cayenne)

Dash salt

Dash black pepper

2 tablespoons Pillsbury Best® all purpose flour

2 tablespoons ranch dressing mix

1 cup chicken stock or broth

2 tablespoons Louisiana hot sauce or other red pepper sauce

3 medium carrots

1 cup crumbled blue cheese (4 oz)

1) Heat oven to 350°F. Bake biscuits as directed on can.

2) Meanwhile, melt 1 tablespoon of the butter. In food processor, place chicken, Cajun seasoning, red pepper, salt, black pepper, 1 tablespoon of the flour, 1 tablespoon of the dry dressing mix and melted butter. Cover; process with 10 to 15 on-and-off pulses until chopped. Shape mixture into 8 patties, 2 ½ inches in diameter.

3) Heat 12-inch nonstick skillet over medium heat. Melt 1 tablespoon of the butter in skillet. Add patties; cook about 5 minutes on each side or until light golden brown. Remove from skillet; cover with foil.

4) Stir ½ cup of the chicken stock into skillet, stirring to loosen bits from bottom of skillet. In small bowl, beat remaining ½ cup chicken stock, remaining 1 tablespoon flour and remaining 1 tablespoon dry dressing mix with wire whisk until blended; beat into mixture in skillet. Heat to boiling. Stir in hot sauce; return patties to skillet. Reduce heat to medium-low. Cover; simmer 6 to 10 minutes, turning patties once, until thermometer inserted in center of patties reads 165°F. Meanwhile, using vegetable peeler, peel carrots into thin strips.

5) Remove patties from skillet. Remove skillet from heat; stir remaining 1 tablespoon butter into sauce. Split biscuits; fill with patties, sauce, carrots and cheese.

1 SANDWICH: Calories 440; Total Fat 20g; Sodium 1780mg; Dietary Fiber 0g; Protein 33g. EXCHANGES: 1-1/2 Starch, 1/2 Other Carbohydrate, 4 Lean Meat, 1-1/2 Fat. CARBOHYDRATE CHOICES: 2.

Apricot-Curry Chicken Sandwiches

PAROMITA TOMERLIN | FLAGLER BEACH, FL

BAKE-OFF® CONTEST 44, 2010

PREP TIME: 45 MINUTES (READY IN 1 HOUR 5 MINUTES)
SERVINGS: 8 SANDWICHES

1 tablespoon curry powder

½ teaspoon ground cinnamon

½ teaspoon ground nutmeg

¼ teaspoon ground cloves

1 teaspoon salt

4 boneless skinless chicken breasts (about 6 oz each)

¼ cup Crisco® pure canola oil

½ small red onion, finely chopped (½ cup)

¼ teaspoon crushed red pepper flakes

1 jalapeño chile, seeded, finely chopped

1 jar (10.25 oz) Smucker's® Low Sugar™ reduced sugar apricot preserves (1 cup)

Dash salt

2 cans (8 oz each) Pillsbury® Crescent Recipe Creations® refrigerated seamless dough sheet

2 slices (¾ oz each) Cheddar cheese, cut into quarters

½ cup Fisher® Chef's Naturals® natural sliced almonds, lightly toasted

1 Eggland's Best egg

1 tablespoon water

1) In small bowl, mix curry powder, cinnamon, nutmeg, cloves and 1 teaspoon salt. Cut each chicken breast in half crosswise to make total of 8 equal portions. Coat chicken evenly with seasoning mixture.

2) In 12-inch nonstick skillet, heat 3 tablespoons of the oil over medium-high heat. Add chicken; cook 3 to 4 minutes on each side or until lightly browned. Remove from heat.

3) In 2-quart saucepan, heat remaining 1 tablespoon oil over medium-high heat. Add onion, red pepper and chile; cook 4 to 6 minutes, stirring frequently, until onion is tender. Reduce heat to medium. Stir in preserves; cook about 5 minutes or until heated. Stir in dash of salt; remove from heat. Cool slightly.

4) Heat oven to 375°F. Line cookie sheet with cooking parchment paper. On work surface, unroll dough sheets. Cut each sheet into quarters. On center of each dough rectangle, place cheese piece; top with 1 teaspoon preserves mixture, 1 teaspoon almonds and chicken piece. In small bowl, beat egg and water until well blended; brush on edges of dough rectangle. Bring up dough over filling; press edges to seal. Place seam side down on cookie sheet.

5) Brush tops with remaining egg mixture; sprinkle with any remaining almonds. Bake 12 to 18 minutes or until golden brown. Serve warm with remaining preserves mixture.

1 SANDWICH: Calories 530; Total Fat 24g; Sodium 860mg; Dietary Fiber 2g; Protein 26g. EXCHANGES: 2-1/2 Starch, 1 Other Carbohydrate, 2-1/2 Lean Meat, 3 Fat. CARBOHYDRATE CHOICES: 3-1/2.

Grilled Ham, Cheddar and Chutney Sandwiches

PREP TIME: 25 MINUTES (READY IN 25 MINUTES)
SERVINGS: 4 SANDWICHES

 EASY

3 tablespoons butter, softened

8 slices whole-grain bread

6 tablespoons mango chutney

8 oz extra-sharp Cheddar cheese, sliced

12 oz thinly sliced smoked ham

1) Heat a griddle or 12-inch nonstick skillet over medium heat.

2) Spread butter on one side of each bread slice. Spread a heaping tablespoon of the chutney on unbuttered side of 4 of the bread slices. Top each with one-fourth of the cheese and ham. Top with remaining bread slices, buttered side up.

3) Place the sandwiches in skillet. Cook uncovered about 3 minutes or until cheese is slightly melted and bread is browned. Turn sandwiches over; cook 3 minutes longer or until the cheese is melted and sandwich is golden brown.

1 SANDWICH: Calories 600; Total Fat 34g; Sodium 1770mg; Dietary Fiber 4g; Protein 39g. EXCHANGES: 1-1/2 Starch, 1 Other Carbohydrate, 4-1/2 Lean Meat, 4 Fat. CARBOHYDRATE CHOICES: 2.

Classic Reuben Panini

Kathy Strahs
San Diego, CA
www.paninihappy.com

PREP TIME: 25 MINUTES (READY IN 25 MINUTES)
SERVINGS: 4 SANDWICHES

 EASY

2 tablespoons butter, softened

8 slices rye bread

¼ cup Thousand Island dressing

1 cup sauerkraut, drained, squeezed dry (from 14.5-oz can)

½ lb corned beef, thinly sliced

8 slices Swiss cheese

1) Heat closed contact grill 5 minutes.

2) Spread butter on one side of each bread slice. On unbuttered side of 1 bread slice, spread 1 tablespoon of the dressing. Top with ¼ cup of the sauerkraut, 2 oz corned beef, 2 slices cheese and remaining bread slice, buttered side up. Repeat for remaining sandwiches.

3) When grill is heated, place sandwiches on grill. Close grill; grill 5 to 6 minutes or until cheese is melted and grill marks appear. Serve immediately.

1 SANDWICH: Calories 500; Total Fat 31g; Sodium 1630mg; Dietary Fiber 4g; Protein 23g. EXCHANGES: 2 Starch, 2-1/2 Medium-Fat Meat, 3-1/2 Fat. CARBOHYDRATE CHOICES: 2.

Make-Ahead Roast Beef Sandwiches

PREP TIME: 15 MINUTES (READY IN 1 HOUR 15 MINUTES)
SERVINGS: 8

  EASY   LOW FAT

SAUCE

¼ cup sour cream

¼ cup mayonnaise or salad dressing

2 tablespoons Dijon mustard

SANDWICHES

1 loaf French bread (1 lb), cut in half horizontally

1 jar (7 or 7.25 oz) roasted red bell peppers, drained, sliced

1 lb thinly sliced cooked roast beef

3 leaves romaine lettuce, torn in half lengthwise

1) In small bowl, mix sour cream, mayonnaise and mustard until blended.

2) Spread half of sour cream mixture on cut side of bottom half of bread; spread remaining mixture on cut side of top half of bread. On bottom half of bread, layer roasted peppers, roast beef and lettuce. Cover with remaining half of bread. Wrap tightly with plastic wrap; refrigerate 1 to 2 hours. When ready to serve, cut sandwich into 8 pieces.

1 SERVING: Calories 300; Total Fat 10g; Sodium 1090mg; Dietary Fiber 2g; Protein 18g. EXCHANGES: 1-1/2 Starch, 1/2 Other Carbohydrate, 1/2 Vegetable, 1-1/2 Medium-Fat Meat, 1/2 Fat. CARBOHYDRATE CHOICES: 2-1/2.

Grilled Cheese Italiano

| PREP TIME: | 20 MINUTES (READY IN 20 MINUTES) | EASY |
| SERVINGS: | 4 SANDWICHES | |

3 tablespoons butter, softened

8 slices whole-grain bread

8 oz fontina or Swiss cheese, shredded (2 cups)

8 thin slices prosciutto or ham

24 fresh basil leaves

8 slices (¼ inch) ripe tomatoes (about 2 medium)

¼ teaspoon salt

¼ teaspoon freshly ground pepper

1) Heat griddle or 12-inch nonstick skillet over medium heat.

2) Spread butter on one side of each bread slice. Layer unbuttered side of 4 of the bread slices with ¼ cup of the cheese, 2 slices of the prosciutto, 6 of the basil leaves and 2 of the tomato slices. Sprinkle with salt and pepper. Top each with ¼ cup of the remaining cheese and remaining bread slice, buttered side up.

3) In hot skillet, heat sandwiches 3 to 5 minutes or until cheese is slightly melted and bread is browned. Turn sandwiches over; heat 3 to 5 minutes longer or until cheese is melted and sandwich is golden brown.

1 SANDWICH: Calories 490; Total Fat 31g; Sodium 1100mg; Dietary Fiber 4g; Protein 26g.
EXCHANGES: 1 Starch, 1/2 Other Carbohydrate, 1/2 Vegetable, 3 High-Fat Meat, 1-1/2 Fat.
CARBOHYDRATE CHOICES: 2.

Hearty Ham and Pear Panini

PREP TIME: 20 MINUTES (READY IN 20 MINUTES)
SERVINGS: 4 SANDWICHES

 EASY

Shreya Sasaki
San Diego, CA
www.recipematcher.com

2 tablespoons yellow mustard

½ loaf focaccia bread (13 to 15 inches long), cut in half horizontally

8 slices (2 oz each) ham

1 medium pear, peeled, thinly sliced

1 cup shredded mozzarella cheese (4 oz)

1 tablespoon olive oil or vegetable oil

1) Heat closed contact grill 5 minutes.

2) Spread mustard on bottom half of bread; layer with ham, pear and cheese. Cover with top half of bread. Lightly brush top of bread with oil. Cut sandwich into fourths.

3) When grill is heated, place sandwiches on grill. Close grill; grill 4 to 6 minutes or until cheese is melted and bread is golden brown.

1 SANDWICH: Calories 540; Total Fat 23g; Sodium 2230mg; Dietary Fiber 3g; Protein 36g. EXCHANGES: 3 Starch, 4 Lean Meat, 2 Fat. CARBOHYDRATE CHOICES: 3.

tip

If you don't have a panini grill, you can "grill" these in a skillet over medium heat for about 3 to 4 minutes per side.

Roast Beef and Bacon Wraps with Spicy Chili Lime Mayo

PREP TIME:	20 MINUTES (READY IN 20 MINUTES)	
SERVINGS:	4 WRAPS	EASY

SPICY CHILI LIME MAYO

⅓ cup mayonnaise or salad dressing

1 tablespoon lime juice

1 teaspoon chili powder

¼ teaspoon ground red pepper (cayenne)

¼ teaspoon salt

SANDWICHES

4 (10 inch) flour tortillas, heated as directed on package

¾ lb thinly sliced cooked roast beef

8 slices bacon, cooked crisply

1 ripe avocado, pitted, peeled and sliced

4 small leaves romaine lettuce

12 thin red onion rings

1) In small bowl, combine mayonnaise, lime juice, chili powder, cayenne and salt. Set aside.

2) Spread ¼ of the mayonnaise mixture over bottom half of each tortilla within 1 inch from edges. Divide roast beef, bacon, avocado, lettuce and onion evenly over bottom half of tortillas. Tuck in sides of tortillas; roll up tightly to enclose filling. Cut in half to serve.

1 WRAP: Calories 520; Total Fat 32g; Sodium 1790mg; Dietary Fiber 3g; Protein 27g. EXCHANGES: 2 Starch, 3 High-Fat Meat, 1-1/2 Fat. CARBOHYDRATE CHOICES: 2.

Portabella Mushroom Burgers

Shreya Sasaki
San Diego, CA
www.recipematcher.com

PREP TIME: 20 MINUTES (READY IN 35 MINUTES)
SERVINGS: 4 SANDWICHES

4 portabella mushroom caps
   (about ¾ lb)

¼ cup balsamic vinegar

2 tablespoons olive or vegetable oil

1 teaspoon dried basil leaves

1 teaspoon dried oregano leaves

1 tablespoon finely chopped garlic

½ teaspoon salt

¼ teaspoon pepper

4 slices provolone cheese

4 burger buns, split

1) Heat gas or charcoal grill.

2) Place mushroom caps in a resealable food-storage plastic bag. In small bowl, whisk together vinegar, oil, basil, oregano, garlic, salt and pepper. Pour over mushrooms; seal bag. Let stand 15 minutes, turning twice.

3) Place mushrooms on grill over medium heat; reserve marinade for basting. Cook, uncovered, brushing with marinade frequently, 5 to 8 minutes. Turn mushrooms over; cook 3 to 6 minutes longer. Top mushrooms with cheese and place burger buns, cut side down, on grill rack. Cook 2 minutes more or until mushrooms are tender and cheese is melted. Serve mushrooms in buns.

1 SANDWICH: Calories 270; Total Fat 13g; Sodium 630mg; Dietary Fiber 2g; Protein 10g. EXCHANGES: 1/2 Starch, 1/2 Other Carbohydrate, 3 Vegetable, 2-1/2 Fat. CARBOHYDRATE CHOICES: 2.

California Wraps

PREP TIME: 25 MINUTES (READY IN 25 MINUTES)
SERVINGS: 4 WRAPS

 EASY

Shreya Sasaki
San Diego, CA
www.recipematcher.com

4 (10 inch) flour tortillas, heated as directed on package

8 to 12 leaves leaf lettuce

12 oz oven-roasted turkey breast slices

12 slices bacon, crisply cooked

1 large tomato, cut into thin wedges

1 avocado, pitted, peeled and cut into thin wedges

1 cup torn arugula

½ cup ranch dressing

1) Lay the tortillas on a flat work surface. Fan the lettuce on top three-fourths of each tortilla; top evenly with turkey, bacon, tomato, avocado, arugula and dressing.

2) Fold up bottom fourth of each tortilla. Roll each sandwich into cone shape. Secure tortillas with toothpicks. Serve immediately.

1 WRAP: Calories 600; Total Fat 35g; Sodium 1140mg; Dietary Fiber 4g; Protein 40g. EXCHANGES: 2 Starch, 1/2 Vegetable, 4-1/2 Lean Meat, 4 Fat. CARBOHYDRATE CHOICES: 2.

tip

To pit an avocado, cut in half lengthwise, cutting around the seed. Twist halves in opposite directions to separate. Slip a spoon under the seed to loosen and remove it. Use a large spoon to loosen flesh from the skin and scoop it out.

Grilled Ham, Cheese and Apple Sandwiches

PREP TIME: 20 MINUTES (READY IN 20 MINUTES)
SERVINGS: 4 SANDWICHES

 EASY

⅓ cup mayonnaise or salad dressing

1 clove garlic, finely chopped

8 slices Italian bread, ½ inch thick

2 tablespoons butter or margarine, softened

½ lb thinly sliced cooked ham (from deli)

1 medium apple, peeled, thinly sliced

1 cup arugula

4 thin slices onion, if desired

4 slices (1 oz each) Swiss cheese

1) In small bowl, mix mayonnaise and garlic. Spread 1 side of each bread slice with butter; spread mayonnaise mixture on unbuttered side. On each of 4 bread slices, buttered sides down, layer ham, apple, arugula, onion, cheese and remaining bread slices, buttered sides up.

2) Heat 12-inch nonstick skillet over medium-low heat 3 to 5 minutes. Place sandwiches in hot skillet; cook uncovered 6 to 9 minutes, turning once, until bread is crisp and cheese is melted.

1 SANDWICH: Calories 450; Total Fat 32g; Sodium 1000mg; Dietary Fiber 1g; Protein 21g. EXCHANGES: 1 Starch, 1/2 Other Carbohydrate, 2-1/2 Lean Meat, 4-1/2 Fat. CARBOHYDRATE CHOICES: 1.

Smoked Turkey and Creamy Artichoke Sandwiches

PREP TIME: 10 MINUTES (READY IN 10 MINUTES)
SERVINGS: 4 SANDWICHES

 EASY   LOW FAT

8 slices marble-rye bread

½ cup refrigerated artichoke dip

½ lb thinly sliced smoked turkey (from deli)

4 thin slices onion

8 thin slices tomato

4 leaves lettuce

1) On each of 4 slices bread, spread 2 tablespoons artichoke dip. Layer each with turkey, onion, tomato, lettuce and remaining bread.

1 SANDWICH: Calories 260; Total Fat 8g; Sodium 1230mg; Dietary Fiber 3g; Protein 16g. EXCHANGES: 2 Starch, 1/2 Vegetable, 1-1/2 Lean Meat, 1/2 Fat. CARBOHYDRATE CHOICES: 2.

Zesty Italian Turkey Burgers

PREP TIME: 20 MINUTES (READY IN 35 MINUTES)
SERVINGS: 2 SANDWICHES

 EASY

2 Pillsbury® Grands!® frozen buttermilk or southern style biscuits (from 25-oz bag)

1 teaspoon zesty Italian dressing

½ lb ground turkey breast

3 tablespoons zesty Italian dressing

1 tablespoon finely chopped red onion

2 slices (1 oz each) provolone cheese, cut in half

2 lettuce leaves

6 red bell pepper strips (about 3x¼ inches)

Additional zesty Italian dressing, if desired

1) Heat oven to 375°F. Bake biscuits as directed on bag; place on cooling rack. Brush biscuits with 1 teaspoon dressing; cool completely. Set aside.

2) Heat gas or charcoal grill. Carefully brush oil on grill rack. Mix turkey, 3 tablespoons dressing and the onion. Shape mixture into 2 patties. Place on grill over medium heat.

3) Cover grill; cook 12 to 15 minutes, carefully turning once, until thermometer inserted in center of patty reads 165°F. Top patties with cheese. Cover and grill about 1 minute longer or until cheese is melted.

4) On 2 serving plates, split biscuits. Place lettuce leaves on bottom halves; top with burgers and bell pepper strips. Drizzle with additional dressing. Top with remaining biscuit halves.

1 SANDWICH: Calories 560; Total Fat 35g; Sodium 1320mg; Dietary Fiber 0g; Protein 34g. EXCHANGES: 2 Starch, 4 Lean Meat, 4 Fat. CARBOHYDRATE CHOICES: 2.

Veggie Wraps

PREP TIME:	20 MINUTES (READY IN 20 MINUTES)	EASY
SERVINGS:	4 WRAPS	

4 flour tortillas (10 inch)

4 oz (half of 8-oz package) cream cheese, softened

1 teaspoon ground cumin

½ teaspoon salt

4 small leaves lettuce

1 medium red bell pepper, cut into thin strips

1 cup sliced fresh mushrooms (3 oz)

½ medium cucumber, cut lengthwise into thin strips

4 medium green onions, chopped (¼ cup)

2 oz pepper Jack cheese, shredded (½ cup)

1) Heat tortillas as directed on package. Meanwhile, in small bowl, mix cream cheese, cumin and salt until blended.

2) On each tortilla, spread 2 tablespoons cream cheese mixture. Layer remaining ingredients evenly over half of each tortilla. Tuck in sides of tortillas; roll up tightly to enclose filling.

1 WRAP: Calories 390; Total Fat 19g; Sodium 950mg; Dietary Fiber 3g; Protein 12g. EXCHANGES: 2 Starch, 1/2 Other Carbohydrate, 1-1/2 Vegetable, 1/2 High-Fat Meat, 2-1/2 Fat. CARBOHYDRATE CHOICES: 3.

Pesto, Mozzarella and Tomato Panini

PREP TIME: 20 MINUTES (READY IN 20 MINUTES)
SERVINGS: 4 SANDWICHES

 EASY

4   ciabatta sandwich rolls

2   tablespoons olive oil

½   cup basil pesto

8   slices mozzarella cheese

1   medium tomato, cut into 8 thin slices

½   teaspoon salt

¼   teaspoon pepper

1) Heat closed contact grill 5 minutes.

2) Cut each roll in half horizontally; brush outside of each half with oil. Spread pesto on inside of both halves. Layer each sandwich with cheese and tomato. Sprinkle with salt and pepper.

3) When grill is heated, place sandwiches on grill. Close grill; grill 4 minutes or until bread is toasty and cheese is melted. Slice sandwiches on diagonal and serve warm.

1 SANDWICH: Calories 430; Total Fat 30g; Sodium 950mg; Dietary Fiber 2g; Protein 15g. EXCHANGES: 1-1/2 Starch, 1-1/2 High-Fat Meat, 3-1/2 Fat. CARBOHYDRATE CHOICES: 2.

tip

If you can't find ciabatta rolls, you can substitute focaccia or simply use 8 slices of country bread.

Tuna Melt

PREP TIME:	25 MINUTES (READY IN 25 MINUTES)	EASY	Larry Cowling
SERVINGS:	4 SANDWICHES		Lanse, MI
			www.cullyskitchen.com

2 cans (5 oz each) solid white tuna in water, drained

⅓ cup mayonnaise or salad dressing

¼ cup finely chopped celery

1 tablespoon finely chopped onion

1 tablespoon chopped fresh parsley

1 teaspoon red wine vinegar

⅛ teaspoon salt

⅛ teaspoon freshly ground pepper

4 slices rye bread

8 slices Swiss cheese

8 slices tomato

1) Set oven control to broil. In medium bowl, mix tuna, mayonnaise, celery, onion, parsley, vinegar, salt and pepper.

2) Place bread slices on baking sheet. Broil about 4 to 6 inches from heat for 1 minute or until lightly toasted.

3) Turn bread over on baking sheet. Spread untoasted side of each slice of bread with about ⅓ cup of the tuna salad, 1 slice of cheese, 2 slices tomato and 1 slice of remaining cheese. Return sandwiches to oven; broil 3 to 5 minutes or until cheese is melted.

1 SANDWICH: Calories 400; Total Fat 24g; Sodium 650mg; Dietary Fiber 2g; Protein 28g.
EXCHANGES: 1 Starch, 1/2 Vegetable, 3-1/2 Lean Meat, 2-1/2 Fat. CARBOHYDRATE CHOICES: 1.

Pesto Tuna Wrap

Shreya Sasaki
San Diego, CA
www.recipematcher.com

PREP TIME:	10 MINUTES (READY IN 10 MINUTES)
SERVINGS:	1 WRAP

 EASY

1 can (5 oz) tuna in water, drained, flaked

2 tablespoons mayonnaise or salad dressing

1 tablespoon basil pesto

1 teaspoon lemon juice

⅛ teaspoon pepper

1 (10 inch) flour tortilla, heated as directed on package

2 leaves leaf lettuce

1 slice provolone cheese, cut in half

5 kalamata olives, cut in half

1) In bowl, gently stir together tuna, mayonnaise, pesto, lemon juice and pepper until well mixed. Spread tuna mixture on tortilla; top with lettuce, cheese and olives. Fold bottom of tortilla up about 2 inches to enclose filling; roll tortilla tightly into compact wrap.

1 WRAP: Calories 660; Total Fat 41g; Sodium 950mg; Dietary Fiber 2g; Protein 45g. EXCHANGES: 2 Starch, 5-1/2 Lean Meat, 4-1/2 Fat. CARBOHYDRATE CHOICES: 2.

Greek Tuna Salad Pita Sandwiches with Feta Cheese

PREP TIME: 20 MINUTES (READY IN 20 MINUTES)
SERVINGS: 6 SANDWICHES

 EASY   LOW FAT

1 tablespoon lemon juice

2 tablespoons olive oil

1 clove garlic, finely chopped

¼ teaspoon salt

1 medium cucumber, peeled, seeded and finely chopped

1 ripe medium tomato, seeded, diced

½ cup crumbled feta cheese (2 oz)

12 kalamata or other large ripe olives, pitted, coarsely chopped (¼ cup)

2 cans (5 oz each) tuna in water, drained, flaked

12 leaves romaine lettuce, torn in half

6 pita (pocket) breads (6 inch), cut in half to form pockets

1) In small bowl, stir together lemon juice, oil, garlic and salt with whisk. In medium bowl, toss cucumber, tomato, cheese, olives and tuna. Pour dressing over salad; toss until coated.

2) Place 1 lettuce leaf half in each pita pocket; top each leaf with ½ cup tuna salad. Serve immediately.

1 SANDWICH: Calories 310; Total Fat 8g; Sodium 600mg; Dietary Fiber 3g; Protein 20g. EXCHANGES: 2 Starch, 2 Vegetable, 1-1/2 Lean Meat, 1/2 Fat. CARBOHYDRATE CHOICES: 2-1/2.

Caramelized Red Onion-Feta Burgers

SUSIE LITTLEWOOD | ROYAL CITY, WA

BAKE-OFF® CONTEST 44, 2010

PREP TIME: 45 MINUTES (READY IN 45 MINUTES)
SERVINGS: 8 SANDWICHES

1 large red onion, sliced (2 ½ cups)

¼ cup red wine vinegar

¼ cup red wine or nonalcoholic red wine

½ cup Smucker's® concord grape jelly

¼ cup sour cream

¼ cup mayonnaise or salad dressing

¾ teaspoon dried dill weed

½ teaspoon onion powder

¼ teaspoon Beau Monde seasoning, if desired

1 medium English (seedless) cucumber, finely diced (1 ½ cups)

1 can (16.3 oz) Pillsbury® Grands!® flaky layers refrigerated original biscuits (8 biscuits)

1 lb lean (at least 80%) ground beef

1 cup crumbled feta cheese (4 oz)

Dash salt

Dash pepper

8 tomato slices

8 lettuce leaves

1) Heat oven to 350°F. In 10-inch skillet, cook onion, vinegar, wine and jelly over medium heat about 20 minutes, stirring frequently, until onion is tender and sauce is reduced and thickened.

2) Meanwhile, in small bowl, mix the sour cream, mayonnaise, dill weed, onion powder, Beau Monde seasoning and cucumber. Refrigerate until ready to serve.

3) Bake biscuits as directed on can. Meanwhile, in large bowl, mix beef, cheese, salt and pepper. Shape mixture into 8 patties, ½ inch thick. Cook patties in grill pan, contact grill or nonstick skillet until meat thermometer inserted in center reads 160°F.

4) Split biscuits. Spread 2 to 3 tablespoons cucumber mixture on bottom of each biscuit. Top with burger, onion mixture and biscuit tops. Serve with tomato, lettuce and remaining cucumber mixture.

1 SANDWICH: Calories 460; Total Fat 24g; Sodium 800mg; Dietary Fiber 1g; Protein 16g. EXCHANGES: 2 Starch, 1 Other Carbohydrate, 1-1/2 Medium-Fat Meat, 3 Fat. CARBOHYDRATE CHOICES: 3.

Chipotle Chicken Quesadillas

PREP TIME: 35 MINUTES (READY IN 35 MINUTES)
SERVINGS: 3

3 tablespoons olive oil

½ red bell pepper, cut into thin strips

½ large onion, thinly sliced

½ cup frozen corn

1 ½ cups shredded cooked chicken

1 cup shredded Monterey Jack cheese (2 oz)

1 tablespoon finely chopped chipotle chile in adobo sauce (from 7-oz can)

2 tablespoons chopped cilantro

6 (8-inch) Old El Paso® flour tortillas

6 tablespoons Old El Paso® salsa

1) In 10-inch nonstick skillet, heat 1 tablespoon of the oil over medium-high heat. Add bell pepper, onion and corn; cook, stirring occasionally, 4 to 5 minutes or until bell pepper and onion are softened. Remove from heat; stir in chicken, cheese, chipotle chile and cilantro.

2) Brush one side of each tortilla with remaining 2 tablespoons oil. With oiled side down, spread 2 tablespoons salsa onto each of 3 tortillas. Spread about 1 cup of chicken mixture on each tortilla over salsa. Top each with remaining tortillas, oiled side up.

3) Heat 10-inch nonstick skillet over medium heat. Cook 1 quesadilla at a time 1 to 2 minutes on each side or until tortilla is golden brown and cheese is melted. Cut each quesadilla in half.

1 SERVING: Calories 650; Total Fat 32g; Sodium 1250mg; Dietary Fiber 4g; Protein 33g. EXCHANGES: 3-1/2 Starch, 1 Vegetable, 3 Lean Meat, 4 Fat. CARBOHYDRATE CHOICES: 4.

Chipotle chiles are smoked, dried jalapeños. They are often sold canned in a vinegary tomato sauce called "adobo." They can be quite hot, so feel free to adjust the amount used to suit your taste. The one tablespoon of chiles in this recipe offers a medium-hot result.

Grilled Mushroom Swiss Burgers

Larry Cowling
Lanse, MI
www.cullyskitchen.com

| PREP TIME: | 35 MINUTES (READY IN 35 MINUTES) |
| SERVINGS: | 6 SANDWICHES |

2 tablespoons butter

1 package (8 oz) sliced fresh mushrooms

3 tablespoons soy sauce

3 large garlic cloves, sliced or finely chopped

1 ½ lb lean (at least 80%) ground beef

½ teaspoon garlic powder

1 teaspoon salt

½ teaspoon pepper

6 slices Swiss cheese

6 burger buns, split

2 medium tomatoes, sliced

1 medium onion, sliced

1) Heat gas or charcoal grill to medium heat.

2) In 12-inch nonstick skillet, melt butter over medium-high heat. Add mushrooms, soy sauce and garlic; cook until mushrooms are tender and liquid evaporates. Set aside; keep warm.

3) Shape beef into 6 (½ inch thick) patties. Sprinkle with garlic powder, salt and pepper. Place patties on grill; cover grill. Cook with medium heat 8 to 10 minutes, turning once, until meat thermometer inserted in center of patties reads 160°F. Place cheese slices on top of burgers; cover and cook 1 to 2 minutes longer or until cheese is melted.

4) Place burgers in buns. Divide cooked mushrooms evenly over burgers. Top with tomatoes and onion.

1 SANDWICH: Calories 440; Total Fat 23g; Sodium 1160mg; Dietary Fiber 2g; Protein 30g. EXCHANGES: 1 Starch, 2-1/2 Vegetable, 3 Medium-Fat Meat, 1-1/2 Fat. CARBOHYDRATE CHOICES: 2.

Blue Cheese Steak Sandwiches

PREP TIME: 45 MINUTES (READY IN 45 MINUTES)
SERVINGS: 4 SANDWICHES

4 tablespoons vegetable oil

2 large onions, thinly sliced (2 cups)

2 tablespoons balsamic vinegar

1 teaspoon salt

1 teaspoon freshly ground pepper

4 oz blue cheese, crumbled (1 cup)

⅓ cup mayonnaise or salad dressing

1 beef flank steak, ¾ to 1 inch thick (1 lb)

4 demi French baguette rolls (5 to 6 inches), cut in half horizontally

1) In 10-inch nonstick skillet, heat 2 tablespoons of the oil over medium heat. Add onions; cook, stirring occasionally, 10 to 12 minutes or until deep golden brown. Add vinegar, ½ teaspoon of the salt and ¼ teaspoon of the pepper; cook 1 minute longer or until liquid has evaporated. Remove from heat; set aside.

2) In small bowl, mix cheese, mayonnaise and remaining ¼ teaspoon pepper. Set aside.

3) Heat gas or charcoal grill. Sprinkle steak with remaining ½ teaspoon of the salt and remaining ½ teaspoon of the pepper. Place steak on grill over medium-high heat. Cover grill; cook for 8- 10 minutes turning once for medium rare or until of desired doneness. Transfer steak to cutting board; let rest 10 minutes.

4) Lightly brush the cut sides of rolls with the remaining 2 tablespoons of the oil. Place the rolls, cut side down, on grill rack. Cook 1 to 2 minutes or until golden.

5) Thinly slice steak across grain on the diagonal. Divide steak among bottom halves of rolls; top each with one-fourth of the onions. Spread cut sides of baguette tops with cheese mixture; place on top of onions. Serve immediately.

1 SANDWICH: Calories 850; Total Fat 43g; Sodium 1750mg; Dietary Fiber 4g; Protein 51g.
EXCHANGES: 3 Starch, 1 Other Carbohydrate, 6 Lean Meat, 4-1/2 Fat. CARBOHYDRATE CHOICES: 4.

Buffalo Chicken Panini

PREP TIME: 35 MINUTES (READY IN 35 MINUTES)
SERVINGS: 8 SANDWICHES

LOW FAT

Kathy Strahs
San Diego, CA
www.paninihappy.com

¾ lb boneless skinless chicken breasts (about 3), cut into ½-inch strips

½ cup Buffalo wing sauce (from 12-oz bottle)

1 tablespoon butter

½ large red onion, sliced into thin rings

1 teaspoon sugar

4 pita fold breads (6 ½-inch diameter)

1 oz blue cheese, crumbled (¼ cup)

1) In 2-quart saucepan, heat chicken and Buffalo wing sauce to boiling over medium-high heat. Reduce heat to low; cover. Simmer 5 to 7 minutes or until chicken is cooked through.

2) Meanwhile, in 10-inch nonstick skillet, melt butter over medium heat. Add onion; cook, stirring frequently, 4 to 6 minutes or until starting to brown. Stir in sugar; reduce heat to low and cook, stirring frequently, 6 minutes longer or until onion is caramelized. Set aside.

3) Heat closed contact grill 5 minutes. Meanwhile, microwave each pita covered with damp paper towel on High 20 to 25 seconds or until soft enough to fold without breaking. Lay pitas flat on work surface. Place one-fourth of the caramelized onion on half of each pita. Using slotted spoon, spoon about ⅓ cup chicken over onion. (Reserve liquid in saucepan to serve with panini). Sprinkle with 1 tablespoon of the cheese. Carefully fold pita over filling. Repeat with remaining pitas.

4) When grill is heated, place sandwich on grill. Close grill; grill 4 to 5 minutes or until cheese is melted and pita is toasted. Serve panini with reserved sauce.

1 SANDWICH: Calories 180; Total Fat 5g; Sodium 800mg; Dietary Fiber 1g; Protein 13g. EXCHANGES: 1 Starch, 1-1/2 Lean Meat, 1/2 Fat. CARBOHYDRATE CHOICES: 1.

Chicken Sandwiches with Gremolata Mayonnaise

PREP TIME: 40 MINUTES (READY IN 40 MINUTES)
SERVINGS: 4 SANDWICHES

GREMOLATA MAYONNAISE

½ cup mayonnaise

¼ cup finely chopped parsley

1 ½ teaspoons grated lemon peel

1 ½ teaspoons minced garlic

SANDWICHES

4 boneless skinless chicken breast halves (4-oz each)

2 tablespoons olive oil

¼ teaspoon salt

⅛ teaspoon pepper

2 small zucchini, cut lengthwise into ¼-inch-thick slices

4 (¼-inch) slices onion

4 sandwich buns, split

4 leaves leaf lettuce

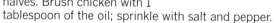

1) Combine all gremolata mayonnaise ingredients; blend well. Set aside. Heat gas or charcoal grill. Place 1 chicken breast half, boned side up, between 2 pieces of plastic wrap or waxed paper. Working from center, gently pound chicken with flat side of meat mallet or rolling pin until about ¼ inch thick; remove wrap. Repeat with remaining chicken breast halves. Brush chicken with 1 tablespoon of the oil; sprinkle with salt and pepper.

2) Place chicken on grill over medium heat. Cover grill; cook 10 to 16 minutes or until chicken is fork-tender and juices run clear, turning once. Meanwhile, brush zucchini and onion slices with remaining tablespoon oil; place on grill. Cook about 10 minutes or until tender, turning occasionally. To toast buns, place cut sides down on grill during last 2 to 4 minutes of cooking time.

3) Spread 1 tablespoon gremolata mayonnaise on bottom half of each bun. Top with lettuce. Place grilled vegetables evenly onto lettuce. Top each sandwich with chicken breast half, 1 tablespoon gremolata mayonnaise and top half of bun.

1 SANDWICH: Calories 550; Total Fat 34g; Sodium 580mg; Dietary Fiber 2g; Protein 31g. EXCHANGES: 1 Starch, 1/2 Other Carbohydrate, 2 Vegetable, 3-1/2 Lean Meat, 4-1/2 Fat. CARBOHYDRATE CHOICES: 2.

Bistro Burgers

PREP TIME: 25 MINUTES (READY IN 25 MINUTES)
SERVINGS: 4 SANDWICHES

 EASY

1 ½ lb. lean ground beef

¼ teaspoon salt

¼ teaspoon pepper

4 kaiser rolls, split

¼ cup purchased creamy mustard-mayonnaise sauce

4 thin slices sweet onion

4 tomato slices

4 oz thinly sliced fresh Parmesan cheese

½ cup fresh basil leaves

1) Heat the grill. In medium bowl, combine the ground beef, salt and pepper; mix well. Shape the mixture into 4 patties, ½ inch thick.

2) When ready to grill, place patties on gas grill over medium heat or on charcoal grill 4 to 6 inches from medium coals. Cook 11 to 13 minutes or until thoroughly cooked, turning once. To toast the rolls, place cut side down on grill during last 1 to 2 minutes of cooking time.

3) Spread cut side of each roll with mustard-mayonnaise sauce. Place patties on bottom halves of rolls. Top each with onion, tomato, cheese and basil. Cover with top halves of rolls.

1 SANDWICH: Calories 590; Total Fat 31g; Sodium 1080mg; Dietary Fiber 1g; Protein 45g. EXCHANGES: 2 Starch, 5-1/2 Medium-Fat Meat, 1/2 Fat. CARBOHYDRATE CHOICES: 2.

Chicken Pesto Panini

PREP TIME: 20 MINUTES (READY IN 20 MINUTES)
SERVINGS: 4 SANDWICHES

 EASY

Shreya Sasaki
San Diego, CA
www.recipematcher.com

1 focaccia bread (2 inches thick), cut into fourths

½ cup basil pesto

1 cup cubed cooked chicken breast

½ cup chopped red bell pepper

2 tablespoons finely chopped red onion

4 slices (1 oz each) provolone cheese

1) Heat closed contact grill 3 to 5 minutes.

2) Cut each piece focaccia in half horizontally. Spread 1 tablespoon pesto on cut sides of each half. Layer bottom halves with one-fourth of the chicken, bell pepper, onion and cheese. Cover with remaining focaccia halves.

3) When grill is heated, place sandwiches on grill. Close grill; grill 3 to 5 minutes or until focaccia is golden brown and cheese is melted.

1 SANDWICH: Calories 760; Total Fat 40g; Sodium 1710mg; Dietary Fiber 4g; Protein 30g. EXCHANGES: 4-1/2 Starch, 2-1/2 Lean Meat, 6 Fat. CARBOHYDRATE CHOICES: 4-1/2.

tip

If you're not a fan of raw onion, go ahead and leave it out or substitute with chopped olives.

Slow Cooker Pulled Pork Wraps with Coleslaw

PREP TIME: 45 MINUTES (READY IN 9 HOURS 45 MINUTES)
SERVINGS: 24

Elizabeth Nyland
Shawnigan Lake, BC
www.guiltykitchen.com

1 boneless pork roast (4 lb)

1 bottle (18 oz) barbecue sauce

COLESLAW

½ head green cabbage, shredded

2 large carrots, shredded (1 cup)

¾ cup mayonnaise

½ cup buttermilk

3 tablespoons sugar

1 ½ tablespoons white wine vinegar

1 tablespoon lime juice

½ teaspoon Dijon mustard

¼ teaspoon onion powder

¼ teaspoon ground mustard

¼ teaspoon salt

¼ teaspoon freshly ground pepper

24 (8-inch) Old El Paso® flour tortillas
for burritos

1) Place pork in 3 ½- to 4-quart slow cooker; pour one bottle barbecue sauce over top. Cover; cook on Low heat setting 9 to 10 hours.

2) Thirty minutes before pork is done, in large bowl, toss cabbage and carrots until mixed. In small bowl, mix remaining ingredients, except tortillas, with whisk until sugar is dissolved. Pour over cabbage mixture; toss until coated.

3) Transfer pork roast to bowl. Shred pork, using 2 forks. Skim the fat off surface of barbecue sauce liquid in slow cooker and pour some sauce over shredded pork to moisten. Stir in more barbecue sauce, if desired.

4) Using slotted spoon, spoon about ⅓ cup pork mixture over tortillas. Top with about ⅓ cup coleslaw; roll up.

1 SERVING: Calories 360; Total Fat 15g; Sodium 590mg; Dietary Fiber 2g; Protein 21g. EXCHANGES: 2 Starch, 1/2 Vegetable, 2 Medium-Fat Meat, 1 Fat. CARBOHYDRATE CHOICES: 2.

Red Pepper Hummus Pita Sandwiches

PREP TIME: 15 MINUTES (READY IN 15 MINUTES)
SERVINGS: 4 (8 SANDWICHES)

 EASY   LOW FAT

HUMMUS

- 1 can (15 oz) Progresso® chick peas (garbanzo beans), drained, rinsed
- 1 tablespoon lemon juice
- 1 tablespoon olive oil
- 2 garlic cloves, chopped
- 1/3 cup drained roasted red bell peppers (from 7.25-oz jar)

SANDWICHES

- 8 lettuce leaves
- 1 cucumber, thinly sliced
- 4 (6 inch) whole wheat pita (pocket) breads, halved

1) In food processor bowl with metal blade, combine chick peas, lemon juice, oil and garlic; process 1 to 2 minutes or until smooth. Add roasted peppers; process 30 to 60 seconds or until peppers are finely chopped.

2) To assemble sandwiches, place lettuce leaf and cucumber slices in each pita bread half. Spoon about 3 tablespoons hummus in each.

1 SERVING: Calories 370; Total Fat 7g; Sodium 360mg; Dietary Fiber 11g; Protein 14g. EXCHANGES: 2-1/2 Starch, 1/2 Other Carbohydrate, 3 Vegetable, 1 Fat. CARBOHYDRATE CHOICES: 4.

New England-Style Shrimp Rolls with Lemon-Herb Mayonnaise

PREP TIME: 20 MINUTES (READY IN 50 MINUTES)
SERVINGS: 4

e EASY

- ⅓ cup mayonnaise or salad dressing
- 1 tablespoon lemon juice
- 1 tablespoon finely chopped fresh parsley
- 1 tablespoon finely chopped fresh basil leaves
- ¾ lb cooked shrimp, cut into ½-inch pieces
- 1 stalk celery, finely chopped (about ½ cup)
- ¼ cup finely chopped sweet onion
- ½ teaspoon seafood seasoning
- ¼ teaspoon salt
- ¼ teaspoon freshly ground pepper
- 2 tablespoons butter, softened
- 4 bratwurst or hoagie buns

1) In medium bowl, stir together mayonnaise, lemon juice, parsley and basil with whisk. Add the shrimp, celery, onion, seafood seasoning, salt and pepper; gently toss until coated. Cover and refrigerate about 30 minutes or until chilled.

2) Heat large heavy skillet over medium-low heat. Lightly butter both sides of each bun. Place in skillet; heat 2 minutes or until buns are golden brown. Turn buns over; toast other side. Divide shrimp salad evenly among toasted buns; serve immediately.

1 SERVING: Calories 390; Total Fat 23g; Sodium 780mg; Dietary Fiber 1g; Protein 22g. EXCHANGES: 1-1/2 Starch, 2-1/2 Lean Meat, 3 Fat. CARBOHYDRATE CHOICES: 1-1/2.

Turkey-BLT Roll-Ups

PREP TIME: 25 MINUTES (READY IN 25 MINUTES)
SERVINGS: 4 ROLL-UPS

 EASY

¼ cup chive-and-onion cream cheese (from 8-oz container)

2 tablespoons mayonnaise

6 slices precooked bacon, cut into small pieces (about ½ cup)

4 Old El Paso® flour tortillas for burritos, 8 inch (from 11.5-oz package)

6 oz thinly sliced cooked turkey

1 cup chopped plum (Roma) tomatoes (about 3 medium)

1 cup shredded lettuce

1) In small bowl, mix cream cheese and mayonnaise. Stir in bacon.

2) Spread cream cheese mixture over each tortilla. Top with turkey, tomatoes and lettuce. Roll up tightly. Serve immediately, or wrap each roll-up in plastic wrap and refrigerate up to 24 hours.

1 ROLL-UP: Calories 370; Total Fat 22g; Sodium 1280mg; Dietary Fiber 0g; Protein 16g. EXCHANGES: 1-1/2 Starch, 1/2 Vegetable, 1-1/2 High-Fat Meat, 2 Fat. CARBOHYDRATE CHOICES: 1-1/2.

Family Heroes

PREP TIME: 10 MINUTES (READY IN 10 MINUTES)
SERVINGS: 4 SANDWICHES

 EASY

¼ cup purchased Thousand Island dressing

4 hoagie buns, split

4 large lettuce leaves

¾ lb. sliced cooked turkey

8 thin slices tomato (about 1 large)

¼ lb. sliced hard salami

1 small cucumber, thinly sliced

4 (¾-oz) slices American cheese, halved

1) Spread the salad dressing evenly on the cut sides of buns.

2) Layer bottom halves of buns with lettuce, turkey, tomato, salami, cucumber and cheese. Cover with top halves of buns.

1 SANDWICH: Calories 600; Total Fat 27g; Sodium 2510mg; Dietary Fiber 3g; Protein 36g.
EXCHANGES: 2 Starch, 1 Other Carbohydrate, 1 Vegetable, 4 Medium-Fat Meat, 1 Fat.
CARBOHYDRATE CHOICES: 3-1/2.

Bacon Burgers

PREP TIME:	30 MINUTES (READY IN 30 MINUTES)	
SERVINGS:	8 SANDWICHES	

 EASY

3 lb. lean ground beef

1 (2.8-oz) pkg. (¾ cup) real bacon pieces

8 whole wheat burger buns, split

8 small leaves leaf lettuce

½ teaspoon seasoned salt

8 (1-oz) slices Cheddar cheese

8 teaspoons barbecue sauce

8 thin slices sweet onion (such as Vidalia®, Walla Walla, Maui or Texas Sweet)

1) Heat gas or charcoal grill. In large bowl, combine ground beef and bacon pieces; mix gently. Shape into 8 (½-inch-thick) patties. Make slight indentation in center of each patty.

2) Place patties on gas grill over medium heat. Cover grill; cook 13 to 15 minutes or until thoroughly cooked, turning once. During last 1 to 2 minutes of cooking time, place buns cut side down on grill; heat until toasted.

3) Place toasted bottoms of buns on large serving platter. Top each with lettuce. While patties are still on grill, sprinkle each with seasoned salt; top each with slice of cheese. Place patties on lettuce-lined buns. Immediately top each with 1 teaspoon barbecue sauce and 1 onion slice. Cover with top halves of buns.

1 SANDWICH: Calories 540; Total Fat 32g; Sodium 880mg; Dietary Fiber 2g; Protein 45g. EXCHANGES: 1/2 Starch, 1/2 Other Carbohydrate, 6 Medium-Fat Meat, 1/2 Fat. CARBOHYDRATE CHOICES: 1.

Beefy Greek Pita Folds

PREP TIME: 20 MINUTES (READY IN 20 MINUTES)
SERVINGS: 4 SANDWICHES

 EASY

1 lb lean (at least 80%) ground beef

1 small onion, cut in half lengthwise, sliced

3 cloves garlic, finely chopped

1 teaspoon dried oregano leaves

½ teaspoon salt

½ cup finely chopped peeled cucumber

½ cup chopped seeded tomato

1 container (8 oz) low-fat plain yogurt (1 cup)

1 teaspoon dried dill weed

¼ cup sliced ripe olives

4 pita fold breads, heated

1) In 10-inch skillet, cook beef, onion, garlic, oregano and ¼ teaspoon of the salt over medium-high heat 5 to 7 minutes, stirring occasionally, until beef is thoroughly cooked; drain.

2) Meanwhile, in medium bowl, mix cucumber, tomato, yogurt, dill and remaining ¼ teaspoon salt. Stir olives into beef mixture.

3) On each of 4 serving plates, place 1 pita bread. Spoon ¼ of beef mixture on half of each pita. Top each with a spoonful of yogurt mixture; fold other half of pita over filling. Serve with remaining yogurt mixture.

1 SANDWICH: Calories 380; Total Fat 15g; Sodium 700mg; Dietary Fiber 2g; Protein 27g.
EXCHANGES: 2 Starch, 1 Vegetable, 2-1/2 Medium-Fat Meat, 1/2 Fat. CARBOHYDRATE CHOICES: 2.

30-Minute Meals

This chapter is a dream for busy cooks because it offers satisfying stir-fries, pizza and more!

SOFT AND CRUNCHY FISH TACOS
PG. 157

FETTUCCINE WITH TWO CHEESES
PG. 150

MARGHERITA PIZZA
PG. 161

VEGETARIAN ITALIAN PASTA
SKILLET DINNER PG. 152

Fettuccine with Two Cheeses

PREP TIME: 25 MINUTES (READY IN 25 MINUTES)
SERVINGS: 4 (1-1/3 CUPS EACH)

e EASY

- 8 oz uncooked fettuccine
- 8 slices bacon, cut into ¼-inch pieces
- ½ cup butter, cut into pieces
- ½ cup half-and-half
- ½ cup shredded Parmesan cheese (2 oz)
- ½ cup crumbled Gorgonzola cheese (2 oz)
- ½ teaspoon cracked black pepper
- 1 tablespoon chopped fresh basil

1) Cook and drain fettuccine as directed on package. Meanwhile, in 10-inch skillet, cook bacon over medium-high heat until crisp; drain on paper towels. Discard drippings.

2) In same skillet, heat butter and half-and-half over medium heat, stirring frequently, until butter is melted and mixture starts to bubble. Reduce heat to low. Simmer 6 minutes, stirring frequently, until slightly thickened; remove from heat. Stir in cheeses, pepper and bacon.

3) In large serving bowl, toss fettuccine with cheese sauce until well coated. Top with basil.

1 SERVING: Calories 640; Total Fat 44g; Sodium 980mg; Dietary Fiber 2g; Protein 22g. EXCHANGES: 2-1/2 Starch, 2 High-Fat Meat, 5-1/2 Fat. CARBOHYDRATE CHOICES: 2-1/2.

Try other cheese combinations, such as shredded Asiago and crumbled blue cheese, in place of the Parmesan and Gorgonzola cheeses.

Greek Chicken with Yogurt Sauce

PREP TIME: 25 MINUTES (READY IN 25 MINUTES)
SERVINGS: 4 (1 CHICKEN BREAST AND 1/4 CUP SAUCE EACH)

 EASY   LOW FAT

SAUCE

- 1 medium cucumber, peeled, seeded and finely chopped
- ¼ cup plain yogurt
- ¼ cup sour cream
- 2 tablespoons chopped fresh parsley
- 2 teaspoons lemon juice
- ¼ teaspoon ground cumin

CHICKEN

- 4 boneless skinless chicken breasts (about 1 ¼ lb)
- ¼ teaspoon salt
- ¼ teaspoon ground cinnamon
- 2 teaspoons vegetable oil
- 2 tablespoons water
  Fresh parsley, if desired

1) In medium bowl, mix all sauce ingredients. Cover; refrigerate until serving time.

2) Sprinkle both sides of chicken with salt and cinnamon. In 10-inch skillet, heat oil over medium-high heat. Cook chicken in oil 10 to 12 minutes, turning occasionally, until golden brown. Reduce heat to low; add water. Cover; cook 2 to 3 minutes longer or until juice of chicken is clear when center of thickest part is cut (165°F).

3) Serve chicken with yogurt sauce. Garnish with parsley.

1 SERVING: Calories 240; Total Fat 10g; Sodium 250mg; Dietary Fiber 0g; Protein 33g. EXCHANGES: 4-1/2 Very Lean Meat, 1-1/2 Fat. CARBOHYDRATE CHOICES: 0.

Vegetarian Italian Pasta Skillet Dinner

PREP TIME: 15 MINUTES (READY IN 25 MINUTES)
SERVINGS: 2 (1-3/4 CUPS EACH)

 EASY   LOW FAT

1 ⅓ cups frozen sausage-style
 soy-protein crumbles

1 cup sliced fresh mushrooms

½ cup coarsely chopped onion
 (1 medium)

1 can (18.5 oz) Progresso® light
 Italian-style vegetable soup

¾ cup uncooked bow-tie (farfalle)
 pasta (2 oz)

2 cups fresh baby spinach leaves

¼ cup shredded mozzarella or
 Parmesan cheese (1 oz)

1) In 12-inch nonstick skillet, cook soy crumbles, mushrooms and onion over medium-high heat 4 to 6 minutes, stirring frequently, until crumbles are hot and vegetables are tender.

2) Stir in soup. Cover; heat to boiling. Stir in pasta; reduce heat to medium-low. Cover; simmer 10 minutes.

3) Add spinach; cook uncovered 3 to 5 minutes, stirring occasionally, until spinach is hot and just begins to wilt. Sprinkle with cheese.

1 SERVING: Calories 340; Total Fat 7g; Sodium 1430mg; Dietary Fiber 8g; Protein 23g. EXCHANGES: 2 Starch, 1/2 Other Carbohydrate, 2 Vegetable, 2 Lean Meat. CARBOHYDRATE CHOICES: 3.

Pork and Corn Hash

PREP TIME: 30 MINUTES (READY IN 30 MINUTES)
SERVINGS: 4 (1-1/4 CUPS EACH)

 EASY

2 tablespoons olive oil

8 small red potatoes (about 1 lb), cut into ½-inch cubes

1 pork tenderloin (about 1 lb), cut into ½-inch pieces

1 jar (12 oz) seasoned gravy for pork

1 can (7 oz) Green Giant® Niblets® whole kernel sweet corn, drained

4 medium green onions with tops, sliced (¼ cup)

⅛ teaspoon pepper

¼ cup chopped fresh parsley

1) In 12-inch nonstick skillet, heat oil over medium-high heat. Cook potatoes in oil 10 to 12 minutes, stirring frequently, until golden brown. Add pork; cook about 5 minutes, stirring frequently.

2) Reduce heat to medium. Add remaining ingredients except parsley. Cook 4 to 6 minutes longer, stirring occasionally, until pork is no longer pink in center. Top with parsley.

1 SERVING: Calories 380; Total Fat 14g; Sodium 540mg; Dietary Fiber 4g; Protein 29g. EXCHANGES: 2 Starch, 1 Vegetable, 3 Lean Meat, 1 Fat. CARBOHYDRATE CHOICES: 2.

Garden-Fresh Alfredo Pizza

PREP TIME: 15 MINUTES (READY IN 30 MINUTES)
SERVINGS: 8 SLICES

 EASY

- 1 package (14 oz) prebaked original Italian pizza crust (11 inch)
- ½ cup refrigerated Alfredo pasta sauce (from 10-oz container)
- 1 plum (Roma) tomato, seeded, coarsely chopped
- ½ cup chopped yellow bell pepper
- 1 small zucchini, sliced (1 cup)
- 1 jar (4.5 oz) Green Giant® sliced mushrooms, drained
- ¼ cup chopped red onion
- ¼ cup chopped fresh basil
- 1 ½ cups shredded Italian cheese blend (6 oz)

tip

To quickly seed a tomato, cut in half lengthwise and use a small spoon to scrape out the seeds from each half.

1) Heat oven to 450°F. Place crust on 12-inch pizza pan or large cookie sheet. Spread Alfredo sauce over crust. Top with remaining ingredients.

2) Bake 10 to 14 minutes or until cheese is melted and crust is golden brown.

1 SLICE: Calories 280; Total Fat 13g; Sodium 470mg; Dietary Fiber 2g; Protein 10g. EXCHANGES: 1-1/2 Starch, 1 Vegetable, 1/2 Medium-Fat Meat, 2 Fat. CARBOHYDRATE CHOICES: 2.

Easy Chicken and Rice

PREP TIME: 30 MINUTES (READY IN 30 MINUTES)
SERVINGS: 6 (ABOUT 1-1/4 CUPS EACH)

 EASY

1 cup uncooked regular long-grain white rice

2 ¼ cups water

2 tablespoons olive oil

1 package (8 oz) sliced fresh mushrooms (about 3 cups)

2 small red or yellow bell peppers, cut into bite-size strips (about 2 cups)

8 medium green onions with tops, finely chopped (½ cup)

3 cloves garlic, finely chopped

1 cup tomato pasta sauce

½ cup Progresso® chicken broth (from 32-oz carton)

2 cups shredded deli rotisserie chicken (from 2-lb chicken)

1 cup shredded Parmesan cheese (4 oz)

3 tablespoons chopped fresh parsley

1) Cook rice in water as directed on package.

2) Meanwhile, in deep 12-inch skillet, heat oil over medium-high heat. Cook the mushrooms, bell peppers, onions and garlic in oil 2 to 3 minutes, stirring frequently, until the vegetables are tender. Remove from heat until rice is cooked.

3) Stir rice, pasta sauce, broth, chicken and ½ cup of the cheese into vegetable mixture; cook over medium-low heat about 3 to 5 minutes, stirring occasionally, until mixture is hot. Sprinkle with remaining ½ cup cheese and the parsley.

1 SERVING: Calories 360; Total Fat 13g; Sodium 840mg; Dietary Fiber 2g; Protein 25g. EXCHANGES: 1-1/2 Starch, 2 Vegetable, 2-1/2 Medium-Fat Meat. CARBOHYDRATE CHOICES: 2.

Spinach and Ham French Bread Pizza

PREP TIME: 20 MINUTES (READY IN 30 MINUTES)
SERVINGS: 6

 EASY

1 loaf (1 lb) French bread

3 tablespoons olive or vegetable oil

1 can (8 oz) pizza sauce

1 cup chopped cooked ham

1 small onion, chopped (¼ cup)

2 tablespoons pine nuts

2 cups chopped fresh spinach (about 2 oz)

12 slices (1 oz each) provolone cheese, cut in half

1) Heat oven to 400°F. Cut loaf of bread in half horizontally; cut each half crosswise into thirds. Place cut sides up on ungreased large cookie sheet; brush with oil. Bake 5 to 6 minutes or until tops are slightly toasted. Remove from oven.

2) Spread pizza sauce evenly over cut sides of each piece of bread. Top evenly with ham, onion, nuts and spinach. Place 4 half slices of cheese on top of each.

3) Bake 7 to 10 minutes or until cheese is melted and pizza is hot.

1 SERVING: Calories 560; Total Fat 27g; Sodium 1400mg; Dietary Fiber 3g; Protein 30g. EXCHANGES: 2-1/2 Starch, 1/2 Other Carbohydrate, 1/2 Vegetable, 3 Lean Meat, 3-1/2 Fat. CARBOHYDRATE CHOICES: 3.

Soft and Crunchy Fish Tacos

PREP TIME: 20 MINUTES (READY IN 20 MINUTES)
SERVINGS: 4 (2 TACOS EACH)

 EASY

8 Old El Paso® flour tortillas for soft tacos & fajitas (6 inch; from 8.2-oz package)

8 Old El Paso® taco shells (from 4.6-oz package)

1 bag (12 oz) broccoli slaw mix (about 4 cups)

⅓ cup light lime vinaigrette dressing or vinaigrette dressing

¼ cup chopped fresh cilantro

1 package (1 oz) Old El Paso® taco seasoning mix

4 tilapia or other mild-flavored, medium-firm fish fillets (about 1 lb)

1 tablespoon vegetable oil

1 cup prepared guacamole

1 cup crumbled cotija or feta cheese, if desired

1) Heat tortillas and taco shells as directed on package. In medium bowl, toss broccoli slaw mix, dressing and cilantro; set aside.

2) In shallow dish, place taco seasoning. Coat both sides of fish with taco seasoning. In 12-inch nonstick skillet, heat oil over medium-high heat. Cook fish in oil 6 minutes, turning once, or until fish flakes easily with fork. Divide fish into 8 pieces.

3) Spread each flour tortilla with 2 tablespoons guacamole. Place hard taco shell on center of flour tortilla. Using slotted spoon, spoon about ¼ cup slaw into each hard taco shell. Place 1 fish piece over slaw in each taco shell. Gently fold tortilla sides up to match taco shell sides. Top with 1 tablespoon cheese.

1 SERVING: Calories 530; Total Fat 21g; Sodium 1630mg; Dietary Fiber 5g; Protein 29g. EXCHANGES: 3 Starch, 1/2 Other Carbohydrate, 1/2 Vegetable, 2-1/2 Lean Meat, 2-1/2 Fat. CARBOHYDRATE CHOICES: 3-1/2.

Chicken and Pasta Fresca

PREP TIME: 20 MINUTES (READY IN 20 MINUTES)
SERVINGS: 4 (1-1/2 CUPS EACH)

 EASY

3 cups uncooked gemelli or rotini pasta (8 oz)

1 tablespoon olive oil

1 medium onion, chopped (½ cup)

½ cup balsamic vinaigrette dressing

2 large tomatoes, chopped (2 cups)

2 cups chopped deli rotisserie chicken (from 2-lb chicken)

1 bag (6 oz) fresh baby spinach leaves

½ cup crumbled feta cheese (2 oz)

1) Cook and drain pasta as directed on package. Meanwhile, in 12-inch nonstick skillet, heat oil over medium-high heat. Cook onion in oil about 2 minutes, stirring frequently. Add dressing, tomatoes and chicken. Cook 2 to 3 minutes, stirring occasionally, until hot. Stir in spinach; cook 1 to 2 minutes or until spinach starts to wilt.

2) In a large serving bowl, toss the cooked pasta with the chicken mixture. Top with cheese.

1 SERVING: Calories 600; Total Fat 27g; Sodium 760mg; Dietary Fiber 5g; Protein 33g. EXCHANGES: 3 Starch, 2-1/2 Vegetable, 2-1/2 Medium-Fat Meat, 2-1/2 Fat. CARBOHYDRATE CHOICES: 4.

tip

For Mediterranean flair, stir some halved kalamata olives into this pasta dish.

Cacciatore Chicken with Polenta

PREP TIME: 30 MINUTES (READY IN 30 MINUTES)
SERVINGS: 4 (3 POLENTA SLICES WITH 1 CUP CHICKEN MIXTURE EACH)

 EASY   LOW FAT

2 teaspoons olive oil

1 roll (1 lb) refrigerated polenta, cut into 12 slices

1 lb boneless skinless chicken breasts, cut into 1-inch pieces

1 medium onion, chopped (½ cup)

½ cup chopped red bell pepper

2 cloves garlic, finely chopped

1 teaspoon Italian seasoning

1 teaspoon sugar

½ teaspoon salt

1 can (14.5 oz) Muir Glen® organic fire roasted diced tomatoes, undrained

1 can (4 oz) Green Giant® mushrooms pieces and stems, drained

¼ cup chopped fresh Italian flat-leaf parsley

1) In 10-inch nonstick skillet, heat 1 teaspoon of the oil over high heat. Cook 6 polenta slices in oil about 5 to 8 minutes, turning once, until golden brown. Repeat with remaining oil and polenta slices. Remove from skillet; cover to keep warm.

2) In same skillet, cook chicken, onion, bell pepper, garlic, Italian seasoning, sugar and salt over medium-high heat 5 minutes, stirring frequently. Stir in the tomatoes and mushrooms. Heat to boiling; reduce heat to medium-low. Simmer uncovered 3 to 5 minutes or until the chicken is no longer pink in center.

3) Serve the chicken mixture over the slices of polenta. Sprinkle with chopped parsley.

1 SERVING: Calories 280; Total Fat 6g; Sodium 980mg; Dietary Fiber 3g; Protein 29g. EXCHANGES: 1-1/2 Starch, 1 Vegetable, 3 Very Lean Meat, 1/2 Fat. CARBOHYDRATE CHOICES: 2.

Greek Chicken Pizza

PREP TIME: 15 MINUTES (READY IN 30 MINUTES)
SERVINGS: 4

 EASY

1 can (13.8 oz) Pillsbury® refrigerated classic pizza crust

1 can (8 oz) pizza sauce

1½ cups shredded mozzarella cheese (6 oz)

2 cups cubed cooked chicken

½ cup thinly sliced red onion

½ cup crumbled feta cheese (2 oz)

¼ cup chopped kalamata olives

1 tablespoon chopped fresh or 1 teaspoon dried oregano leaves

1) Heat oven to 425°F. Spray large cookie sheet with cooking spray. Unroll dough on cookie sheet; starting at center, press dough into 13x9-inch rectangle.

2) Spread pizza sauce over dough to within ½ inch of edges. Top with remaining ingredients.

3) Bake 12 to 15 minutes or until the pizza crust is golden brown and the cheese is melted.

1 SERVING: Calories 610; Total Fat 24g; Sodium 1410mg; Dietary Fiber 3g; Protein 44g. EXCHANGES: 2-1/2 Starch, 1 Other Carbohydrate, 1/2 Vegetable, 5 Lean Meat, 1-1/2 Fat. CARBOHYDRATE CHOICES: 4.

Margherita Pizza

PREP TIME: 15 MINUTES (READY IN 30 MINUTES)
SERVINGS: 20

❸ EASY   **⑪ LOW FAT**

2 teaspoons cornmeal

1 can (13.8 oz) Pillsbury® refrigerated classic pizza crust

2 teaspoons olive oil

2 cloves garlic, finely chopped

1 ½ cups shredded mozzarella cheese (6 oz)

¼ cup shredded Parmesan cheese (1 oz)

20 slices (¼ inch thick) plum (Roma) tomatoes (about 6 medium)

⅓ cup thin strips fresh basil leaves

1) Move oven rack to lowest position. Heat oven to 425°F. Spray 15x10-inch baking pan with cooking spray; sprinkle with cornmeal.

2) Unroll dough; place in pan. Starting at center, press out dough to edge of pan. Brush dough with oil; sprinkle evenly with garlic.

3) Bake crust 6 to 8 minutes or until set and dry. Remove from oven. Sprinkle cheeses over partially baked crust. Arrange tomato slices over cheese. Sprinkle with half of the basil.

4) Bake 12 to 17 minutes longer or until crust is deep golden brown. Sprinkle with remaining basil. Cut into 20 squares. Serve warm.

1 SERVING: Calories 90; Total Fat 3g; Sodium 210mg; Dietary Fiber 0g; Protein 4g. EXCHANGES: 1/2 Starch, 1/2 Vegetable, 1/2 Fat. CARBOHYDRATE CHOICES: 1.

tip

Make sure your oven is hot before baking pizza. The crust has to bake and brown very quickly. A slow or underheated oven will not force moisture out of the crust, making the toppings and crust soggy.

Buffalo Chicken-Style Pizza

PREP TIME: 15 MINUTES (READY IN 30 MINUTES)
SERVINGS: 8

 EASY

1 can (11 oz) Pillsbury® refrigerated thin pizza crust

½ cup Buffalo wing sauce

1 ½ cups chopped cooked chicken

¼ cup finely chopped celery

¼ cup finely chopped onion

½ cup crumbled blue cheese (2 oz), if desired

1 ½ cups finely shredded Colby-Monterey Jack cheese blend (6 oz)

½ cup ranch dressing

1) Heat oven to 400°F. Grease 15x10-inch or larger dark or nonstick cookie sheet with shortening. Unroll dough on cookie sheet; starting at center, press dough into 15x10-inch rectangle.

2) Spread ¼ cup of the Buffalo wing sauce over dough to within ½ inch of edges. In medium bowl, mix chicken, celery, onion and remaining ¼ cup Buffalo wing sauce. Spoon evenly over crust. Sprinkle with cheeses.

3) Bake 12 to 14 minutes or until crust is golden brown and cheese is melted. Serve with ranch dressing.

1 SERVING: Calories 320; Total Fat 19g; Sodium 940mg; Dietary Fiber 1g; Protein 15g. EXCHANGES: 1-1/2 Starch, 1-1/2 Lean Meat, 2-1/2 Fat. CARBOHYDRATE CHOICES: 1-1/2.

Beef and Potato Skillet Dinner with Roasted Red Pepper Sauce

PREP TIME: 30 MINUTES (READY IN 30 MINUTES)
SERVINGS: 4 (ABOUT 1-3/4 CUPS EACH)

 EASY

1 jar (7 or 7.25 oz) roasted red bell peppers, drained

½ cup half-and-half

4 teaspoons vegetable oil

1 bag (20 oz) refrigerated cooked diced potatoes with onions

1 lb boneless beef sirloin steak, cut into thin strips

½ teaspoon salt

¼ teaspoon pepper

1 bag (12 oz) Green Giant® Valley Fresh Steamers™ frozen broccoli florets, thawed

1 teaspoon chopped fresh tarragon leaves

1) In food processor or blender, place roasted peppers and half-and-half. Cover and process on medium-high speed 30 seconds until smooth. Set aside.

2) In deep 12-inch nonstick skillet, heat 2 teaspoons of the oil over medium-high heat. Add potatoes. Cover; cook 10 to 12 minutes, stirring frequently, until tender. Remove from skillet; cover to keep warm.

3) In same skillet, heat remaining 2 teaspoons oil over medium-high heat. Cook beef, salt and pepper in oil 2 to 3 minutes, stirring frequently, until beef is browned.

4) Add broccoli and potatoes. Pour reserved red pepper sauce over mixture; gently toss to coat. Reduce heat to low. Simmer, uncovered, 2 to 3 minutes or until broccoli is crisp-tender. Sprinkle with tarragon.

1 SERVING: Calories 400; Total Fat 12g; Sodium 360mg; Dietary Fiber 6g; Protein 35g. EXCHANGES: 2 Starch, 2 Vegetable, 3-1/2 Lean Meat. CARBOHYDRATE CHOICES: 2-1/2.

Italian Chicken Pot Pie with Basil Biscuits

PREP TIME: 30 MINUTES (READY IN 30 MINUTES)
SERVINGS: 6 (ABOUT 1 CHICKEN MIXTURE AND 3 BISCUITS EACH)

 EASY   LOW FAT

1 tablespoon olive oil

1 medium onion, chopped (½ cup)

1 clove garlic, finely chopped

3 small zucchini, cut into ½-inch pieces (about 2 cups)

2 cups shredded deli rotisserie chicken (from 2-lb chicken)

1 can (15 oz) tomato sauce

1 can (15 oz) Progresso® cannellini beans, drained, rinsed

1 can (14.5 oz) diced tomatoes with Italian-style herbs, undrained

¼ teaspoon salt

¼ teaspoon cracked black pepper

1 cup Original Bisquick® mix

⅔ cup yellow cornmeal

¾ cup milk

¼ cup chopped fresh basil

1) In deep 12-inch skillet, heat oil over medium-high heat. Cook onion and garlic in oil 2 to 3 minutes, stirring occasionally, until onion is soft. Stir in zucchini, chicken, tomato sauce, beans, tomatoes, salt and pepper. Heat to boiling; reduce heat to medium-low. Cover; simmer 5 minutes.

2) Meanwhile, in medium bowl, mix Bisquick mix, cornmeal, milk and basil just until moistened. Drop dough by 18 rounded tablespoonfuls onto hot chicken mixture. Cover; cook 8 minutes.

1 SERVING: Calories 380; Total Fat 10g; Sodium 1060mg; Dietary Fiber 7g; Protein 23g. EXCHANGES: 2 Starch, 1/2 Other Carbohydrate, 2 Vegetable, 2 Medium-Fat Meat. CARBOHYDRATE CHOICES: 3.

tip

Cornmeal can be white, yellow or blue, depending on which strain of corn is used. All three types can be used interchangeably in recipes.

Asian Beef Noodle Bowls

PREP TIME: 20 MINUTES (READY IN 20 MINUTES)
SERVINGS: 4 (1-1/4 CUPS EACH)

 EASY

4 oz uncooked angel hair pasta (capellini), broken in half

8 oz fresh sugar snap peas

5 teaspoons vegetable oil

1 lb boneless beef sirloin steak, cut into ¼-inch strips

1 medium carrot, thinly sliced (½ cup)

½ cup teriyaki baste and glaze (from 12-oz bottle)

4 medium green onions with tops, sliced (¼ cup)

½ cup honey-roasted peanuts, chopped

1) Cook pasta as directed on package. Meanwhile, snip off stem ends of sugar snap peas and remove strings if desired. Drain pasta; cover to keep warm.

2) In 12-inch nonstick skillet, heat 3 teaspoons of the oil over medium-high heat. Stir-fry beef in oil about 2 to 3 minutes, until no longer pink. Remove from skillet; keep warm.

3) In same skillet, heat remaining 2 teaspoons oil over medium-high heat. Stir-fry peas and carrot in oil about 3 to 4 minutes, until crisp-tender. Stir in pasta, beef and teriyaki baste and glaze; toss until well blended.

4) Serve in bowls; sprinkle with onions and peanuts.

1 SERVING: Calories 520; Total Fat 20g; Sodium 1500mg; Dietary Fiber 5g; Protein 43g. EXCHANGES: 1-1/2 Starch, 1/2 Other Carbohydrate, 1-1/2 Vegetable, 5 Lean Meat, 1 Fat. CARBOHYDRATE CHOICES: 3.

Fettuccine with Beef and Peppers

PREP TIME: 20 MINUTES (READY IN 20 MINUTES)
SERVINGS: 4 (1-1/2 CUPS EACH)

🅔 EASY

1 package (9 oz) refrigerated fettuccine

1 lb lean (at least 80%) ground beef

1 medium green bell pepper, cut into thin bite-size strips

1 medium red bell pepper, cut into thin bite-size strips

½ cup half-and-half

⅓ cup basil pesto

½ teaspoon salt

⅛ teaspoon pepper

1) Cook and drain fettuccine as directed on package.

2) Meanwhile, in 12-inch skillet, cook beef over medium-high heat 5 to 7 minutes, stirring occasionally, until thoroughly cooked; drain. Add bell peppers; cook 4 to 6 minutes, stirring frequently, until crisp-tender.

3) Add fettuccine and remaining ingredients. Reduce heat to medium; cook 3 to 5 minutes, stirring occasionally, until thoroughly heated.

1 SERVING: Calories 590; Total Fat 31g; Sodium 540mg; Dietary Fiber 3g; Protein 30g. EXCHANGES: 3 Starch, 1 Vegetable, 2-1/2 Medium-Fat Meat, 3-1/2 Fat. CARBOHYDRATE CHOICES: 3

Mom's Skillet Goulash

PREP TIME: 30 MINUTES (READY IN 30 MINUTES)
SERVINGS: 6 (1-1/2 CUPS EACH)

🅔 EASY   🅕 LOW FAT

2 ⅔ cups uncooked rotini pasta (8 oz)

1 lb lean (at least 80%) ground beef

1 ½ cups chopped celery

1 large onion, chopped (1 cup)

2 cans (14.5 oz each) diced tomatoes, undrained

1 can (10 ¾ oz) condensed tomato soup

1 teaspoon dried basil leaves

½ teaspoon salt

¼ teaspoon pepper

1) Cook and drain pasta as directed on package.

2) Meanwhile, in 12-inch nonstick skillet, cook beef, celery and onion over medium-high heat 5 to 7 minutes, stirring occasionally, until beef is thoroughly cooked; drain.

3) Stir in the pasta and remaining ingredients. Heat to boiling; reduce the heat to medium-low. Simmer, uncovered, 10 minutes or until thickened and bubbly.

1 SERVING: Calories 350; Total Fat 10g; Sodium 750mg; Dietary Fiber 4g; Protein 21g. EXCHANGES: 2 Starch, 1/2 Other Carbohydrate, 2 Vegetable, 1-1/2 Lean Meat, 1 Fat. CARBOHYDRATE CHOICES: 3.

Chicken with Chipotle Alfredo Sauce

PREP TIME: 30 MINUTES (READY IN 30 MINUTES)
SERVINGS: 4 (3/4 CUP PASTA AND 1/2 CUP CHICKEN MIXTURE EACH)

 EASY

2 cups uncooked penne pasta (6 oz)

1 tablespoon olive oil

1 lb boneless skinless chicken breasts, cut into ½-inch pieces

2 cloves garlic, finely chopped

1 chipotle chile in adobo sauce (from 7-oz can), finely chopped

1 jar (16 oz) Alfredo pasta sauce

2 tablespoons chopped fresh cilantro

1) Cook and drain pasta as directed on package.

2) Meanwhile, in 10-inch skillet, heat oil over medium-high heat. Cook chicken and garlic in oil 5 to 7 minutes, stirring occasionally, until chicken is no longer pink in center. Stir in chile and Alfredo sauce; cook 2 minutes, stirring frequently.

3) Serve the chicken mixture over the cooked pasta; sprinkle with cilantro.

1 SERVING: Calories 740; Total Fat 44g; Sodium 530mg; Dietary Fiber 2g; Protein 41g. EXCHANGES: 3 Starch, 4-1/2 Lean Meat, 6 Fat. CARBOHYDRATE CHOICES: 3.

To keep cilantro fresh for a few days, cut the stems and place in a container in an inch or two of water. Cover loosely with a plastic bag and refrigerate.

Easy Cheesy Beef and Bow-Ties

PREP TIME: 20 MINUTES (READY IN 20 MINUTES)
SERVINGS: 4 (1-1/3 CUPS EACH)

 EASY

2 ½ cups uncooked bow-tie (farfalle)
pasta (5 oz)

1 lb lean (at least 80%) ground beef

1 can (10 ¾ oz) condensed Cheddar
cheese soup

1 cup Old El Paso® thick 'n chunky
salsa

8 medium green onions, chopped
(½ cup)

1 ½ cups shredded American-Cheddar
cheese blend (6 oz)

1) Cook and drain pasta as directed on package.

2) Meanwhile, in 12-inch nonstick skillet, cook beef over medium-high heat 5 to 7 minutes, stirring occasionally, until thoroughly cooked; drain. Stir in the soup, salsa and 6 tablespoons of the onions. Heat to boiling. Reduce heat to medium-low; cook 5 minutes.

3) Stir in pasta; cook 3 to 5 minutes, stirring occasionally, until thoroughly heated. Sprinkle with cheese; cook just until melted. Sprinkle with remaining 2 tablespoons onions.

1 SERVING: Calories 600; Total Fat 35g; Sodium 1460mg; Dietary Fiber 1g; Protein 38g. EXCHANGES: 2-1/2 Starch, 4 High-Fat Meat. CARBOHYDRATE CHOICES: 2.

Gingered Rice and Beef

PREP TIME: 30 MINUTES (READY IN 30 MINUTES)
SERVINGS: 4 (1-1/3 CUPS EACH)

 EASY

1 lb extra-lean (at least 90%) ground beef

1 tablespoon grated gingerroot

1 box (6.2 oz) fried rice-flavor rice and vermicelli mix (with seasoning packet)

2 cups water

1 medium red bell pepper, coarsely chopped (1 cup)

2 cups Green Giant Select® Valley Fresh Steamers™ frozen sugar snap peas (from 12-oz bag)

1) In 12-inch nonstick skillet, cook beef and gingerroot over medium-high heat 5 to 7 minutes, stirring occasionally, until beef is thoroughly cooked; drain.

2) Add rice and vermicelli mix with contents of seasoning packet; cook and stir 2 minutes. Add water; heat to boiling. Reduce heat to low. Cover; simmer 10 minutes, stirring occasionally.

3) Stir in bell pepper and sugar snap peas. Cover; simmer 5 to 10 minutes longer, stirring occasionally, until rice and vegetables are tender.

1 SERVING: Calories 370; Total Fat 11g; Sodium 950mg; Dietary Fiber 4g; Protein 28g. EXCHANGES: 2-1/2 Starch, 1 Vegetable, 2-1/2 Lean Meat, 1/2 Fat. CARBOHYDRATE CHOICES: 2-1/2.

Asian Pork and Vegetable Stir-Fry

PREP TIME: 30 MINUTES (READY IN 30 MINUTES)
SERVINGS: 2

 EASY   LOW FAT

½ cup uncooked instant brown rice

1 cup water

1 boneless pork loin chop (4 oz), cut into thin bite-size strips

2 cups sliced fresh mushrooms (about 5 oz)

1 medium onion, cut into thin wedges

½ teaspoon garlic powder

1 can (18.5 oz) Progresso® light homestyle vegetable and rice soup

1 tablespoon stir-fry sauce

1 cup fresh snow pea pods

2 tablespoons sliced almonds, if desired

1) In 1-quart saucepan, cook the rice in water as directed on the package, omitting butter.

2) Meanwhile, in 12-inch nonstick skillet, place pork, mushrooms and onion; sprinkle with garlic powder. Cook over high heat 4 to 6 minutes, stirring frequently, until pork begins to brown. Stir in soup and stir-fry sauce; heat to boiling. Stir in pea pods. Cook over high heat 5 to 7 minutes, stirring occasionally, until pea pods are crisp-tender.

3) Serve the pork mixture over rice; sprinkle with almonds.

1 SERVING: Calories 310; Total Fat 5g; Sodium 1050mg; Dietary Fiber 8g; Protein 20g. EXCHANGES: 1-1/2 Starch, 1/2 Other Carbohydrate, 2-1/2 Vegetable, 1-1/2 Lean Meat. CARBOHYDRATE CHOICES: 3.

Pizza Skillet Hot Dish

PREP TIME: 30 MINUTES (READY IN 30 MINUTES)
SERVINGS: 4 (1-1/4 CUPS EACH)

 EASY

½ lb lean (at least 80%) ground beef

2 oz sliced pepperoni, chopped
(½ cup)

1 jar (16 oz) tomato pasta sauce

1 cup water

1 package (7 oz) ready-cut spaghetti
(short curved spaghetti)

¼ cup sliced ripe olives

½ green bell pepper, cut into bite-size
strips

1 cup shredded mozzarella cheese
(4 oz)

1) In 12-inch skillet, cook the beef over medium-high heat 5 to 7 minutes, stirring occasionally, until thoroughly cooked. Add the pepperoni; cook 1 minute. Drain.

2) Stir in pasta sauce, water and uncooked spaghetti. Heat to boiling; stir. Reduce heat to medium-low. Cover; cook 10 to 15 minutes or until spaghetti is desired doneness, stirring occasionally.

3) Gently stir in the olives. Arrange pepper strips over the top. Sprinkle with cheese. Remove from heat. Cover; let stand 3 to 5 minutes or until the cheese is melted.

1 SERVING: Calories 610; Total Fat 24g; Sodium 1240mg; Dietary Fiber 4g; Protein 30g. EXCHANGES: 3 Starch, 1-1/2 Other Carbohydrate, 3 Medium-Fat Meat, 1-1/2 Fat. CARBOHYDRATE CHOICES: 4-1/2.

Meatball Primavera

PREP TIME: 15 MINUTES (READY IN 15 MINUTES)
SERVINGS: 4 (2-1/2 CUPS EACH)

🄴 EASY

8 oz uncooked fettuccine, broken in half

½ cup thin red onion wedges

2 small zucchini or yellow summer squash (or 1 of each), cut into 2x½-inch strips

4 plum (Roma) tomatoes, chopped (about 1 cup)

24 frozen cooked meatballs (from 16-oz bag), thawed

½ cup basil pesto

1) Cook and drain fettuccine as directed on package.

2) Meanwhile, in 12-inch nonstick skillet, cook onion over medium heat 2 to 3 minutes, stirring frequently, until crisp-tender. Add zucchini; cook and stir 2 minutes. Stir in tomatoes and meatballs; cook 3 to 5 minutes, stirring occasionally, until thoroughly heated.

3) Add the fettuccine and pesto; cook and stir just until thoroughly heated.

1 SERVING: Calories 610; Total Fat 31g; Sodium 750mg; Dietary Fiber 5g; Protein 28g. EXCHANGES: 3 Starch, 2 Vegetable, 2 Medium-Fat Meat, 4 Fat. CARBOHYDRATE CHOICES: 3-1/2.

Barbecue Beef and Vegetable Skillet

PREP TIME: 25 MINUTES (READY IN 25 MINUTES)
SERVINGS: 5 (1-1/2 CUPS EACH)

EASY   **LOW FAT**

1 lb lean (at least 80%) ground beef

3 cups frozen seasoned chunky-style hash brown potatoes (from 20-oz bag)

3 cups Green Giant® Valley Fresh Steamers™ frozen cut green beans (from 12-oz bag)

1 cup frozen bell pepper and onion stir-fry

1 cup barbecue sauce

½ cup water

1) In 12-inch skillet, cook beef over medium-high heat 5 to 7 minutes, stirring occasionally, until thoroughly cooked; drain.

2) Stir in potatoes, green beans and bell pepper and onion stir-fry. Reduce heat to medium. Cover; cook 8 to 12 minutes or until vegetables are tender, stirring occasionally. Stir in barbecue sauce and water. Cover; simmer 3 to 5 minutes or until thoroughly heated.

1 SERVING: Calories 380; Total Fat 10g; Sodium 1000mg; Dietary Fiber 5g; Protein 20g. EXCHANGES: 1-1/2 Starch, 1-1/2 Other Carbohydrate, 2 Vegetable, 1-1/2 Medium-Fat Meat, 1/2 Fat. CARBOHYDRATE CHOICES: 3-1/2.

Pork, Broccoli and Noodle Skillet

PREP TIME: 30 MINUTES (READY IN 30 MINUTES)
SERVINGS: 5 (1-1/2 CUPS EACH)

 EASY

4 cups uncooked dumpling egg noodles (8 oz)

1 bag (12 oz) Green Giant Select® Valley Fresh Steamers™ frozen broccoli florets

1 tablespoon butter or margarine

1 lb pork tenderloin, cut crosswise into ¼-inch slices

1 cup sliced fresh mushrooms (3 oz)

1 clove garlic, finely chopped

1 jar (12 oz) mushroom gravy

1 tablespoon Worcestershire sauce

1) In 4-quart Dutch oven or saucepan, cook the noodles as directed on package, adding the broccoli during last 3 to 5 minutes of cooking time. Cook until the noodles and broccoli are tender; drain. Return to saucepan; cover to keep warm.

2) In 12-inch nonstick skillet, melt butter over medium-high heat. Cook pork in butter 3 to 5 minutes, stirring frequently, until browned. Add mushrooms and garlic; cook 2 to 4 minutes, stirring frequently, until mushrooms are tender.

3) Stir in gravy and Worcestershire sauce. Cook over medium-high heat, stirring frequently, until bubbly and thickened. Add pork mixture to noodles and broccoli; toss gently to coat.

1 SERVING: Calories 390; Total Fat 17g; Sodium 710mg; Dietary Fiber 4g; Protein 25g. EXCHANGES: 2 Starch, 1/2 Vegetable, 2-1/2 Lean Meat, 1-1/2 Fat. CARBOHYDRATE CHOICES: 2.

Black Beans, Chicken and Rice

PREP TIME: 30 MINUTES (READY IN 30 MINUTES)
SERVINGS: 4 (1-1/2 CUPS EACH)

 EASY

2 teaspoons vegetable oil

1 cup uncooked regular long-grain white rice

1 ½ teaspoons ground cumin

1 teaspoon chili powder

2 cups cubed cooked chicken

2 cups frozen bell pepper and onion stir-fry, coarsely chopped

1 can (15 oz) black beans, drained, rinsed

1 ¾ cups Progresso® chicken broth (from 32-oz carton)

2 tablespoons water

½ cup shredded Cheddar cheese (2 oz)

1) In 12-inch skillet, heat oil over medium-high heat. Cook and stir rice, cumin and chili powder in oil 1 minute. Stir in all remaining ingredients except cheese. Heat to boiling. Reduce heat; cover and simmer 15 to 18 minutes, stirring occasionally, until liquid is absorbed and rice is tender.

2) Remove skillet from heat. Uncover and fluff mixture with fork. Sprinkle with cheese. Cover; let stand 1 to 2 minutes or until cheese is melted before serving.

1 SERVING: Calories 510; Total Fat 11g; Sodium 1020mg; Dietary Fiber 10g; Protein 37g. EXCHANGES: 4 Starch, 1 Vegetable, 3 Lean Meat. CARBOHYDRATE CHOICES: 4.

tip

Use fresh red, yellow and green bell pepper strips, and 1/4 cup of chopped onion, in place of the frozen stir-fry mixture.

GREEK-STYLE BEEF AND PASTA
PG. 188

Fresh Pasta Dishes

From easy skillet recipes to satisfying stir-fries, you'll find all your favorite pasta dishes here!

TEX-MEX MACARONI AND CHEESE
PG. 191

THAI PEANUT RAMEN
PG. 187

EASY NOODLES NIÇOISE
PG. 193

Bacon-Tomato-Spinach Ravioli Toss

PREP TIME: 20 MINUTES (READY IN 20 MINUTES)
SERVINGS: 4 (1-1/4 CUPS EACH)

 EASY

2 packages (9 oz each) refrigerated cheese-filled ravioli

6 slices packaged precooked bacon (from 2.1-oz package), broken into ½-inch pieces

3 cups fresh baby spinach leaves (from 6-oz bag)

1 cup grape tomatoes, cut in half

½ cup balsamic vinaigrette dressing

¼ teaspoon freshly ground pepper

1) In 5-quart Dutch oven, cook ravioli as directed on package; drain and return to Dutch oven. Meanwhile, on microwavable plate, microwave bacon 30 to 45 seconds on High until crisp.

2) Add bacon, spinach, tomatoes and dressing to ravioli. Cook over medium heat until warmed and spinach is partially wilted. Sprinkle with pepper.

1 SERVING: Calories 500; Total Fat 18g; Sodium 660mg; Dietary Fiber 3g; Protein 22g. EXCHANGES: 4 Starch, 1 Vegetable, 1 High-Fat Meat, 1-1/2 Fat. CARBOHYDRATE CHOICES: 4.

Chicken-Artichoke Pasta with Herbs

PREP TIME: 25 MINUTES (READY IN 25 MINUTES)
SERVINGS: 4

 EASY

¼ cup chopped fresh parsley

2 tablespoons chopped fresh chives

1 tablespoon chopped fresh tarragon leaves

4 cups uncooked medium egg noodles (8 oz)

1 tablespoon olive oil

1 package (14 oz) uncooked chicken breast tenders (not breaded), cut into 1 ½-inch pieces

1 can (14 oz) Progresso® artichoke hearts, drained, quartered

3 large cloves garlic, finely chopped

⅓ cup white wine or chicken broth

1 cup whipping cream

½ teaspoon salt

1 ¼ cups shredded Parmesan cheese (5 oz)

1) In small bowl, mix parsley, chives and tarragon; set aside. Cook and drain noodles as directed on package. Meanwhile, in 10-inch nonstick skillet, heat oil over medium-high heat. Cook chicken in oil 5 to 7 minutes, stirring frequently, until no longer pink in center. Remove chicken; cover to keep warm.

2) Add artichokes to skillet; cook 1 minute. Add garlic; cook 30 seconds. Stir in wine. Heat to boiling; boil 30 seconds or until liquid begins to reduce. Add cream; boil until slightly thickened, about 5 minutes. Remove from heat. Reserve 1 tablespoon of the herb mixture. Stir chicken, salt, 1 cup of the cheese and the remaining herb mixture into sauce. Serve with noodles; top with reserved herbs and remaining ¼ cup cheese.

1 SERVING: Calories 753; Total Fat 40g; Sodium 1600mg; Dietary Fiber 4g; Protein 42g. EXCHANGES: 2-1/2 Starch, 1/2 Other Carbohydrate, 1 Vegetable, 4-1/2 Lean Meat, 6-1/2 Fat. CARBOHYDRATE CHOICES: 3.

Beef-Mushroom Teriyaki Noodles

PREP TIME: 20 MINUTES (READY IN 20 MINUTES)
SERVINGS: 4 (1-3/4 CUPS EACH)

 EASY LOW FAT

5 cups fine egg noodles (8 oz)

2 green onions

1 tablespoon vegetable oil

1 package (8 oz) sliced fresh mushrooms (about 3 cups)

1 cup matchstick carrots

1 cup red bell pepper strips

1 lb boneless beef top sirloin, cut into thin bite-size strips

½ cup teriyaki marinade and sauce (from 10-oz bottle)

2 teaspoons cornstarch

1) Cook and drain noodles as directed on package.

2) Meanwhile, diagonally slice onions; set green tops aside. In 12-inch nonstick skillet, heat oil over medium-high heat. Cook mushrooms, carrots, pepper strips and white portion of onions in oil 5 minutes, stirring occasionally, until soft. Remove mixture from skillet to bowl; set aside.

3) In same skillet, cook beef 1 to 2 minutes or just until meat begins to brown. Drain and return to skillet. In small bowl, mix teriyaki marinade and cornstarch until blended. Stir teriyaki mixture and mushroom mixture into skillet. Heat to boiling over medium heat, stirring constantly, until sauce is thickened.

4) In large serving bowl, toss noodles with beef mixture and reserved green onion tops. Serve immediately.

1 SERVING: Calories 425; Total Fat 9g; Sodium 270mg; Dietary Fiber 2g; Protein 42g. EXCHANGES: 2-1/2 Starch, 1/2 Other Carbohydrate, 1/2 Vegetable, 3 Lean Meat, 1 Fat. CARBOHYDRATE CHOICES: 3.

tip

Teriyaki marinade and sauce has a thin consistency. For the best results, do not substitute teriyaki baste and glaze in this recipe.

Creamy Chicken Primavera

PREP TIME: 30 MINUTES (READY IN 30 MINUTES)
SERVINGS: 6

 EASY

6 oz uncooked linguine

1 lb uncooked chicken breast strips for stir-fry

1 cup sliced fresh mushrooms (3 oz)

1 cup ready-to-eat baby-cut carrots, quartered lengthwise

½ medium red bell pepper, cut into thin bite-size strips

1 box (9 oz) Green Giant® Simply Steam® frozen sugar snap peas

½ cup water

1 jar (16 oz) Alfredo pasta sauce

¼ cup dry white wine or milk

3 tablespoons chopped fresh basil leaves

Shredded Parmesan cheese, if desired

1) Cook and drain linguine as directed on package; cover to keep warm.

2) Meanwhile, spray 12-inch skillet with cooking spray; heat over medium-high heat. Add chicken; cook 4 to 6 minutes, stirring frequently, until no longer pink in center.

3) Add mushrooms, carrots, bell pepper, peas and ½ cup water to skillet. Heat to boiling; reduce heat. Cover; simmer 6 to 8 minutes or until vegetables are crisp-tender. Drain.

4) Stir Alfredo sauce, wine and basil into chicken mixture. Cook 2 to 4 minutes, stirring occasionally, until thoroughly heated. Serve over linguine. Sprinkle with cheese.

1 SERVING: Calories 490; Total Fat 27g; Sodium 460mg; Dietary Fiber 4g; Protein 28g. EXCHANGES: 2 Starch, 1 Vegetable, 3 Very Lean Meat, 4-1/2 Fat. CARBOHYDRATE CHOICES: 2.

Penne with Shrimp and Vegetables

PREP TIME: 20 MINUTES (READY IN 20 MINUTES)
SERVINGS: 6 SERVINGS (1-1/2 CUPS EACH)

 EASY

2 ¼ cups uncooked penne pasta (8 oz)

3 tablespoons butter

1 package (8 oz) sliced fresh mushrooms (about 3 cups)

3 cloves garlic, finely chopped

1 cup whipping cream

1 container (10 oz) refrigerated Alfredo pasta sauce

1 small zucchini, cut in half lengthwise, then cut into ½-inch slices

8 oz fresh thin asparagus spears, trimmed, cut into 1 ½-inch pieces (2 cups)

¼ teaspoon crushed red pepper flakes

1 lb cooked, deveined peeled large shrimp, thawed if frozen, tail shells removed

½ teaspoon salt

1) Cook and drain pasta as directed on package.

2) Meanwhile, in 5-quart Dutch oven, melt butter over medium-high heat. Cook mushrooms in butter 7 to 8 minutes, stirring frequently, until softened and liquid is evaporated. Add garlic; cook 30 seconds. Add whipping cream; cook and stir 3 to 4 minutes or until slightly thickened.

3) Stir in Alfredo sauce. Add zucchini, asparagus and pepper flakes. Cook 3 minutes, stirring frequently. Add shrimp. Cook and stir 1 minute or until asparagus is crisp-tender and shrimp are thoroughly heated.

4) Add the cooked pasta to the shrimp mixture and toss to combine. Season with salt.

1 SERVING: Calories 590; Total Fat 37g; Sodium 710mg; Dietary Fiber 3g; Protein 24g. EXCHANGES: 1-1/2 Starch, 1/2 Other Carbohydrate, 2 Vegetable, 2 Very Lean Meat, 7 Fat. CARBOHYDRATE CHOICES: 3.

Pizza Pasta

PREP TIME: 20 MINUTES (READY IN 20 MINUTES)
SERVINGS: 4 (1-1/4 CUPS EACH)

 EASY

1 package (9 oz) refrigerated three-cheese-filled tortellini

1 medium green bell pepper, chopped (1 cup)

6 oz sliced pepperoni (from 8-oz package), chopped (about 1 ¾ cups)

1 jar (25.5 oz) Muir Glen® tomato pasta sauce (any flavor)

1 cup shredded mozzarella cheese (4 oz)

Fresh basil leaves, if desired

1) In 5-quart Dutch oven, cook tortellini with bell pepper as directed on tortellini package. Drain and return to Dutch oven.

2) Stir pepperoni and pasta sauce into tortellini mixture; cook over medium heat until thoroughly heated. Top individual servings with cheese. Garnish with basil.

1 SERVING: Calories 510; Total Fat 31g; Sodium 1450mg; Dietary Fiber 4g; Protein 25g. EXCHANGES: 1-1/2 Starch, 1/2 Other Carbohydrate, 1/2 Vegetable, 2-1/2 High-Fat Meat, 2 Fat. CARBOHYDRATE CHOICES: 2.

tip

Refrigerated pasta has a shorter cooking time than dry pasta, making it a great choice for nights when you need to make dinner quickly.

Salami-Pesto Fusilli

| PREP TIME: | 20 MINUTES (READY IN 20 MINUTES) | | EASY |
| SERVINGS: | 4 (1-1/2 CUPS EACH) | | |

2 cups uncooked fusilli pasta (8 oz)

1 container (7 oz) refrigerated basil pesto

1 ½ cups quartered cherry tomatoes

5 oz hard salami, cut into ½-inch cubes (about 1 cup)

⅔ cup shredded Parmesan cheese

1) Cook and drain pasta as directed on package.

2) In large bowl, toss hot pasta with pesto, tomatoes and salami. Sprinkle with cheese.

1 SERVING: Calories 730; Total Fat 43g; Sodium 1640mg; Dietary Fiber 5g; Protein 29g. EXCHANGES: 3-1/2 Starch, 1 Vegetable, 1 Medium-Fat Meat, 1 High-Fat Meat, 5-1/2 Fat. CARBOHYDRATE CHOICES: 4.

tip Genoa and cotto are among the best-known Italian salamis. Genoa is made of pork and veal, seasoned with garlic, pepper and red wine. Cotto is made of pork and beef, seasoned with garlic and studded with peppercorns. Use your favorite salami in this recipe.

Tex-Mex Macaroni and Cheese

PREP TIME: 20 MINUTES (READY IN 20 MINUTES)
SERVINGS: 6 (1-1/3 CUPS EACH)

 EASY

---

3 cups uncooked elbow macaroni (12 oz)

2 tablespoons butter

2 tablespoons all-purpose flour

2 cups half-and-half

3 cups shredded sharp Cheddar cheese (12 oz)

1 teaspoon ground cumin

½ teaspoon salt

¼ teaspoon pepper

1 jar (12 oz) roasted red bell peppers, drained, chopped

1 can (4 oz) Old El Paso® whole green chiles, drained, chopped

1 cup crushed nacho-flavored tortilla chips

1) Cook and drain macaroni as directed on package.

2) Meanwhile, in 3-quart saucepan, melt butter over medium heat. Stir in flour with whisk until smooth; cook 1 minute. Add half-and-half, cheese, cumin, salt and pepper; cook and stir until cheese is melted.

3) Add cooked macaroni, roasted peppers and chiles; toss to combine. Serve in bowls; sprinkle with crushed tortilla chips.

1 SERVING: Calories 700; Total Fat 37g; Sodium 1000mg; Dietary Fiber 4g; Protein 26g. EXCHANGES: 3 Starch, 1-1/2 Other Carbohydrate, 2-1/2 High-Fat Meat, 3 Fat. CARBOHYDRATE CHOICES: 4.

Chicken Pesto Linguine

PREP TIME: 15 MINUTES (READY IN 15 MINUTES)
SERVINGS: 4 (1-1/2 CUPS EACH)

 EASY

1 package (9 oz) refrigerated linguine

1 cup red bell pepper slices

1 cup Green Green Giant® Valley Fresh Steamers™ frozen sweet peas (from 12-oz bag)

1 container (7 oz) refrigerated basil pesto

2 packages (6 oz each) refrigerated grilled chicken breast strips

1 cup crumbled Gorgonzola cheese (4 oz)

1) Fill 5-quart Dutch oven two-thirds full of water; heat to boiling. Add linguine, red bell pepper and peas; boil 2 to 3 minutes or until tender. Drain and return to Dutch oven.

2) Stir pesto, chicken and cheese into linguine mixture; cook over medium heat until thoroughly heated.

1 SERVING: Calories 490; Total Fat 29g; Sodium 460mg; Dietary Fiber 4g; Protein 37g. EXCHANGES: 1-1/2 Starch, 1-1/2 Other Carbohydrate, 2 Vegetable, 2-1/2 Very Lean Meat, 1 High-Fat Meat, 4 Fat. CARBOHYDRATE CHOICES: 2.

Easy Noodles Niçoise

PREP TIME: 15 MINUTES (READY IN 15 MINUTES)
SERVINGS: 4

 EASY

2 cups fresh green beans, cut into 1-inch pieces (about 8 oz)

8 oz uncooked vermicelli

¾ cup Caesar dressing

1 can (12 oz) white albacore tuna, drained

12 pitted kalamata or ripe olives

4 hard-cooked eggs, sliced

¼ cup sliced radishes

1) Fill 5-quart Dutch oven two-thirds full of water; heat to boiling. Add beans; boil 1 minute. Add vermicelli; boil 6 minutes. Drain. Rinse with cold water to cool; drain and return to Dutch oven. Add ½ cup of the dressing and toss to coat.

2) Divide vermicelli mixture evenly among 4 serving plates. Mound one-fourth of the tuna in center of each plate; surround with olives, eggs and radishes. Drizzle remaining ¼ cup dressing over salads.

1 SERVING: Calories 670; Total Fat 34g; Sodium 1090mg; Dietary Fiber 5g; Protein 34g. EXCHANGES: 3-1/2 Starch, 1 Vegetable, 3 Lean Meat, 4-1/2 Fat. CARBOHYDRATE CHOICES: 4.

Basil Pork and Asian Noodles

PREP TIME: 25 MINUTES (READY IN 25 MINUTES)
SERVINGS: 4

 EASY   LOW FAT

8 oz uncooked angel hair (capellini) pasta

2 teaspoons dark sesame oil

1 tablespoon sesame seed

1 lb pork tenderloin, cut in half lengthwise, thinly sliced

1 medium onion, cut into thin wedges

½ cup stir-fry sauce

2 tablespoons honey

2 cups Green Giant® Valley Fresh Steamers™ Select® frozen sugar snap peas (from 12-oz bag)

¼ cup sliced fresh basil leaves

1) Cook and drain pasta as directed on package. Add oil; toss to coat. Cover to keep warm.

2) Meanwhile, heat wok or 12-inch nonstick skillet over medium-high heat. Add sesame seed; cook and stir 2 to 3 minutes or until golden brown (watch carefully to prevent burning). Remove from wok; set aside.

3) Spray same wok with cooking spray. Add pork and onion; cook and stir over medium-high heat 3 to 4 minutes or until pork is browned.

4) Add stir-fry sauce, honey and sugar snap peas; mix well. Reduce heat to medium; cook 3 to 4 minutes, stirring occasionally, until peas are crisp-tender. Add basil; cook and stir 1 minute. Serve over pasta. Sprinkle with toasted sesame seeds.

1 SERVING: Calories 510; Total Fat 8g; Sodium 1320mg; Dietary Fiber 5g; Protein 34g. EXCHANGES: 3-1/2 Starch, 1 Other Carbohydrate, 1 Vegetable, 1 Very Lean Meat, 2 Lean Meat. CARBOHYDRATE CHOICES: 5.

Minty Linguine with Grilled Chicken

PREP TIME: 30 MINUTES (READY IN 30 MINUTES)
SERVINGS: 4

 EASY

4 boneless skinless chicken breasts (1 ¼ lb)

½ cup olive oil

1 teaspoon garlic-pepper blend

⅔ cup lightly packed fresh mint leaves

2 tablespoons lemon juice

½ teaspoon salt

¼ teaspoon pepper

8 oz uncooked linguine

1 box (9 oz) Green Giant® Simply Steam® frozen baby sweet peas

1 cup small fresh mozzarella cheese balls (6 oz)

¼ cup chopped fresh chives

1) Heat gas or charcoal grill. Brush both sides of chicken with 1 tablespoon of the olive oil; sprinkle with garlic-pepper blend. In blender, place remaining oil, the mint, lemon juice, salt and pepper. Cover; blend until smooth. Set aside.

2) Place chicken on grill over medium heat. Cover grill; cook 10 to 12 minutes, turning once, until juice of chicken is clear when center of thickest part is cut (165°F). Remove chicken from grill to cutting board. Loosely cover; let stand 3 minutes.

3) Meanwhile, cook and drain linguine as directed on package, adding peas during last 3 minutes of cooking time. Toss linguine and peas with reserved mint mixture and the mozzarella; cover to keep warm.

4) Slice chicken crosswise. Place linguine mixture on platter or individual plates; arrange chicken on top. Sprinkle with chives.

1 SERVING: Calories 850; Total Fat 44g; Sodium 930mg; Dietary Fiber 6g; Protein 54g. EXCHANGES: 3 Starch, 1/2 Other Carbohydrate, 1 Vegetable, 5 Very Lean Meat, 1 Medium-Fat Meat, 7 Fat. CARBOHYDRATE CHOICES: 4.

Mediterranean Pasta with Shrimp

PREP TIME: 20 MINUTES (READY IN 20 MINUTES)
SERVINGS: 5 (1-1/2 CUPS EACH)

 EASY

2 ½ cups uncooked bow-tie (farfalle) pasta (about 5 oz)

1 lb uncooked deveined peeled medium shrimp (thawed if frozen), tail shells removed

1 medium red bell pepper, chopped (1 cup)

3 cups lightly packed fresh spinach (about 3 oz), stems removed, torn into pieces

2 tablespoons chopped fresh or 2 teaspoons dried basil leaves

½ teaspoon salt

⅓ cup sliced pitted kalamata olives or 1 can (2 ¼ oz) sliced ripe olives, drained

1 cup crumbled feta cheese (4 oz)

2 tablespoons olive or vegetable oil

1) In 5-quart Dutch oven, cook pasta as directed on package, adding shrimp and bell pepper during last 2 minutes of cooking time. Cook until pasta is tender and shrimp are pink. Drain and return to Dutch oven.

2) Add spinach, basil, salt and olives to pasta mixture; heat over medium heat until hot. Toss with cheese and oil.

1 SERVING : Calories 340; Total Fat 13g; Sodium 860mg; Dietary Fiber 3g; Protein 23g. EXCHANGES: 2 Starch, 1 Vegetable, 2 Very Lean Meat, 2 Fat. CARBOHYDRATE CHOICES: 2.

Kalamata olives are plump and juicy with a powerful flavor, bright acidity and high salt content. However, if you don't have them on hand, your favorite olive variety will work for this recipe.

Spinach and Bacon Mac 'n Cheese

PREP TIME: 25 MINUTES (READY IN 25 MINUTES)
SERVINGS: 6 (1 CUP EACH)

 EASY

3 cups uncooked bow-tie (farfalle) pasta (8 oz)

½ lb sliced bacon, coarsely chopped

2 tablespoons butter

1 small clove garlic, finely chopped

¼ cup all-purpose flour

¼ teaspoon salt

¼ teaspoon pepper

2 cups milk

2 cups shredded sharp Cheddar cheese (8 oz)

1 bag (6 oz) fresh baby spinach leaves, coarsely chopped

1) In 5-quart Dutch oven, cook and drain pasta as directed on package. Return to Dutch oven; cover to keep warm.

2) Meanwhile, in 10-inch skillet, cook bacon over medium heat 5 to 8 minutes, stirring often, until crisp; remove to paper towels. Drain, reserving 2 tablespoons drippings.

3) In 3-quart saucepan, heat butter and reserved bacon drippings over medium heat until butter is melted. Add garlic; cook 30 seconds or until fragrant. Stir in flour, salt and pepper with whisk until smooth. Stir in milk; heat to boiling. Stir in cheese until melted and sauce is smooth.

4) Pour cheese sauce over pasta; stir until coated. Stir in spinach. Reserve ¼ cup of the bacon; stir remaining bacon into pasta mixture.

5) Divide pasta mixture among 6 serving bowls; garnish with reserved bacon.

1 SERVING: Calories 470; Total Fat 24g; Sodium 810mg; Dietary Fiber 2g; Protein 23g. EXCHANGES: 2 Starch, 1/2 Other Carbohydrate, 1 Vegetable, 2 High-Fat Meat, 1-1/2 Fat. CARBOHYDRATE CHOICES: 3.

Southwest Chicken and Linguine

PREP TIME: 20 MINUTES (READY IN 20 MINUTES)
SERVINGS: 4 (1-1/2 CUPS EACH)

 EASY

1 package (9 oz) refrigerated linguine

1 can (14.5 oz) diced tomatoes with green chiles or jalapeño chiles, undrained

1 package (9 oz) frozen cooked southwestern-seasoned chicken breast strips, thawed

1 cup shredded Monterey Jack cheese (4 oz)

1 medium avocado, pitted, peeled and chopped, if desired

1) Cook and drain fettuccine as directed on package. Meanwhile, in 3-quart saucepan, cook tomatoes and chicken over medium heat, stirring occasionally, until thoroughly heated. Stir in fettuccine. Sprinkle individual servings with cheese and avocado.

1 SERVING: Calories 380; Total Fat 12g; Sodium 1120mg; Dietary Fiber 2g; Protein 29g. EXCHANGES: 2-1/2 Starch, 2-1/2 Very Lean Meat, 1/2 High-Fat Meat, 1 Fat. CARBOHYDRATE CHOICES: 2-1/2.

Herbed Veggie-Chicken Fettuccine

PREP TIME: 30 MINUTES (READY IN 30 MINUTES)
SERVINGS: 6

EASY

12 oz uncooked fettuccine

1 tablespoon olive or vegetable oil

1 medium onion, chopped (½ cup)

1 ½ lb boneless skinless chicken breasts, cut into 1-inch pieces

1 small green bell pepper, cut into bite-size strips

2 cloves garlic, finely chopped

½ teaspoon salt

¼ teaspoon pepper

3 small zucchini, cut in half lengthwise, sliced

3 large tomatoes, seeded, chopped

3 tablespoons chopped fresh basil leaves

2 tablespoons chopped fresh oregano leaves

½ cup shredded Parmesan cheese (2 oz)

1) Cook and drain fettuccine as directed on package; cover to keep warm.

2) Meanwhile, in 12-inch nonstick skillet, heat oil over medium-high heat. Cook onion in oil 2 to 3 minutes, stirring occasionally, until tender.

3) Stir in chicken, bell pepper, garlic, salt and pepper. Cook 5 to 6 minutes, stirring occasionally, until chicken is no longer pink in center. Stir in zucchini, tomatoes, basil and oregano. Cook 5 to 6 minutes, stirring occasionally, until zucchini is tender.

4) Place fettuccine on serving platter; top with chicken mixture and cheese. Serve with additional Parmesan cheese if desired.

1 SERVING: Calories 440; Total Fat 12g; Sodium 670mg; Dietary Fiber 4g; Protein 37g. EXCHANGES: 2 Starch, 1/2 Other Carbohydrate, 1-1/2 Vegetable, 4 Lean Meat. CARBOHYDRATE CHOICES: 3.

Dilled Shrimp 'n Peas with Linguine

PREP TIME: 20 MINUTES (READY IN 20 MINUTES)
SERVINGS: 4 (1-3/4 CUPS EACH)

EASY

2 cups fresh sugar snap peas (8 oz)

1 package (9 oz) refrigerated linguine

¼ cup butter or margarine

3 cloves garlic, finely chopped

24 uncooked large shrimp (1 lb), peeled (tail shells removed), deveined

½ cup dry white wine or chicken broth

2 teaspoons grated lemon peel

2 tablespoons chopped fresh dill weed

½ cup shredded Parmesan cheese (2 oz)

1) Fill 5-quart Dutch oven two-thirds full of water; heat to boiling. Meanwhile, remove strings from sugar snap peas, if desired. Add peas to boiling water; boil 3 minutes. Add linguine; boil 2 to 3 minutes longer or until peas and linguine are tender.

2) Meanwhile, in 12-inch nonstick skillet, melt butter over medium-high heat. Cook and stir garlic and shrimp in butter 1 minute. Stir in wine and lemon peel; cook 2 minutes or until shrimp are pink.

3) Drain linguine and peas; place in large serving bowl. Add shrimp mixture and dill; toss to combine. Sprinkle with cheese. Serve immediately.

1 SERVING: Calories 390; Total Fat 17g; Sodium 510mg; Dietary Fiber 2g; Protein 20g. EXCHANGES: 2 Starch, 1 Vegetable, 1 Very Lean Meat, 1/2 Lean Meat, 3 Fat. CARBOHYDRATE CHOICES: 2-1/2.

Creole Shrimp Pasta

PREP TIME: 30 MINUTES (READY IN 30 MINUTES)
SERVINGS: 4

 EASY   LOW FAT

1 ¼ cups uncooked orzo or rosamarina pasta (8 oz)

2 tablespoons olive oil

1 large onion, chopped (1 cup)

2 stalks celery, thinly sliced (1 cup)

2 small yellow or green bell peppers or 1 of each, chopped (1 cup)

3 large cloves garlic, finely chopped

1 can (28 oz) Muir Glen® organic diced tomatoes, undrained

2 teaspoons Cajun seasoning

1 lb uncooked deveined peeled medium shrimp, thawed if frozen, tail shells removed

1) Cook and drain orzo as directed on package.

2) Meanwhile, in 12-inch nonstick skillet, heat oil over medium-high heat. Cook onion and celery in oil 3 to 5 minutes, stirring frequently, until vegetables begin to soften. Add bell peppers; cook 2 to 3 minutes. Add garlic; cook 30 seconds or until fragrant.

3) Stir in tomatoes and Cajun seasoning. Heat to boiling. Add shrimp. Cook and stir over medium-high heat until shrimp are pink and vegetables are crisp-tender.

4) To serve, spoon ¾ cup orzo into each of 4 shallow bowls; top each with 1 ½ cups shrimp mixture. Garnish with chopped fresh parsley, if desired.

1 SERVING: Calories 460; Total Fat 9g; Sodium 1430mg; Dietary Fiber 6g; Protein 29g. EXCHANGES: 3-1/2 Starch, 1/2 Other Carbohydrate, 1 Vegetable, 2-1/2 Very Lean Meat, 1 Fat. CARBOHYDRATE CHOICES: 4.

tip Orzo, tiny rice-shaped pasta, is a nice alternative to the traditional rice served with shrimp Creole. Feel free to substitute cooked long-grain white rice, however, if you prefer.

Sesame Chicken Lo Mein

PREP TIME: 25 MINUTES (READY IN 25 MINUTES)
SERVINGS: 3 (1-1/2 CUPS EACH)

 EASY

- 1 lb boneless skinless chicken breasts, cut into bite-size strips
- 1 teaspoon sesame oil
- 1 bag (19 oz) Green Giant® Create a Meal!® frozen stir-fry lo mein meal starter
- 1 cup fresh snow pea pods, trimmed
- ¼ cup cashew pieces

1) Spray 12-inch nonstick skillet with cooking spray; heat over medium-high heat. Add chicken; cook and stir 4 to 5 minutes or until no longer pink in center.

2) Add oil, frozen vegetables and sauce packet (from meal starter) and snow peas to skillet with chicken; cook and stir 7 to 10 minutes or until vegetables are crisp-tender. Sprinkle with cashews.

1 SERVING: Calories 420; Total Fat 12g; Sodium 920mg; Dietary Fiber 3g; Protein 41g. EXCHANGES: 1 Starch, 1 Other Carbohydrate, 1 Vegetable, 5 Very Lean Meat, 2 Fat. CARBOHYDRATE CHOICES: 2-1/2.

Sun-Dried Tomato Chicken Alfredo

PREP TIME: 35 MINUTES (READY IN 35 MINUTES)
SERVINGS: 5

1 tablespoon olive oil

4 boneless skinless chicken breasts (about 1 lb)

1 medium onion, chopped (½ cup)

1 box (6.8 oz) Betty Crocker® Chicken Helper® fettuccine Alfredo

1 cup hot water

1 cup half-and-half

¼ cup chopped dry-pack sun-dried tomatoes

¼ cup chopped fresh basil leaves

1) In 10-inch skillet, heat oil over medium-high heat. Cook chicken and onion in oil 15 to 18 minutes, stirring onion frequently and turning chicken once, until onion is tender and juice of chicken is clear when center of thickest part is cut (at least 165°F). Remove from heat; cover to keep warm.

2) Meanwhile, fill 2-quart saucepan two-thirds full of water; heat to boiling. Stir in the pasta (from Chicken Helper box). Gently boil uncovered about 15 minutes, stirring occasionally, until the pasta is tender. Drain and cover to keep warm.

3) In same saucepan, mix hot water, half-and-half, tomatoes and sauce mix (from Chicken Helper box). Heat to boiling; reduce heat. Cover; simmer 10 minutes, stirring occasionally, until sauce is slightly thickened.

4) Cut chicken into slices. Divide pasta evenly among serving plates; top with chicken, onion and sauce mixture. Sprinkle with basil.

1 SERVING: Calories 350; Total Fat 12g; Sodium 860mg; Dietary Fiber 2g; Protein 27g. EXCHANGES: 2 Starch, 3-1/2 Lean Meat. CARBOHYDRATE CHOICES: 2.

Turkey Scaloppine with Vegetables

PREP TIME: 30 MINUTES (READY IN 30 MINUTES)
SERVINGS: 6

 EASY   LOW FAT

1 ½ lb turkey tenderloins

5 teaspoons olive oil

2 teaspoons chopped fresh rosemary leaves

2 teaspoons chopped fresh lemon thyme or thyme leaves

2 cloves garlic, crushed

1 ½ cups ready-to-eat baby-cut carrots

1 small onion, cut into eighths, separated

½ teaspoon salt

¼ teaspoon pepper

¼ cup dry white wine or chicken broth

12 oz uncooked angel hair (capellini) pasta

2 tablespoons grated Parmesan cheese

1 tablespoon dried parsley flakes

1 ½ cups fresh sugar snap peas, trimmed

1) Cut turkey tenderloins diagonally into ½-inch slices. In 12-inch nonstick skillet, heat 2 teaspoons of the oil over medium-high heat. Add rosemary, thyme and garlic; cook and stir 2 minutes. Add turkey slices; cook 2 minutes. Turn slices; cook 2 minutes longer.

2) Stir in carrots, onion, salt, pepper and wine. Reduce heat to medium-low. Cover; cook 10 to 15 minutes, stirring occasionally, until turkey is no longer pink in center and carrots are crisp-tender.

3) Meanwhile, cook and drain pasta as directed on package. In large bowl, gently toss warm pasta, cheese, parsley and remaining 3 teaspoons oil. Cover to keep warm. Stir sugar snap peas into turkey mixture. Heat to boiling. Reduce heat to medium-low. Cover; cook 5 minutes longer, or until peas are crisp-tender. Serve turkey mixture with pasta.

1 SERVING: Calories 440; Total Fat 7g; Sodium 530mg; Dietary Fiber 4g; Protein 37g. EXCHANGES: 3-1/2 Starch, 1 Vegetable, 3-1/2 Very Lean Meat, 1/2 Fat. CARBOHYDRATE CHOICES: 3-1/2.

Fiesta Spaghetti

MICHELLE SANTOS | AUSTIN, TX

 BAKE-OFF® CONTEST 40, 2002

PREP TIME: 30 MINUTES (READY IN 30 MINUTES)
SERVINGS: 8

 EASY

1 package (16 oz) spaghetti

2 tablespoons olive oil

1 medium onion, chopped (½ cup)

1 medium red bell pepper, chopped (1 cup)

1 lb lean (at least 80%) ground beef

⅓ cup sugar

1 package (1 oz) Old El Paso® taco seasoning mix

1 can (28 oz) crushed tomatoes, undrained

1 can (8 oz) Muir Glen® organic tomato sauce

1 can (11 oz) Green Giant® Mexicorn® whole kernel corn with red and green peppers, drained

1 jar (4.5 oz) Green Giant® sliced mushrooms, drained

Grated Parmesan cheese, if desired

1) Cook and drain spaghetti as directed on package.

2) Meanwhile, in 12-inch skillet, heat oil over medium heat. Cook onion and bell pepper in oil 3 to 4 minutes, stirring occasionally, until tender. Remove from skillet. Add beef; cook 8 to 10 minutes, stirring frequently, until thoroughly cooked; drain.

3) Return onion and bell pepper to skillet. Stir in sugar, taco seasoning mix, tomatoes, tomato sauce, corn and mushrooms. Heat to boiling. Reduce heat to low; simmer 5 minutes, stirring occasionally. Serve over spaghetti. Sprinkle with grated Parmesan cheese, if desired.

1 SERVING: Calories 500; Total Fat 12g; Sodium 1080mg; Dietary Fiber 6g; Protein 22g. EXCHANGES: 3-1/2 Starch, 1 Other Carbohydrate, 1 Vegetable, 1-1/2 Medium-Fat Meat, 1/2 Fat. CARBOHYDRATE CHOICES: 5.

Creamy Chicken–Asparagus Pasta

| PREP TIME: | 25 MINUTES (READY IN 25 MINUTES) |
| SERVINGS: | 4 (1-3/4 CUPS EACH) |

 EASY

⅓ cup pine nuts

10 uncooked lasagna noodles (about 8 oz), broken into 2-inch pieces

1 bunch asparagus (about 1 lb), trimmed, cut diagonally into 1 ½-inch pieces

1 jar (15 oz) Alfredo pasta sauce

⅓ cup refrigerated basil pesto (from 7-oz container)

2 cups shredded cooked chicken

¼ teaspoon salt

⅓ cup shredded Parmesan cheese

1 small tomato, chopped (½ cup)

1) To toast pine nuts, sprinkle in ungreased heavy skillet. Cook over medium heat 3 to 5 minutes, stirring frequently until nuts begin to brown, then stirring constantly until nuts are light brown. Remove from skillet to plate; set aside to cool.

2) Cook and drain noodles as directed on package, adding asparagus during last 3 minutes of cooking time.

3) Meanwhile, in 3-quart saucepan, heat Alfredo sauce to boiling. Stir in pesto with whisk. Stir in chicken and salt.

4) Reserve ¼ cup asparagus for garnish. Stir noodles and remaining asparagus into Alfredo-pesto mixture. Cook and stir over medium heat until hot. Sprinkle with toasted pine nuts and cheese and chopped tomato; garnish with reserved asparagus.

1 SERVING: Calories 817; Total Fat 46g; Sodium 1051mg; Dietary Fiber 5g; Protein 46g. EXCHANGES: 4 Starch, 1/2 Vegetable, 2-1/2 Lean Meat, 1/2 Medium-Fat Meat, 6-1/2 Fat. CARBOHYDRATE CHOICES: 4.

Sausage and Veggie Spaghetti

PREP TIME: 20 MINUTES (READY IN 20 MINUTES)
SERVINGS: 4

 EASY

8 oz uncooked spaghetti

1 lb bulk Italian pork sausage

1 medium onion, chopped (½ cup)

1 large yellow bell pepper, cut into strips

1 medium zucchini, sliced

1 jar (14 oz) tomato pasta sauce (any flavor)

½ cup shredded Parmesan cheese (2 oz)

1) Cook and drain spaghetti as directed on package.

2) Meanwhile, in 12-inch skillet, cook sausage and onion over medium heat until sausage is no longer pink, stirring occasionally and breaking sausage into small chunks. Add bell pepper and zucchini; cook and stir until vegetables are crisp-tender, about 2 minutes. Drain, if desired.

3) Stir pasta sauce into sausage mixture; heat to boiling over medium heat.

4) To serve, place ¾ cup spaghetti on each of 4 plates. Top each with 1 cup meat sauce and 2 tablespoons cheese.

1 SERVING: Calories 630; Total Fat 24g; Sodium 1340mg; Dietary Fiber 6g; Protein 27g. EXCHANGES: 3-1/2 Starch, 1 Other Carbohydrate, 2 Vegetable, 1-1/2 High-Fat Meat, 2 Fat. CARBOHYDRATE CHOICES: 5.

tip

If your family likes a little heat in their food, use spicy Italian pork sausage instead of the regular kind.

Enchilada Lasagna

PREP TIME: 25 MINUTES (READY IN 1 HOUR 35 MINUTES)
SERVINGS: 8

1 ½ lb lean (at least 80%) ground beef

1 medium onion, chopped

3 cloves garlic, chopped

2 cans (10 oz each) Old El Paso® enchilada sauce

2 teaspoons ground cumin

1 teaspoon salt

1 egg, beaten

1 ½ cups cottage cheese

1 can (4 oz) Old El Paso® whole green chiles, drained, chopped

12 no-boil lasagna noodles

4 cups shredded Mexican cheese blend (16 oz)

1 can (14.5 oz) organic diced tomatoes, drained

1) Heat oven to 350°F. Spray 13x9-inch (3-quart) glass baking dish with cooking spray. In 12-inch nonstick skillet, cook the beef, onion and garlic over medium-high heat 7 to 10 minutes, stirring occasionally, until the beef is thoroughly cooked; drain. Stir in 1 can of enchilada sauce, the cumin and salt; set aside. In small bowl, mix the egg, cottage cheese and chiles; set aside.

2) Using remaining can of enchilada sauce, ladle ⅓ cup of the sauce into baking dish. Top with 4 noodles, half of the beef mixture (about 1 ¾ cups), ½ of the cottage cheese mixture (about 1 cup) and 1 cup of the shredded cheese. Repeat layers. Top with remaining 4 noodles. Pour remaining enchilada sauce over noodles. Spoon tomatoes over sauce.

3) Cover; bake 45 minutes. Uncover; sprinkle with remaining 2 cups shredded cheese. Bake 10 to 15 minutes longer or until edges are bubbly. Let stand 10 minutes before cutting.

1 SERVING: Calories 570; Total Fat 30g; Sodium 1520mg; Dietary Fiber 2g; Protein 38g. EXCHANGES: 2 Starch, 1/2 Other Carbohydrate, 2-1/2 Lean Meat, 2 High-Fat Meat, 1 Fat. CARBOHYDRATE CHOICES: 2-1/2.

Cajun Pasta with Smoked Sausage

PREP TIME: 25 MINUTES (READY IN 25 MINUTES)
SERVINGS: 6 (1-1/2 CUPS EACH)

 EASY

8 oz uncooked fettuccine

2 tablespoons vegetable oil

1 large onion, chopped (1 cup)

2 medium red or green bell peppers, thinly sliced

3 cloves garlic, finely chopped

1 package (14 oz) smoked sausage, cut into ½-inch slices

1 can (28 oz) Muir Glen® organic fire roasted crushed tomatoes, undrained

1 tablespoon Cajun seasoning

½ cup whipping cream

½ cup shredded Parmesan cheese (2 oz)

1) In 5-quart Dutch oven, cook and drain fettuccine as directed on package. Return to Dutch oven; cover to keep warm.

2) Meanwhile, in 12-inch nonstick skillet, heat oil over medium-high heat. Cook onion, bell peppers and garlic in oil 3 to 4 minutes, stirring frequently, until vegetables are crisp-tender. Add sausage; cook 3 to 4 minutes, stirring frequently, until vegetables are tender.

3) Stir tomatoes and Cajun seasoning into sausage mixture. Stir in whipping cream; cook uncovered 5 to 8 minutes, stirring occasionally, or until mixture is thickened.

4) Add sausage mixture to fettuccine in Dutch oven; toss to combine. Sprinkle with cheese and chopped fresh parsley, if desired.

1 SERVING: Calories 560; Total Fat 35g; Sodium 1890mg; Dietary Fiber 4g; Protein 18g. EXCHANGES: 1-1/2 Starch, 1 Other Carbohydrate, 1 Vegetable, 1/2 Lean Meat, 1 High-Fat Meat, 5 Fat. CARBOHYDRATE CHOICES: 3.

Reliable Slow Cooker Recipes

Enjoy a little spare time by letting your slow cooker create these hearty, home-style recipes for you.

WINTER SQUASH AND PORK STEW
PG. 212

COUNTRY-STYLE PORK RIBS
PG. 217

GREEN CHILE STEW
PG. 218

NEW HOPPIN' JOHN
PG. 226

Italian Bistro Hot Beef Sandwiches

PREP TIME: 10 MINUTES (READY IN 7 HOURS 20 MINUTES)
SERVINGS: 8 SANDWICHES

 EASY   LOW FAT

2 medium onions, sliced

1 beef rump roast (3 lb)

2 tablespoons balsamic vinegar

1 tablespoon Italian seasoning

1 teaspoon black pepper

½ teaspoon salt

¼ teaspoon ground red pepper (cayenne)

1 cup reduced-sodium beef broth

8 French rolls or hoagie buns, split, toasted

1) Spray 3 ½ - to 4-quart slow cooker with cooking spray. Place onions in slow cooker. Place beef roast on onions. Brush roast with vinegar, turning to coat evenly. Sprinkle with seasonings. Pour broth around roast.

2) Cover; cook on Low heat setting 7 to 9 hours or until meat is tender.

3) Remove roast to cutting board. Cover with foil; let stand 5 to 10 minutes. Meanwhile, strain onions from cooking juices; place in serving dish. Ladle cooking juices into 8 small cups. Slice beef; serve on rolls. Serve each sandwich with onions and cups of juice for dipping.

1 SANDWICH: Calories 350; Total Fat 6g; Sodium 510mg; Dietary Fiber 2g; Protein 43g. EXCHANGES: 2 Starch, 4 Very Lean Meat, 1 Lean Meat. CARBOHYDRATE CHOICES: 2.

Home-Style Greek Sandwiches

PREP TIME: 30 MINUTES (READY IN 3 HOURS 10 MINUTES)
SERVINGS: 10 SANDWICHES

SANDWICHES

2 lb lean (at least 80%) ground beef

1 medium red onion, chopped (1 cup)

1 tablespoon Worcestershire sauce

1 tablespoon dried minced garlic

1 tablespoon dried oregano leaves

2 teaspoons ground cumin

¼ teaspoon salt

¼ teaspoon pepper

1 can (10 oz) beef consommé

10 pita (pocket) breads (6 inch),
cut in half to form pockets

YOGURT SAUCE

1 cup plain low-fat yogurt

½ cucumber, peeled, chopped
(about ½ cup)

1 clove garlic, finely chopped

1 teaspoon fresh lemon juice

TOPPINGS

1 ¼ cups chopped tomatoes
(about 2 medium)

2 ½ cups shredded lettuce

¾ cup crumbled feta cheese (6 oz)

1) Spray 3 ½- to 4-quart slow cooker with cooking spray. In 12-inch nonstick skillet, cook beef and onion over medium-high heat 8 to 10 minutes, stirring occasionally, until beef is browned; drain. In slow cooker, stir together beef mixture and remaining sandwich ingredients except pita.

2) Cover; cook on Low heat setting 3 to 4 hours. Meanwhile, in small bowl, stir all sauce ingredients. Cover; refrigerate until serving time.

3) Warm pita breads as directed on package. Using slotted spoon, fill each pita half with 3 to 4 tablespoons hot beef mixture; add 1 rounded tablespoon yogurt sauce. Top with tomatoes, lettuce and cheese.

1 SERVING: Calories 400; Total Fat 15g; Sodium 840mg; Dietary Fiber 2g; Protein 26g. EXCHANGES: 2 Starch, 1/2 Skim Milk, 1/2 Vegetable, 2 Medium-Fat Meat, 1/2 Fat. CARBOHYDRATE CHOICES: 2-1/2.

tip

Consommé is a clarified broth and is often sold as double strength. If you wish, substitute 1-1/4 cups beef broth or stock for consommé.

Eggplant Stew with Polenta

PREP TIME: 30 MINUTES (READY IN 4 HOURS 30 MINUTES)
SERVINGS: 4 (2 CUPS STEW AND 3 SLICES POLENTA EACH)

5 tablespoons olive oil

1 medium eggplant (about 1 lb), peeled, cut into 1-inch cubes

1 medium onion, halved, thinly sliced

2 medium zucchini, cut into ½-inch slices

1 green bell pepper, cut into ½-inch strips

1 red bell pepper, cut into ½-inch strips

1 can (28 oz) crushed tomatoes, undrained

1 teaspoon Italian seasoning

1 teaspoon dried basil leaves

1 teaspoon dried minced garlic

½ teaspoon salt

½ teaspoon coarse ground black pepper

1 roll (1 lb) refrigerated polenta, cut into 12 slices

1) Spray 4- to 5-quart slow cooker with cooking spray. In 12-inch skillet, heat 2 tablespoons of the oil over medium-high heat. Cook the eggplant and onion in oil 5 minutes, stirring occasionally, until almost tender. Spoon into slow cooker.

2) In same skillet, heat 1 tablespoon oil over medium-high heat. Cook zucchini and bell peppers in oil 3 minutes, stirring occasionally. Spoon into slow cooker. Add remaining ingredients except polenta and remaining oil; stir well.

3) Cover; cook on Low heat setting 4 to 6 hours.

4) In 12-inch nonstick skillet, heat remaining 2 tablespoons oil over medium-high heat. Cook polenta slices in oil 4 to 6 minutes on each side until golden brown. Place polenta on serving plates; top with stew.

1 SERVING: Calories 660; Total Fat 17g; Sodium 2500mg; Dietary Fiber 15g; Protein 16g. EXCHANGES: 4 Starch, 2-1/2 Other Carbohydrate, 2-1/2 Vegetable, 3 Fat. CARBOHYDRATE CHOICES: 7.

Country-Style Pork Ribs

PREP TIME:	10 MINUTES (READY IN 9 HOURS 10 MINUTES)
SERVINGS:	6

e EASY

3 lb country-style pork loin ribs

2 cups ketchup

½ cup cider vinegar

⅓ cup packed dark brown sugar

3 tablespoons spicy brown mustard

3 tablespoons Worcestershire sauce

1 tablespoon liquid smoke

1 tablespoon chili powder

1 teaspoon salt

1 teaspoon coarse ground black pepper

1) Spray 4- to 5-quart slow cooker with cooking spray. Place ribs in slow cooker. In medium bowl, mix all remaining ingredients. Pour over ribs.

2) Cover; cook on Low heat setting 9 to 10 hours.

1 SERVING: Calories 850; Total Fat 55g; Sodium 1740mg; Dietary Fiber 1g; Protein 54g. EXCHANGES: 1/2 Starch, 2 Other Carbohydrate, 3 Lean Meat, 4-1/2 Medium-Fat Meat, 4-1/2 Fat. CARBOHYDRATE CHOICES: 2.

Green Chile Stew

PREP TIME: 15 MINUTES (READY IN 9 HOURS 15 MINUTES)
SERVINGS: 6 (1-1/3 CUPS EACH)

 EASY

2 lb boneless pork loin, cut into 1 ½-inch cubes

1 medium onion, chopped (½ cup)

1 jalapeño chile, seeded, chopped

1 can (4.5 oz) Old El Paso® chopped green chiles

1 can (14.5 oz) Muir Glen® organic diced tomatoes, undrained

1 can (15 oz) pinto beans, drained, rinsed

1 cup Green Giant® Valley Fresh Steamers™ Extra Sweet Niblets® frozen corn (from 12-oz bag), thawed

3 cloves garlic, finely chopped

2 teaspoons dried oregano leaves

2 teaspoons ground cumin

¼ teaspoon salt

¼ teaspoon pepper

⅓ cup Old El Paso® salsa verde

½ cup Progresso® chicken broth (from 32-oz carton)

GARNISHES

½ cup sour cream

¼ cup chopped green onions

1 cup shredded Cheddar cheese

1) Spray 3 ½- to 4-quart slow cooker with cooking spray. In slow cooker, place all ingredients except garnish; stir well.

2) Cover; cook on Low heat setting 9 to 10 hours.

3) Ladle stew into bowls. Garnish with sour cream, green onions and cheese.

1 SERVING: Calories 500; Total Fat 23g; Sodium 750mg; Dietary Fiber 7g; Protein 45g. EXCHANGES: 1-1/2 Starch, 1/2 Other Carbohydrate, 3 Lean Meat, 2-1/2 Medium-Fat Meat. CARBOHYDRATE CHOICES: 2.

tip

Salsa verde is a flavorful but fairly mild salsa. Look for jars of this green salsa in the Mexican-foods section of your grocery store.

Carnitas Soft Tacos

PREP TIME: 15 MINUTES (READY IN 9 HOURS 25 MINUTES)
SERVINGS: 8 (2 TACOS EACH)

 EASY

1 medium onion, sliced

2 teaspoons dried minced garlic

1 teaspoon ground cumin

1 teaspoon coarse ground black pepper

½ teaspoon salt

¼ cup fresh lime juice (from 1 large lime)

1 boneless pork butt or shoulder blade roast (3 lb)

1 can (4.5 oz) Old El Paso® chopped green chiles

1 can (10 oz) Old El Paso® green enchilada sauce

½ cup chopped fresh cilantro

2 packages (11 oz each) Old El Paso® flour tortillas for burritos (16 tortillas; 8 inch)

Salsa, if desired

1) Spray 4- to 5-quart slow cooker with cooking spray. Place onion in slow cooker. In small bowl, mix dried minced garlic, cumin, pepper, salt and 2 tablespoons of the lime juice to form paste. Pat mixture on top and sides of pork roast (if roast comes tied or in netting, remove before rubbing with spice mixture). Place roast on onion. Top with chiles. Pour enchilada sauce around roast.

2) Cover; cook on Low heat setting 9 to 10 hours or until meat is tender.

3) Remove pork; when cool enough to handle, shred with 2 forks. Return meat to slow cooker; stir in cilantro and remaining 2 tablespoons lime juice. Heat tortillas as directed on package. With slotted spoon, spoon ⅔ cup pork mixture on each tortilla. Serve with salsa.

1 SERVING: Calories 610; Total Fat 28g; Sodium 1020mg; Dietary Fiber 0g; Protein 42g. EXCHANGES: 2-1/2 Starch, 1/2 Other Carbohydrate, 1/2 Lean Meat, 4-1/2 Medium-Fat Meat, 1/2 Fat. CARBOHYDRATE CHOICES: 3.

Sesame Ginger Chicken

PREP TIME: 15 MINUTES (READY IN 6 HOURS 30 MINUTES)
SERVINGS: 6

 EASY

12 boneless skinless chicken thighs
(about 2 lb)

1 bag (16 oz) ready-to-eat baby-cut
carrots, cut in half lengthwise

2 tablespoons grated gingerroot

½ cup Progresso® chicken broth
(from 32-oz carton)

¼ cup honey

2 teaspoons sesame oil

1 teaspoon dried minced garlic

¼ cup soy sauce

3 tablespoons cold water

3 tablespoons cornstarch

1 tablespoon sesame seed, toasted

2 green onions, sliced with tops

tip

To toast sesame seed and enhance the flavor, sprinkle in an ungreased heavy skillet. Cook over medium-low heat for 5 to 7 minutes, stirring frequently until browning begins, then stir constantly until golden brown.

1) Spray 3 ½- to 4-quart slow cooker with cooking spray. Place chicken in slow cooker. Add carrots; sprinkle with gingerroot. In small bowl, stir broth, honey, oil and dried minced garlic. Pour over chicken and carrots.

2) Cover; cook on Low heat setting for 6 to 8 hours.

3) With slotted spoon, remove chicken and carrots to serving platter; cover to keep warm. Strain cooking liquid; pour into 1-quart saucepan. In small bowl, mix soy sauce, water and cornstarch until smooth; add to liquid in saucepan. Cook and stir over high heat until thickened and sauce begins to bubble.

4) To serve, pour the sauce over chicken and carrots. Garnish with sesame seed and onions.

1 SERVING: Calories 360; Total Fat 14g; Sodium 810mg; Dietary Fiber 2g; Protein 33g. EXCHANGES: 1 Starch, 1/2 Other Carbohydrate, 1/2 Vegetable, 4 Lean Meat, 1/2 Fat. CARBOHYDRATE CHOICES: 1-1/2.

Cuban Sandwiches with Cilantro-Lime Mayonnaise

PREP TIME: 15 MINUTES (READY IN 8 HOURS 25 MINUTES)
SERVINGS: 12

 EASY

SANDWICHES

- 2 large sweet onions, thinly sliced
- 2 teaspoons dried minced garlic
- 1 ½ teaspoons ground cumin
- 1 teaspoon salt
- 1 teaspoon coarse ground black pepper
- 1 can (10 oz) frozen margarita mix, thawed
- 1 boneless pork butt or shoulder blade roast (3 ½ to 4 lb)
- ¼ cup chopped fresh cilantro
- 2 loaves ciabatta bread (12 oz each)
- 6 to 8 large leaves leaf lettuce

CILANTRO-LIME MAYONNAISE

- 1 cup light mayonnaise
- 2 tablespoons fresh lime juice
- 1 clove garlic, finely chopped
- 2 tablespoons chopped fresh cilantro

1) Spray 4- to 5-quart slow cooker with cooking spray. Place onions in slow cooker. In small bowl, mix dried minced garlic, cumin, salt, pepper and 1 tablespoon of the margarita mix to form paste. Pat mixture on top and sides of roast (if roast comes tied or in netting, remove before rubbing with spice mixture). Place roast on onions. Pour remaining margarita mix around roast.

2) Cover; cook on Low heat setting 8 to 10 hours or until meat is tender.

3) Remove pork; when cool enough to handle, shred with 2 forks. Return meat to slow cooker; stir in ¼ cup cilantro.

4) In small bowl, mix Cilantro-Lime Mayonnaise ingredients. Slice each loaf of ciabatta bread in half horizontally. With slotted spoon, spoon pork mixture onto bottom halves of bread. Top each with 3 to 4 lettuce leaves. Spread about ½ cup Cilantro-Lime Mayonnaise on top halves of bread; place over lettuce. Cut into slices. Discard liquid in slow cooker.

1 SERVING: Calories 590; Total Fat 27g; Sodium 730mg; Dietary Fiber 2g; Protein 38g. EXCHANGES: 2-1/2 Starch, 1/2 Other Carbohydrate, 1/2 Vegetable, 4 Medium-Fat Meat, 1 Fat. CARBOHYDRATE CHOICES: 3.

Slow Cooker Turkey Breast

PREP TIME: 20 MINUTES (READY IN 7 HOURS 20 MINUTES)
SERVINGS: 8

 EASY   LOW FAT

3   medium red potatoes, cut into
    1-inch pieces (about 4 cups)

8   medium carrots, cut into 1-inch
    pieces (about 2 cups)

1   small onion, cut into wedges
    (½ cup)

1   bone-in whole turkey breast with
    gravy packet (5 to 6 lb), thawed if
    frozen

1) Spray 5- to 6-quart slow cooker with
   cooking spray. In slow cooker, mix the
   potatoes, carrots, onion and the gravy
   from turkey breast. Place turkey breast
   on top.

2) Cover; cook on Low heat setting 7 to 8
   hours or until vegetables are tender and
   thermometer inserted in center of turkey
   reads 165°F.

1 SERVING: Calories 340; Total Fat 2g; Sodium 640mg;
Dietary Fiber 3g; Protein 56g. EXCHANGES: 1 Starch,
1 Vegetable, 7 Very Lean Meat. CARBOHYDRATE
CHOICES: 1-1/2.

To serve with
cranberry-orange
relish, add the grated
peel of 1 fresh orange
(about 1 tablespoon)
to 1 can (14 to 16 oz)
of whole berry
cranberry sauce.

Wild Rice Stuffing

PREP TIME: 20 MINUTES (READY IN 6 HOURS 20 MINUTES)
SERVINGS: 22 (1/2 CUP EACH)

 EASY LOW FAT

1 cup uncooked whole-grain wild rice
(not cracked or broken)

1 cup sliced fresh mushrooms (3 oz)

1 medium onion, chopped (½ cup)

1 medium stalk celery, chopped
(½ cup)

1 medium carrot, chopped (½ cup)

2 tablespoons butter or margarine,
cut into small pieces

1 carton (32 oz) Progresso® chicken
broth

5 cups herb-seasoned stuffing cubes

1) Spray 5- to 6-quart slow cooker with cooking spray. In slow cooker, combine all ingredients except stuffing; mix well.

2) Cover; cook on Low heat setting 5 hours.

3) Gently stir stuffing into rice mixture. Cover; cook 45 to 60 minutes longer or until stuffing is moist and tender. Gently stir just before serving.

1 SERVING: Calories 100; Total Fat 1.5g; Sodium 460mg; Dietary Fiber 1g; Protein 3g. EXCHANGES: 1 Starch. CARBOHYDRATE CHOICES: 1.

New Hoppin' John

PREP TIME: 10 MINUTES (READY IN 8 HOURS 20 MINUTES)
SERVINGS: 4 (1-1/2 CUPS EACH)

 EASY

2 smoked pork hocks (about 1 ¼ lb)

1 ¾ cups Progresso® reduced-sodium chicken broth (from 32-oz carton)

1 tablespoon dried chopped onion

2 cans (15.8 oz each) black-eyed peas, drained, rinsed

½ lb smoked sausage, cut in half lengthwise, then cut crosswise into 1-inch pieces

½ cup uncooked instant rice

1) Spray 3 ½- to 4-quart slow cooker with cooking spray. Place pork hocks in cooker. Add 1 cup of the broth (refrigerate remaining broth). Top pork with onion, peas and sausage.

2) Cover; cook on Low heat setting 8 to 10 hours.

3) Remove pork from cooker; place on cutting board. Pull meat from bones, using 2 forks; discard bones, skin and fat. Return pork to cooker. Add remaining broth and the rice. Increase heat setting to High. Cover; cook 10 minutes or until rice is tender.

1 SERVING: Calories 510; Total Fat 20g; Sodium 1290mg; Dietary Fiber 8g; Protein 29g. EXCHANGES: 3 Starch, 1/2 Other Carbohydrate, 3 Medium-Fat Meat, 1/2 Fat. CARBOHYDRATE CHOICES: 3-1/2.

Rustic Italian Chicken

PREP TIME: 40 MINUTES (READY IN 6 HOURS 40 MINUTES)
SERVINGS: 6

12 boneless skinless chicken thighs (about 2 lb)

2 large carrots, cut into ½-inch slices

1 medium red bell pepper, chopped (1 cup)

1 cup sliced fresh mushrooms (3 oz)

3 cloves garlic, finely chopped

1 tablespoon Italian seasoning

½ teaspoon salt

½ teaspoon pepper

1 can (28 oz) crushed tomatoes, undrained

3 ½ cups uncooked penne pasta (about 12 oz)

Shredded Parmesan cheese, if desired

Chopped fresh Italian (flat-leaf) parsley, if desired

1) Spray 3 ½- to 4-quart slow cooker with cooking spray. Place the chicken in slow cooker. Top with the remaining ingredients except pasta, cheese and parsley.

2) Cover; cook on Low heat setting 6 to 8 hours. About 30 minutes before chicken is done, cook and drain pasta as directed on package.

3) Serve chicken with pasta. Garnish with cheese and parsley.

1 SERVING: Calories 550; Total Fat 14g; Sodium 910mg; Dietary Fiber 6g; Protein 43g. EXCHANGES: 3-1/2 Starch, 1/2 Other Carbohydrate, 1/2 Vegetable, 1/2 Very Lean Meat, 4 Lean Meat. CARBOHYDRATE CHOICES: 4.

tip

If you enjoy spicy food, add ¼ teaspoon crushed red pepper flakes with the other seasonings in the recipe.

Caribbean Pork Stew with Peppers

PREP TIME: 20 MINUTES (READY IN 6 HOURS 20 MINUTES)
SERVINGS: 4 (1-1/4 CUPS STEW AND 1 CUP RICE EACH)

e EASY

⅓ cup all-purpose flour

1 teaspoon salt

½ teaspoon pepper

2 lb boneless pork loin, cut into 1-inch cubes

2 tablespoons vegetable oil

1 medium yellow onion, chopped (½ cup)

1 medium green bell pepper, cut into 1-inch pieces

1 medium red bell pepper, cut into 1-inch pieces

2 cloves garlic, finely chopped

½ teaspoon ground cinnamon

½ teaspoon ground ginger

¼ teaspoon crushed red pepper flakes

1 ¼ cups orange juice

1 ½ cups uncooked regular long-grain white rice

3 cups water

1) In large resealable food-storage plastic bag, place flour, salt and pepper. Add pork; seal bag and shake to coat. In 12-inch skillet, heat oil over medium-high heat. Brown pork cubes in oil on all sides, working in batches if necessary.

2) Spray 3 ½- to 4-quart slow cooker with cooking spray. With slotted spoon, remove pork from skillet to slow cooker. Stir in all remaining ingredients except rice and water.

3) Cover; cook on Low heat setting 6 to 8 hours. About 25 minutes before pork is done, cook the rice in water as directed on package. Serve the stew over rice.

1 SERVING: Calories 800; Total Fat 26g; Sodium 1500mg; Dietary Fiber 3g; Protein 58g. EXCHANGES: 4-1/2 Starch, 1/2 Fruit, 1/2 Other Carbohydrate, 1/2 Vegetable, 6 Lean Meat, 1 Fat. CARBOHYDRATE CHOICES: 5-1/2.

A melon baller works very well when you need to easily clean out the seeds and membranes from bell pepper halves.

Bacon-Topped Macaroni and Cheese

PREP TIME: 25 MINUTES (READY IN 2 HOURS 25 MINUTES)
SERVINGS: 6 (1-1/3 CUPS EACH)

3 cups uncooked elbow macaroni (about 12 oz)

¼ cup butter or margarine, cut into pieces

1 can (12 oz) evaporated milk

1 ½ cups half-and-half

3 cups shredded mild Cheddar cheese (12 oz)

8 oz (half of 16-oz loaf) prepared cheese product, cut into cubes

2 teaspoons Dijon mustard

¼ teaspoon salt

¼ teaspoon pepper

½ cup chopped packaged precooked bacon (about 8 slices from 2.1-oz package)

1) Spray 3 ½- to 4-quart slow cooker with cooking spray. Cook and drain macaroni as directed on package, using minimum cook time. Place macaroni in slow cooker; immediately add butter and stir until melted.

2) Add evaporated milk, half-and-half, 2 ½ cups of the Cheddar cheese, the cubed cheese, mustard, salt and pepper; stir to blend well.

3) Cover; cook on Low heat setting 2 to 3 hours, stirring once halfway through cooking time. During last 15 minutes of cooking, sprinkle with remaining ½ cup Cheddar cheese and the bacon.

1 SERVING: Calories 850; Total Fat 50g; Sodium 1670mg; Dietary Fiber 3g; Protein 39g. EXCHANGES: 3 Starch, 1 Low-Fat Milk, 1/2 Milk, 1/2 Medium-Fat Meat, 2 High-Fat Meat, 4 Fat. CARBOHYDRATE CHOICES: 4.

Buffalo Sloppy Joes

PREP TIME: 20 MINUTES (READY IN 3 HOURS 20 MINUTES)
SERVINGS: 18 SANDWICHES

 EASY

SLOPPY JOES

- 2 lb ground beef
- 1 large onion, chopped (1 cup)
- 6 stalks celery, thinly sliced (3 cups)
- 1 can (8 oz) Muir Glen® organic tomato sauce
- 1 can (6 oz) Muir Glen® organic tomato paste
- ½ cup Buffalo wing sauce
- 1 tablespoon cider vinegar
- 2 teaspoons chili powder
- 18 hamburger buns, split, toasted

BLUE CHEESE SAUCE

- 1 container (8 oz) sour cream
- ⅔ cup crumbled blue cheese
- 1 green onion, finely chopped (1 tablespoon)
- 2 teaspoons Buffalo wing sauce

1) Spray 3 ½- to 4-quart slow cooker with cooking spray. In 12-inch nonstick skillet, cook beef and onion over medium-high heat 8 to 10 minutes, stirring occasionally, until beef is browned; drain. Spoon beef mixture into slow cooker. Add remaining sloppy joe ingredients except buns; stir well.

2) Cover; cook on Low heat setting 3 to 4 hours.

3) In small bowl, mix sauce ingredients. To serve, spoon ⅓ cup sloppy joe mixture on bottom half of each bun. Spread 1 tablespoon sauce on top half of each bun; place over meat.

1 SANDWICH: Calories 270; Total Fat 12g; Sodium 580mg; Dietary Fiber 2g; Protein 15g. EXCHANGES: 1-1/2 Starch, 1/2 Vegetable, 1-1/2 Lean Meat, 1-1/2 Fat. CARBOHYDRATE CHOICES: 2.

Tex-Mex Pot Roast

PREP TIME: 15 MINUTES (READY IN 7 HOURS 20 MINUTES)
SERVINGS: 10

 e EASY   **lf** LOW FAT

1 medium onion, halved, sliced

1 beef rump roast or boneless arm roast (3 lb)

2 cloves garlic, finely chopped

1 teaspoon chili powder

½ teaspoon salt

¼ teaspoon pepper

1 can (10 oz) diced tomatoes with green chiles, undrained

¼ cup beef broth

¼ cup red wine or additional beef broth

3 tablespoons cornstarch

¼ cup cold water

1) Spray 4- to 5-quart slow cooker with cooking spray. Place onion in slow cooker. Place beef roast on onion. Sprinkle with garlic, chili powder, salt and pepper. Pour tomatoes, broth and wine over roast.

2) Cover; cook on Low heat setting 7 to 9 hours.

3) Remove roast to cutting board; cover to keep warm. Ladle cooking liquid into 2-quart saucepan; heat to boiling. In small bowl, combine cornstarch and water to form smooth paste; stir into boiling liquid. Cook and stir 1 minute or until thickened. Slice beef; serve with gravy.

1 SERVING: Calories 180; Total Fat 4g; Sodium 260mg; Dietary Fiber 0g; Protein 30g. EXCHANGES: 1/2 Starch, 3-1/2 Very Lean Meat, 1/2 Lean Meat. CARBOHYDRATE CHOICES: 1/2.

Beans 'n Wieners

PREP TIME: 10 MINUTES (READY IN 5 HOURS 10 MINUTES)
SERVINGS: 8 (1 CUP EACH)

 EASY

1 lb hot dogs, each cut into 4 pieces

3 cans (15 oz each) pork and beans in tomato sauce, undrained

½ cup ketchup

1 small onion, finely chopped (¼ cup)

¼ cup molasses

2 teaspoons yellow mustard

1) Spray 3 ½- to 4-quart slow cooker with cooking spray. In slow cooker, mix all ingredients.

2) Cover; cook on Low heat setting 5 to 6 hours.

1 SERVING: Calories 400; Total Fat 18g; Sodium 1570mg; Dietary Fiber 9g; Protein 15g. EXCHANGES: 2 Starch, 1 Other Carbohydrate, 1-1/2 High-Fat Meat, 1 Fat. CARBOHYDRATE CHOICES: 3.

Country-Style Ribs and Sauerkraut

PREP TIME:	10 MINUTES (READY IN 8 HOURS 10 MINUTES)
SERVINGS:	6

 EASY

2 lb boneless country-style pork ribs

1 medium cooking apple, sliced

1 small onion, sliced

1 can (14 oz) sauerkraut, drained, rinsed

3 tablespoons packed brown sugar

1 teaspoon caraway seed

¼ cup dry white wine or apple juice

1) Spray 3 ½- to 4-quart slow cooker with cooking spray. In slow cooker, place ribs, apple and onion. Top with sauerkraut, brown sugar and caraway seed; mix lightly. Pour wine over top.

2) Cover; cook on Low heat setting 8 to 10 hours.

1 SERVING: Calories 340; Total Fat 18g; Sodium 390mg; Dietary Fiber 2g; Protein 31g. EXCHANGES: 1 Other Carbohydrate, 1 Lean Meat, 3 Medium-Fat Meat. CARBOHYDRATE CHOICES: 1.

Key West Ribs

PREP TIME: 10 MINUTES (READY IN 7 HOURS 10 MINUTES)
SERVINGS: 4

 EASY

2 ½ lb country-style pork loin ribs

1 small onion, finely chopped (¼ cup)

¼ cup barbecue sauce

1 teaspoon grated orange peel

1 teaspoon grated lime peel

½ teaspoon salt

¼ cup orange juice

2 tablespoons lime juice

1) Spray 3 ½- to 4-quart slow cooker with cooking spray. Place ribs in slow cooker. In small bowl, mix remaining ingredients. Pour over ribs.

2) Cover; cook on Low heat setting 7 to 9 hours. Spoon the sauce over ribs when serving.

1 SERVING: Calories 570; Total Fat 33g; Sodium 560mg; Dietary Fiber 0g; Protein 58g. EXCHANGES: 1/2 Starch, 4 Lean Meat, 4 Medium-Fat Meat. CARBOHYDRATE CHOICES: 1.

Porketta with Two Potatoes

PREP TIME: 15 MINUTES (READY IN 8 HOURS 15 MINUTES)
SERVINGS: 6

 EASY

2 medium dark-orange sweet potatoes, peeled, cut into ½-inch cubes (about 2 ½ cups)

2 Yukon Gold potatoes, cut into ½-inch cubes (about 2 ½ cups)

2 teaspoons fennel seed, crushed

1 teaspoon dried oregano leaves

1 teaspoon paprika

½ teaspoon garlic powder

½ teaspoon salt

¼ teaspoon pepper

1 boneless pork loin roast (2 lb)

1 cup Progresso® chicken broth (from 32-oz carton)

1) Spray 3 ½- to 4-quart slow cooker with cooking spray. Place potatoes in slow cooker. In small bowl, mix fennel seed, oregano, paprika, garlic powder, salt and pepper. Rub into pork roast. Place pork on potatoes. Pour broth over pork and potatoes.

2) Cover; cook on Low heat setting 8 to 10 hours.

3) Remove roast to cutting board; cut into slices. Serve with potatoes.

1 SERVING: Calories 340; Total Fat 12g; Sodium 420mg; Dietary Fiber 3g; Protein 36g. EXCHANGES: 1 Starch, 1 Vegetable, 2-1/2 Very Lean Meat, 2 Medium-Fat Meat. CARBOHYDRATE CHOICES: 1-1/2.

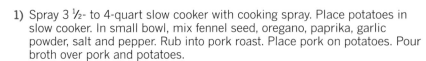

Southwestern Spice-Rubbed Turkey Thighs

PREP TIME:	5 MINUTES (READY IN 7 HOURS 5 MINUTES)
SERVINGS:	4

 EASY

2 turkey thighs (¾ to 1 lb each), skin removed

1 tablespoon olive oil

1 teaspoon Cajun seasoning

¼ cup Old El Paso® thick 'n chunky salsa

¼ cup sour cream

1) Spray 4- to 5-quart slow cooker with cooking spray. Brush turkey thighs with oil; rub with Cajun seasoning. Place in single layer in slow cooker.

2) Cover; cook on Low heat setting 7 to 8 hours.

3) Remove the turkey to cutting board; cut into slices. Serve with salsa and sour cream.

1 SERVING: Calories 310; Total Fat 13g; Sodium 530mg; Dietary Fiber 0g; Protein 46g. EXCHANGES: 2-1/2 Very Lean Meat, 4 Lean Meat. CARBOHYDRATE CHOICES: 0.

Slow-Cooked Lasagna

PREP TIME: 30 MINUTES (READY IN 4 HOURS)
SERVINGS: 8

1 lb lean (at least 80%) ground beef

1 jar (26 to 28 oz) tomato pasta sauce

1 can (8 oz) no-salt-added tomato sauce

8 no-boil lasagna noodles (from 9-oz package)

1 jar (16 oz) Alfredo pasta sauce

3 cups shredded mozzarella cheese (12 oz)

¼ cup grated Parmesan cheese

1) In 10-inch skillet, cook beef over medium-high heat 5 to 7 minutes, stirring frequently, until thoroughly cooked; drain.

2) Spray 4- to 5-quart slow cooker with cooking spray. Spread ¾ cup of the tomato pasta sauce in bottom of slow cooker. Stir remaining tomato pasta sauce and the tomato sauce into cooked beef.

3) Layer 3 noodles over sauce in slow cooker, breaking noodles as necessary. Spread evenly with ⅓ of the Alfredo sauce. Sprinkle with 1 cup of the mozzarella cheese. Spread evenly with ⅓ of the beef mixture. Repeat layers twice, using 2 noodles in last layer. Sprinkle the Parmesan cheese over top.

4) Cover; cook on Low heat setting 3 hours 30 minutes to 4 hours 30 minutes. Cut into wedges to serve, if desired.

1 SERVING: Calories 640; Total Fat 38g; Sodium 1010mg; Dietary Fiber 3g; Protein 31g. EXCHANGES: 2 Starch, 1/2 Other Carbohydrate, 1/2 Vegetable, 1-1/2 Lean Meat, 2 Medium-Fat Meat, 4-1/2 Fat. CARBOHYDRATE CHOICES: 3.

Slow-Simmered Beef Stew

PREP TIME: 15 MINUTES (READY IN 8 HOURS 15 MINUTES)
SERVINGS: 4 (1-3/4 CUPS EACH)

 EASY

1 ½ cups ready-to-eat baby-cut carrots

2 medium potatoes, peeled, cut into 1-inch pieces

1 medium stalk celery, cut into 1-inch pieces

1 lb beef stew meat

1 package (1.5 oz) beef stew seasoning mix

1 cup water

1 cup Green Giant® Valley Fresh Steamers™ Niblets® frozen corn (from 12-oz bag), thawed

1 cup Green Giant® Valley Fresh Steamers™ frozen cut green beans (from 12-oz bag), thawed

1) Spray 3 ½- to 4-quart slow cooker with cooking spray. In slow cooker, layer carrots, potatoes and celery.

2) In resealable plastic food-storage bag, place the beef and seasoning mix; seal bag and shake to coat. Place beef on vegetables in slow cooker; sprinkle with any remaining seasoning mix. Add water. Layer corn and green beans on top.

3) Cover; cook on Low heat setting 8 to 10 hours. Stir before serving.

1 SERVING: Calories 360; Total Fat 13g; Sodium 1000mg; Dietary Fiber 4g; Protein 25g. EXCHANGES: 2 Starch, 1-1/2 Vegetable, 2 Lean Meat, 1 Fat. CARBOHYDRATE CHOICES: 2.

INDIAN-STYLE VEGETABLE CASSEROLE
PG. 246

Hearty
Casseroles

These filling one-dish dinners—from lasagna to pot pie—are sure to please your hungry family!

SLOPPY JOE-TATER NUGGET
HOT DISH
PG. 268

SAUSAGE WITH WHITE BEANS
AND ROSEMARY
PG. 251

MEXICAN MANICOTTI
PG. 262

Scampi-Style Halibut

PREP TIME: 15 MINUTES (READY IN 30 MINUTES)
SERVINGS: 4

 EASY

2 large shallots, sliced (about ½ cup)

1 small red bell pepper, cut into thin bite-size strips (about 1 cup)

1 can (14 oz) Progresso® artichoke hearts, drained, halved

¼ cup fresh lemon juice

5 tablespoons butter, melted

1 teaspoon garlic-pepper blend

½ cup Progresso® panko crispy bread crumbs

4 halibut fillets (about 6 oz each), skin removed

2 tablespoons chopped fresh parsley

1) Heat oven to 450°F. Spray 11x7-inch (2-quart) glass baking dish with cooking spray.

2) In medium bowl, mix the shallots, bell pepper, artichokes, lemon juice, 3 tablespoons of the butter and the garlic-pepper blend. Spoon into baking dish.

3) In small bowl, mix bread crumbs and remaining 2 tablespoons butter. Pat 2 tablespoons crumb mixture on top of each fillet. Place fillets on vegetables in baking dish.

4) Bake uncovered 12 to 15 minutes or until fish flakes easily with fork and crumb topping is golden brown. Sprinkle with parsley.

1 SERVING: Calories 400; Total Fat 18g; Sodium 570mg; Dietary Fiber 7g; Protein 36g. EXCHANGES: 1-1/2 Starch, 1/2 Vegetable, 4 Very Lean Meat, 3 Fat. CARBOHYDRATE CHOICES: 1-1/2.

Wild About Mushrooms

PREP TIME: 25 MINUTES (READY IN 55 MINUTES)
SERVINGS: 8

1 box (1 lb) fettuccine

3 tablespoons olive oil

1 lb assorted wild mushrooms
(crimini, oyster, portabella, shiitake),
sliced

1 large onion, cut into wedges
(about 1 ½ cups)

1 teaspoon dried thyme leaves

1 teaspoon salt

¼ teaspoon pepper

2 tablespoons all-purpose flour

1 ½ cups Progresso® chicken broth
(from 32-oz carton)

1 ½ cups whipping cream

¼ cup chopped fresh parsley

4 oz chèvre (goat) cheese, crumbled
(1 cup)

1 cup shredded Parmesan cheese (4 oz)

1) Heat oven to 400°F. Spray 13x9-inch (3-quart) glass baking dish with cooking spray.

2) Cook and drain fettuccine as directed on package. Meanwhile, in 12-inch nonstick skillet, heat oil over medium-high heat. Cook mushrooms, onion, thyme, salt and pepper in oil 10 minutes, stirring occasionally, until tender. Remove from heat. Stir in flour; gradually stir in broth. Heat to boiling; boil 1 minute. Remove from heat; stir in whipping cream.

3) Add cooked fettuccine and parsley to skillet; toss. Add goat cheese; toss gently. Spoon into baking dish.

4) Cover; bake 15 minutes. Uncover; sprinkle with Parmesan cheese. Bake 10 to 15 minutes longer or until thoroughly heated and bubbly.

1 SERVING: Calories 550; Total Fat 33g; Sodium 1020mg; Dietary Fiber 3g; Protein 18g. EXCHANGES: 2-1/2 Starch, 1/2 Milk, 1/2 Vegetable, 1/2 Medium-Fat Meat, 5 Fat. CARBOHYDRATE CHOICES: 3.

Country Chicken Bacon Pot Pie

PREP TIME: 30 MINUTES (READY IN 1 HOUR)
SERVINGS: 4

6 slices bacon, cut into ½-inch pieces

1 lb boneless skinless chicken thighs, cut into 1-inch pieces

¼ teaspoon salt

¼ teaspoon pepper

1 large onion, cut into wedges (about 1 ½ cups)

1 ½ cups frozen sliced carrots (from 16-oz bag), thawed, drained

1 can (14.75 oz) Green Giant® cream style sweet corn

½ cup Progresso® chicken broth (from 32-oz carton)

2 tablespoons country-style Dijon mustard

1 Pillsbury® refrigerated pie crust, softened as directed on box

1 tablespoon milk

¼ cup shredded Parmesan cheese (2 oz)

1 tablespoon chopped fresh parsley, if desired

1) Heat oven to 400°F. Spray 11x7-inch 2-quart glass baking dish with cooking spray. Place cookie sheet on lowest oven rack to catch any spills.

2) In 10-inch nonstick skillet, cook bacon over medium-high heat, stirring frequently, until crisp; remove with slotted spoon to paper towels to drain. Discard all but 1 tablespoon drippings.

3) Cook chicken, salt and pepper in bacon drippings over medium-high heat 4 minutes, stirring occasionally. Add onion and cook over medium heat 5 minutes, stirring occasionally, until onion is tender and chicken is no longer pink in center.

4) Stir in carrots, corn, broth and mustard. Heat to boiling; boil 1 minute. Remove from heat. Stir in bacon. Spoon into casserole.

5) Remove pie crust from pouch; unroll and cut into 1 ½-inch-wide strips. Lay 3 longest strips lengthwise over filling. Lay remaining 4 strips crosswise, trimming to fit pan. Brush crust strips with milk.

6) Bake 30 to 35 minutes or until crust is golden and filling is bubbly. Sprinkle cheese evenly over crust strips. Bake 1 to 2 minutes longer or until cheese is melted. Sprinkle with parsley.

1 SERVING: Calories 630; Total Fat 33g; Sodium 1550mg; Dietary Fiber 3g; Protein 36g. EXCHANGES: 2-1/2 Starch, 1/2 Other Carbohydrate, 1/2 Vegetable, 4 Lean Meat, 4 Fat. CARBOHYDRATE CHOICES: 3.

Corn Dog Casserole

PREP TIME: 15 MINUTES (READY IN 40 MINUTES)
SERVINGS: 6

e EASY

1 can (28 oz) baked beans, undrained

1 package (16 oz) cocktail-size hot dogs

½ cup barbecue sauce

1 small onion, chopped (¼ cup)

1 box (8.5 oz) corn muffin mix

⅓ cup milk

1 egg

1) Heat oven to 375°F. In large saucepan, mix beans, hot dogs, barbecue sauce and onion. Cook over medium-high heat, stirring frequently until bubbly. Pour into ungreased 2-quart casserole.

2) In medium bowl, stir muffin mix, milk and egg just until combined. Spoon batter evenly over hot bean mixture.

3) Bake 20 to 25 minutes or until topping is golden brown.

1 SERVING: Calories 610; Total Fat 29g; Sodium 2020mg; Dietary Fiber 8g; Protein 18g. EXCHANGES: 2-1/2 Starch, 2 Other Carbohydrate, 1/2 Vegetable, 1 Lean Meat, 1/2 High-Fat Meat, 4 Fat. CARBOHYDRATE CHOICES: 4-1/2.

Herb-Crusted Chicken Ratatouille

PREP TIME: 30 MINUTES (READY IN 1 HOUR 10 MINUTES)
SERVINGS: 6

3 tablespoons olive oil

1 ¼ lb boneless skinless chicken breasts, cut into thin strips

½ teaspoon salt

¼ teaspoon pepper

1 small eggplant (about 12 oz), cut in half, then into ½-inch slices (about 3 cups)

1 medium zucchini (about 9 oz), cut into ½-inch slices (about 2 cups)

1 large onion, chopped (1 cup)

1 ½ teaspoons dried basil leaves

1 ½ teaspoons dried oregano leaves

2 cloves garlic, finely chopped

1 can (14.5 oz) Muir Glen® organic diced tomatoes, undrained

1 can (8 oz) Muir Glen® organic tomato sauce

1 Pillsbury® refrigerated pie crust, softened as directed on box

1 tablespoon butter, melted

½ teaspoon grated lemon peel

1) Heat oven to 400°F. Spray 11x7-inch (2-quart) glass baking dish with cooking spray.

2) In 12-inch nonstick skillet, heat 1 tablespoon of the oil over medium-high heat. Cook chicken, salt and pepper in oil 4 minutes, stirring occasionally (chicken will not be fully cooked). Remove with slotted spoon to bowl. In same skillet, heat 1 tablespoon of the oil over medium-high heat. Cook eggplant, zucchini, onion, 1 teaspoon of the basil and 1 teaspoon of the oregano in oil 4 minutes, stirring occasionally.

3) Add remaining 1 tablespoon oil. Cook 4 minutes longer, stirring occasionally, until vegetables are tender. Add garlic; cook and stir 1 minute. Stir in tomatoes and tomato sauce. Heat to boiling. Return chicken to skillet, discarding any juices in bowl. Remove from heat. Spoon into baking dish.

4) Remove pie crust from pouch; unroll on work surface. Brush with butter; sprinkle with lemon peel and remaining ½ teaspoon basil and ½ teaspoon oregano, gently pressing into crust. Using pizza wheel or sharp knife, cut crust into various shaped (1x2-inch) pieces. Arrange pieces of crust over casserole, slightly overlapping edges if necessary.

5) Bake 35 to 40 minutes or until chicken is no longer pink and crust is golden brown.

1 SERVING: Calories 400; Total Fat 20g; Sodium 790mg; Dietary Fiber 4g; Protein 25g. EXCHANGES: 1-1/2 Starch, 1-1/2 Vegetable, 2-1/2 Lean Meat, 2-1/2 Fat. CARBOHYDRATE CHOICES: 2.

Layered Beefy Mac 'n Cheese

PREP TIME: 30 MINUTES (READY IN 1 HOUR)
SERVINGS: 6 (1-1/2 CUPS EACH)

2 cups uncooked elbow macaroni
   (8 oz)

1 lb lean (at least 80%) ground beef

1 teaspoon salt

⅛ teaspoon pepper

2 tablespoons butter or margarine

2 tablespoons all-purpose flour

2 cups milk

½ cup Progresso® chicken broth
   (from 32-oz carton)

3 cups shredded Cheddar cheese
   (12 oz)

1 cup soft bread crumbs
   (about 2 slices bread)

1) Heat oven to 350°F. Spray 2-quart casserole with cooking spray. Cook and drain macaroni as directed on package, using minimum cook time. Meanwhile, in 10-inch skillet, cook beef, ½ teaspoon of the salt and the pepper over medium-high heat 5 to 7 minutes, stirring occasionally, until beef is thoroughly cooked; drain, if desired.

2) In 2-quart saucepan, melt butter over medium heat. Stir in flour; cook and stir 1 minute until bubbly. Add milk; cook and stir 5 to 6 minutes until mixture thickens slightly. Stir in broth and remaining ½ teaspoon salt. Remove from heat; stir in cheese. Fold in cooked macaroni.

3) Spoon one-third of the macaroni mixture (about 1 ⅓ cups) into casserole; top with half of the beef (about 1 ½ cups). Layer with another third of the macaroni mixture, remaining beef and remaining macaroni mixture. Top with bread crumbs.

4) Bake uncovered 25 to 30 minutes or until bread crumbs are golden brown.

1 SERVING: Calories 630; Total Fat 34g; Sodium 1130mg; Dietary Fiber 2g; Protein 37g. EXCHANGES: 2-1/2 Starch, 1/2 Other Carbohydrate, 4 High-Fat Meat. CARBOHYDRATE CHOICES: 3.

Spicy Unstuffed Peppers Casserole

PREP TIME: 25 MINUTES (READY IN 45 MINUTES)
SERVINGS: 10 (1 BISCUIT AND ABOUT 1 CUP BEEF MIXTURE EACH)

1 box (6.2 oz) fast-cooking long-grain and wild rice mix (with seasoning packet)

1 ½ lb lean (at least 80%) ground beef

1 tablespoon olive oil

2 large red, green or yellow bell peppers, cut into 1-inch pieces (about 4 cups)

3 cloves garlic, finely chopped

1 can (14.5 oz) Muir Glen® organic diced tomatoes, undrained

2 chipotle chiles in adobo sauce (from 7-oz can), finely chopped

1 can (12 oz) Pillsbury® Grands!® Jr. Golden Layers® refrigerated buttermilk biscuits

1) Heat oven to 375°F. Spray 13x9-inch (3-quart) glass baking dish with cooking spray.

2) Cook rice as directed on package. Meanwhile, in 12-inch nonstick skillet, cook beef over medium-high heat 5 to 7 minutes, stirring occasionally, until thoroughly cooked. Remove beef from skillet; drain well.

3) In same skillet, heat oil over medium heat. Cook bell peppers in oil 7 minutes, stirring occasionally, until crisp-tender. Add garlic; cook and stir 1 minute. Stir in tomatoes, chiles and cooked beef. Heat to boiling; remove from heat.

4) Separate dough into 10 biscuits. Spread cooked rice evenly in bottom of baking dish. Spoon hot beef mixture over rice. Top with biscuits. Bake immediately to ensure that bottoms of biscuits bake completely.

5) Bake uncovered 18 to 20 minutes or until thoroughly heated and biscuits are golden.

1 SERVING: Calories 310; Total Fat 13g; Sodium 760mg; Dietary Fiber 1g; Protein 16g. EXCHANGES: 2 Starch, 1/2 Vegetable, 1/2 Lean Meat, 1 Medium-Fat Meat, 1 Fat. CARBOHYDRATE CHOICES: 2.

Sausage with White Beans and Rosemary

PREP TIME: 15 MINUTES (READY IN 40 MINUTES)
SERVINGS: 5

 EASY

1 lb bulk Italian pork sausage

2 cloves garlic, finely chopped

1 can (15 oz) Progresso® cannellini beans, drained, rinsed

1 can (14.5 oz) Muir Glen® organic diced tomatoes, undrained

2 cups frozen pearl onions (from 1-lb bag), thawed

1 tablespoon chopped fresh rosemary leaves

1 can (12 oz) Pillsbury® Grands!® Jr. Golden Layers® refrigerated buttermilk biscuits

1) Heat oven to 375°F. Spray 2-quart round casserole with cooking spray.

2) In 12-inch nonstick skillet, cook sausage over medium-high heat 8 minutes, stirring occasionally, until no longer pink. Add garlic; cook and stir 1 minute. Stir in beans, tomatoes, onions and rosemary. Heat to boiling over high heat; remove from heat. Spoon into casserole.

3) Separate dough into 10 biscuits; arrange over casserole. Bake 20 to 25 minutes or until thoroughly heated and biscuits are golden brown.

1 SERVING: Calories 560; Total Fat 26g; Sodium 1900mg; Dietary Fiber 5g; Protein 24g. EXCHANGES: 2-1/2 Starch, 1 Other Carbohydrate, 1/2 Vegetable, 1/2 Very Lean Meat, 2 High-Fat Meat, 1-1/2 Fat. CARBOHYDRATE CHOICES: 4.

Sausage, Rice and Beans

PREP TIME: 10 MINUTES (READY IN 40 MINUTES)
SERVINGS: 6 (1 CUP EACH)

 EASY

1 box (6.2 oz) fast-cooking long-grain and wild rice mix (with seasoning packet)

1 ¾ cups boiling water

1 can (14.75 oz) Green Giant® cream style sweet corn

1 lb smoked chorizo or kielbasa sausage, cut diagonally into ½-inch slices

1 large green bell pepper, chopped (1 ½ cups)

1 can (15 oz) Progresso® black beans, drained, rinsed

1) Heat oven to 375°F. Spray 2-quart round casserole with cooking spray.

2) In casserole, stir rice mix, contents of seasoning packet and boiling water; stir in corn. Add sausage, bell pepper and beans; stir carefully (casserole will be full).

3) Cover tightly with foil; bake 25 to 30 minutes or until rice is tender.

1 SERVING: Calories 570; Total Fat 30g; Sodium 1700mg; Dietary Fiber 7g; Protein 27g. EXCHANGES: 3 Starch, 1/2 Vegetable, 1 Lean Meat, 1-1/2 Medium-Fat Meat, 3-1/2 Fat. CARBOHYDRATE CHOICES: 3.

 tip

Chorizo is a coarsely ground fresh or smoked pork sausage that has Mexican, Spanish and Portuguese origins. It's traditionally made with paprika or chili powder, which gives it a spicy flavor and reddish color.

Lickety-Split Alfredo-Style Mac 'n Cheese

PREP TIME: 25 MINUTES (READY IN 55 MINUTES)
SERVINGS: 8

3   cups uncooked elbow macaroni (12 oz)

1   cup matchstick-cut or shredded carrots (from 10-oz bag)

1   bag (12 oz) Green Giant® Valley Fresh Steamers™ Select® frozen broccoli florets, thawed

2   containers (10 oz each) refrigerated Alfredo pasta sauce

¾   cup freshly shredded Parmesan cheese (6 oz)

¾   cup Progresso® panko crispy bread crumbs

3   tablespoons butter or margarine, melted

1) Heat oven to 375°F. Spray 13x9-inch (3-quart) glass baking dish with cooking spray.

2) In 5-quart Dutch oven, heat 4 quarts water to boiling. Add macaroni; cook 4 minutes. Stir in carrots; cook 2 minutes longer or until tender. Drain. Return macaroni and carrots to Dutch oven. Stir in broccoli, Alfredo sauce and ½ cup of the cheese. Spoon into baking dish.

3) In small bowl, mix bread crumbs, remaining ¼ cup cheese and the butter; sprinkle evenly over casserole.

4) Bake uncovered 25 to 30 minutes or until thoroughly heated and topping is golden.

1 SERVING: Calories 600; Total Fat 34g; Sodium 840mg; Dietary Fiber 3g; Protein 21g. EXCHANGES: 3 Starch, 1/2 Milk, 1/2 Vegetable, 1 Lean Meat, 5 Fat. CARBOHYDRATE CHOICES: 3-1/2.

Shortcut Vegetable Lasagna

PREP TIME: 40 MINUTES (READY IN 2 HOURS)
SERVINGS: 8

1 tablespoon olive oil

4 medium green onions, sliced (¼ cup)

2 medium zucchini, shredded (about 3 cups)

2 medium carrots, shredded (about 1 cup)

1 medium sweet potato, peeled, shredded (about 1 cup)

1 package (8 oz) sliced fresh mushrooms (about 3 cups)

2 cloves garlic, finely chopped

1 egg

1 container (15 oz) light ricotta cheese

1 cup shredded Swiss cheese (4 oz)

¼ cup grated Parmesan cheese

1 teaspoon dried basil leaves

1 jar (16 oz) Alfredo pasta sauce

1 ½ cups water

9 uncooked lasagna noodles

1 cup shredded mozzarella cheese (4 oz)

2 tablespoons chopped fresh parsley

1) Heat oven to 350°F. Spray 13x9-inch (3-quart) glass baking dish with cooking spray.

2) In 12-inch nonstick skillet, heat oil over medium-high heat. Cook onions, zucchini, carrots, sweet potato, mushrooms and garlic in oil 6 to 8 minutes, stirring occasionally, until mushrooms are tender. Drain off any excess liquid.

3) In medium bowl, beat egg. Stir in ricotta cheese, Swiss cheese, Parmesan cheese and basil. In separate medium bowl, mix Alfredo sauce and water.

4) Arrange 3 uncooked noodles in bottom of baking dish. Top with ⅓ of sauce mixture (about 1 cup), ½ of ricotta mixture and ½ of vegetable mixture. Repeat layers once. Top with remaining 3 noodles and remaining sauce mixture. Sprinkle with mozzarella cheese. Spray sheet of foil with cooking spray; cover baking dish tightly with foil, sprayed side down.

5) Bake 1 hour to 1 hour 10 minutes or until bubbly around edges. Sprinkle with parsley. Let stand 10 minutes before serving.

1 SERVING: Calories 540; Total Fat 33g; Sodium 470mg; Dietary Fiber 3g; Protein 25g. EXCHANGES: 2 Starch, 1 Vegetable, 1/2 Lean Meat, 2 Medium-Fat Meat, 4 Fat. CARBOHYDRATE CHOICES: 2.

Spicy Caribbean Burrito Bake

PREP TIME: 15 MINUTES (READY IN 1 HOUR)
SERVINGS: 8

 EASY   LOW FAT

2 cups uncooked instant white rice

2 cups water

2 cups shredded cooked chicken

1 can (15 oz) Progresso® black beans, drained, rinsed

1 ripe avocado, pitted, peeled and chopped

2 chipotle chiles in adobo sauce (from 7-oz can), finely chopped

½ cup orange marmalade

½ cup sour cream

1 tablespoon fresh lime juice

1 tablespoon Jamaican jerk seasoning (dry)

8 whole wheat tortillas (8 inch)

4 medium green onions, chopped (¼ cup)

1) Heat oven to 375°F. Spray 13x9-inch (3-quart) glass baking dish with cooking spray.

2) In 2-quart saucepan, cook rice in water as directed on package.

3) Meanwhile, in large bowl, toss chicken, beans, avocado and chiles. In small bowl, stir marmalade, sour cream, lime juice and jerk seasoning. Add to chicken mixture; toss until evenly coated.

4) Spoon ½ cup cooked rice down center of each tortilla; top each with ½ cup chicken mixture. Roll up tortillas; place seam side down in baking dish and tuck ends under.

5) Cover; bake 45 minutes or until thoroughly heated. Garnish with onions.

1 SERVING: Calories 430; Total Fat 10g; Sodium 850mg; Dietary Fiber 9g; Protein 19g. EXCHANGES: 2-1/2 Starch, 1-1/2 Other Carbohydrate, 1/2 Vegetable, 1-1/2 Lean Meat, 1 Fat. CARBOHYDRATE CHOICES: 4-1/2.

Bacon-Alfredo Casserole

PREP TIME: 35 MINUTES (READY IN 1 HOUR 35 MINUTES)
SERVINGS: 12

1 box (1 lb) spaghetti

½ cup butter

⅓ cup all-purpose flour

1 teaspoon salt

½ teaspoon pepper

1 quart half-and-half

8 slices bacon, crisply cooked, crumbled

1 bag (12 oz) Green Giant® Valley Fresh Steamers™ frozen sweet peas, thawed

1 ½ cups grated Parmesan cheese

1 egg, slightly beaten

2 tablespoons chopped fresh parsley

1) Heat oven to 350°F. Spray 13x9-inch (3-quart) glass baking dish with cooking spray.

2) In 5-quart Dutch oven, cook and drain spaghetti as directed on package; set aside. In same Dutch oven, melt butter over medium heat. Stir in flour, salt and pepper. Cook and stir over medium heat until smooth and bubbly. Gradually stir in half-and-half. Heat to boiling, stirring constantly; boil 1 minute. Remove from heat.

3) Add cooked spaghetti, bacon, peas and 1 cup of the cheese; toss to coat spaghetti. Stir in egg. Spoon into baking dish. Sprinkle with remaining ½ cup cheese.

4) Bake uncovered 20 minutes or until set and edges are bubbly. Sprinkle with parsley. Cut into squares to serve.

1 SERVING: Calories 480; Total Fat 25g; Sodium 820mg; Dietary Fiber 3g; Protein 19g. EXCHANGES: 2-1/2 Starch, 1/2 Other Carbohydrate, 1/2 Lean Meat, 1 Medium-Fat Meat, 3-1/2 Fat. CARBOHYDRATE CHOICES: 3.

Chicken Pot Pie with Flaky Crust

PREP TIME: 40 MINUTES (READY IN 1 HOUR 35 MINUTES)
SERVINGS: 4

1 sheet frozen puff pastry (from 17.3-oz package), thawed

1 tablespoon olive or vegetable oil

¾ lb boneless skinless chicken breasts, cut into ½-inch pieces

1 large onion, coarsely chopped (1 cup)

1 cup quartered ready-to-eat baby-cut carrots

¾ cup Green Giant® Valley Fresh Steamers™ frozen sweet peas (from 12-oz bag)

1 jar (12 oz) chicken gravy

½ cup sour cream

2 tablespoons cornstarch

¼ teaspoon dried thyme leaves

¼ teaspoon pepper

1 egg, beaten, if desired

1) Heat oven to 375°F. On lightly floured surface, unroll puff pastry. With rolling pin, roll pastry into 11-inch square. Cut off corners to make 11-inch round. Cut slits or small designs in several places in pastry; set aside.

2) In 10-inch skillet, heat oil over medium-high heat. Cook chicken in oil about 4 minutes, stirring frequently, until no longer pink in center. Add onion and carrots; cook 5 minutes, stirring frequently, until crisp-tender. Remove from heat; stir in peas.

3) In medium bowl, beat remaining ingredients except egg with wire whisk until well blended. Stir into chicken mixture in skillet. Spoon into 9 ½-inch deep-dish glass pie plate. Place pastry over filling, allowing pastry to hang over edge.

4) Bake 20 minutes. Brush crust with egg. Cover edge of crust with strips of foil to prevent excessive browning.

5) Bake 20 to 25 minutes longer or until crust is golden brown. Let stand 10 minutes before serving.

1 SERVING: Calories 610; Total Fat 37g; Sodium 720mg; Dietary Fiber 3g; Protein 27g. EXCHANGES: 1 Starch, 1-1/2 Other Carbohydrate, 1 Vegetable, 3 Very Lean Meat, 7 Fat. CARBOHYDRATE CHOICES: 3.

tip

Use a miniature cookie or canapé cutter to make steam holes in the pastry. Save the pastry cutouts and place on top of the pastry after brushing it with egg. Bake as directed.

Speedy Stir-Fry Casserole

PREP TIME: 15 MINUTES (READY IN 35 MINUTES)
SERVINGS: 4 (1-1/2 CUPS EACH)

e EASY

1 cup instant whole-grain brown rice

1 cup water

1 tablespoon olive oil

1 lb boneless skinless chicken breasts, cut into thin strips

1 bag (1 lb) frozen broccoli stir-fry vegetable blend, thawed

1 cup Cascadian Farm® frozen organic shelled edamame (from 10-oz bag), thawed

½ cup stir-fry sauce

¼ cup Progresso® chicken broth (from 32-oz carton)

1 cup chow mein noodles

1) Heat oven to 375°F. Spray 8-inch square (2-quart) glass baking dish with cooking spray.

2) Cook rice in water as directed on package. Meanwhile, in 12-inch nonstick skillet, heat oil over medium-high heat. Cook chicken in oil 6 minutes, stirring occasionally, or until no longer pink in center. Stir in cooked rice and remaining ingredients except noodles; heat to boiling. Spoon into baking dish. Sprinkle with noodles.

3) Bake uncovered 15 to 20 minutes or until thoroughly heated.

1 SERVING: Calories 430; Total Fat 13g; Sodium 1230mg; Dietary Fiber 5g; Protein 35g. EXCHANGES: 2-1/2 Starch, 1 Vegetable, 1-1/2 Very Lean Meat, 2 Lean Meat, 1 Fat. CARBOHYDRATE CHOICES: 3.

Tuna Melt Pot Pie

PREP TIME: 20 MINUTES (READY IN 55 MINUTES)
SERVINGS: 6 (1-1/2 CUPS EACH)

 EASY

3 cups uncooked rotini pasta (9 oz)

1 can (10 ¾ oz) condensed Cheddar cheese soup

½ cup milk

1 large tomato, chopped (1 cup)

1 cup shredded Cheddar cheese (4 oz)

2 tablespoons grated Parmesan cheese

1 can (12 oz) solid white tuna in water, drained, flaked

1 can (2.8 oz) French-fried onions

1) Heat oven to 375°F. Spray 9 ½-inch glass deep-dish pie plate with cooking spray.

2) Cook and drain pasta as directed on package. In large bowl, mix soup and milk. Stir in cooked pasta, tomato and cheeses. Gently fold in tuna. Spoon into pie plate.

3) Cover with foil; bake 30 minutes. Uncover; sprinkle onions evenly over top. Bake 5 minutes longer or until onions are light golden brown.

1 SERVING: Calories 490; Total Fat 20g; Sodium 1070mg; Dietary Fiber 3g; Protein 29g. EXCHANGES: 2-1/2 Starch, 1/2 Milk, 1/2 Vegetable, 2 Lean Meat, 1/2 High-Fat Meat, 1 Fat. CARBOHYDRATE CHOICES: 3.

tip

All the flavors of a favorite diner sandwich are captured in this home-style, family-pleasing casserole. Don't have Cheddar cheese soup? Try it with cream of mushroom instead!

Hot Tamale Pot Pie

PREP TIME: 25 MINUTES (READY IN 50 MINUTES)
SERVINGS: 6

2 tablespoons olive oil

1 lb boneless skinless chicken breasts, cut into 1-inch pieces

½ teaspoon salt

¼ teaspoon pepper

1 large onion, chopped (1 cup)

2 cloves garlic, finely chopped

1 teaspoon ground cumin

1 can (15 oz) Progresso® black beans, drained, rinsed

1 cup Old El Paso® salsa verde

3 tablespoons chopped fresh cilantro

1 roll (1 lb) refrigerated polenta, cut into ¼-inch slices

½ cup shredded sharp Cheddar cheese (2 oz)

½ cup shredded Monterey Jack cheese (2 oz)

1) Heat oven to 400°F. Spray 11x7-inch (2-quart) glass baking dish with cooking spray.

2) In 12-inch nonstick skillet, heat 1 tablespoon of the oil over medium-high heat. Cook chicken, salt and pepper in oil 8 minutes, stirring occasionally, until chicken is no longer pink in center. Remove with slotted spoon to bowl. In same skillet, heat remaining 1 tablespoon oil over medium heat. Cook onion in oil 3 minutes, stirring occasionally, until tender. Add garlic and cumin; cook and stir 1 minute.

3) Return chicken to skillet, discarding any juices in bowl. Stir in beans, salsa and 2 tablespoons of the cilantro. Heat to boiling; remove from heat. Spoon into baking dish. Arrange sliced polenta over hot chicken mixture. Sprinkle evenly with cheeses and remaining 1 tablespoon cilantro.

4) Cover; bake 20 minutes. Uncover; bake 5 minutes longer or until thoroughly heated and cheese is melted.

1 SERVING: Calories 370; Total Fat 14g; Sodium 980mg; Dietary Fiber 7g; Protein 28g. EXCHANGES: 2 Starch, 1/2 Vegetable, 2-1/2 Lean Meat, 1/2 High-Fat Meat. CARBOHYDRATE CHOICES: 2.

Moroccan Chicken-Lentil Casserole

PREP TIME: 30 MINUTES (READY IN 1 HOUR 10 MINUTES)
SERVINGS: 6

LOW FAT

CASSEROLE

4 cups water

1 cup dried lentils, sorted, rinsed

2 tablespoons olive oil

1 lb boneless skinless chicken breasts, cut into 1-inch pieces

1 ½ teaspoons salt

1 teaspoon chili powder

½ teaspoon ground cinnamon

½ teaspoon ground cumin

¼ teaspoon pepper

1 large onion, chopped (1 cup)

2 cloves garlic, finely chopped

½ cup Progresso® chicken broth (from 32-oz carton)

½ cup red wine or additional chicken broth

1 can (15 oz) Progresso® chick peas (garbanzo beans), drained, rinsed

TOPPING

1 medium red apple, diced (1 cup)

¼ cup dried apricots, chopped

1 tablespoon lemon juice

1 teaspoon sugar

¼ teaspoon ground ginger

¼ cup slivered almonds, toasted

1) In 3-quart saucepan, heat water to boiling. Stir in lentils; return to boiling. Reduce heat to medium. Cover; cook 30 to 45 minutes or until desired tenderness is reached. Drain if necessary.

2) About 15 minutes before lentils are done, heat oven to 375°F. Spray 11x7-inch (2-quart) glass baking dish with cooking spray.

3) In 12-inch nonstick skillet, heat 1 tablespoon of the oil over medium-high heat. Cook chicken, ½ teaspoon of the salt, the chili powder, cinnamon, cumin and pepper in oil 6 to 8 minutes, stirring occasionally, until chicken is no longer pink in center. Remove with slotted spoon to bowl. Reduce heat to medium. Cook onion in remaining 1 tablespoon oil 3 minutes, stirring occasionally, until tender. Add garlic; cook and stir 1 minute.

4) Stir in broth, wine, cooked lentils, chick peas and remaining 1 teaspoon salt. Heat to boiling over high heat; remove from heat. Return chicken to skillet, discarding any juices in bowl. Spoon into baking dish.

5) In medium bowl, toss all topping ingredients except almonds. Sprinkle topping over casserole.

6) Cover; bake 20 minutes or until apples are just tender. Sprinkle with almonds. Let stand 5 minutes before serving.

1 SERVING: Calories 400; Total Fat 9g; Sodium 790mg; Dietary Fiber 11g; Protein 31g. EXCHANGES: 3 Starch, 1/2 Vegetable, 1/2 Very Lean Meat, 2-1/2 Lean Meat. CARBOHYDRATE CHOICES: 3.

Three-Cheese Beef Pasta Shells

PREP TIME: 25 MINUTES (READY IN 1 HOUR 20 MINUTES)
SERVINGS: 8 (3 SHELLS EACH)

24 uncooked jumbo pasta shells

1 lb lean (at least 80%) ground beef

1 jar (26 oz) chunky tomato pasta sauce

¼ cup water

1 container (8 oz) chives-and-onion cream cheese spread

1 ½ cups shredded Italian cheese blend (6 oz)

½ cup grated Parmesan cheese

1 egg

1 to 2 tablespoons chopped fresh parsley, if desired

tip

For the best results, cook the pasta shells just until al dente (still slightly firm). They will be easier to stuff and won't become overcooked during the baking time.

1) Heat oven to 350°F. Cook and drain pasta shells as directed on package. Rinse with cold water to cool; drain well.

2) In 10-inch skillet, cook beef over medium-high heat 5 to 7 minutes, until thoroughly cooked; drain. Cool slightly. In large bowl, mix pasta sauce and water. Pour 1 cup of the mixture into ungreased 13x9-inch (3-quart) glass baking dish.

3) In medium bowl, mix cream cheese, 1 cup of the Italian cheese blend, the Parmesan cheese, egg and cooked beef. Spoon 1 heaping tablespoon mixture into each pasta shell. Arrange stuffed shells over sauce in baking dish. Pour remaining sauce over top, covering shells completely.

4) Cover; bake 40 to 45 minutes or until bubbly and cheese filling is set. Uncover; sprinkle with remaining ½ cup Italian cheese blend. Bake about 10 minutes longer or until cheese is melted. Sprinkle with parsley.

1 SERVING: Calories 490; Total Fat 26g; Sodium 1170mg; Dietary Fiber 3g; Protein 25g. EXCHANGES: 2 Starch, 1/2 Other Carbohydrate, 2-1/2 Medium-Fat Meat, 2-1/2 Fat. CARBOHYDRATE CHOICES: 2-1/2.

Creamy Tuna-Broccoli Casserole

PREP TIME: 20 MINUTES (READY IN 50 MINUTES)
SERVINGS: 6

 EASY   LOW FAT

3 cups uncooked rotini pasta (about 10 oz)

3 cups Green Giant® Valley Fresh Steamers™ frozen broccoli cuts (from 12-oz bag)

1 can (6 oz) albacore tuna in water, drained

1 can (18 oz) Progresso® vegetable classics creamy mushroom soup

¼ cup milk

1 ½ cups garlic bagel chips (from 6-oz bag), broken into pieces

1) Heat oven to 350°F. In 3-quart saucepan, cook pasta as directed on package, using minimum cook time and adding broccoli during last 5 minutes of cooking time. Drain and return to saucepan.

2) Stir in tuna, soup and milk. Spoon mixture into ungreased 8-inch square (2-quart) glass baking dish.

3) Bake uncovered 15 minutes. Sprinkle with bagel chips. Bake 10 to 15 minutes longer or until chips are lightly browned and casserole is hot.

1 SERVING: Calories 420; Total Fat 8g; Sodium 700mg; Dietary Fiber 6g; Protein 20g. EXCHANGES: 3-1/2 Starch, 1/2 Other Carbohydrate, 1 Vegetable, 1 Very Lean Meat, 1 Fat. CARBOHYDRATE CHOICES: 4-1/2.

Sloppy Joe-Tater Nugget Hot Dish

PREP TIME: 20 MINUTES (READY IN 1 HOUR 10 MINUTES)
SERVINGS: 5 (1-1/3 CUPS EACH)

 EASY

1 lb lean (at least 80%) ground beef

¾ cup chopped onions (about 2 medium)

½ cup chopped celery (1 medium stalk)

1 can (15.5 or 16 oz) sloppy joe sauce

1 can (10-3/4 oz) condensed cream of chicken soup

1 cup Green Giant® Valley Fresh Steamers™ Niblets® frozen corn (from 12-oz bag), thawed

1 bag (32 oz) frozen potato nuggets (4 cups)

1) Heat oven to 375°F. In 10-inch nonstick skillet, cook beef, onions and celery over medium heat 8 to 10 minutes, stirring frequently, until beef is thoroughly cooked; drain.

2) Stir in sloppy joe sauce, soup and corn. Spoon mixture into ungreased 11x7-inch (2-quart) glass baking dish. Place potato nuggets in single layer on top.

3) Bake uncovered 40 to 50 minutes or until bubbly around edges and potatoes are golden brown.

1 SERVING: Calories 700; Total Fat 30g; Sodium 2460mg; Dietary Fiber 9g; Protein 23g. EXCHANGES: 4 Starch, 1 Other Carbohydrate, 2 Vegetable, 1/2 Very Lean Meat, 1/2 Medium-Fat Meat, 5 Fat. CARBOHYDRATE CHOICES: 5-1/2.

Southwestern Turkey-Tater Casserole

PREP TIME: 25 MINUTES (READY IN 1 HOUR 5 MINUTES)
SERVINGS: 6 (1-1/3 CUPS EACH)

1 lb lean (at least 90%) ground turkey

2 teaspoons chili powder

1 teaspoon ground cumin

2 cups Green Giant® Valley Fresh Steamers™ frozen cut green beans (from 12-oz bag)

1 can (18 oz) Progresso® vegetable classics creamy mushroom soup

1 can (14.5 oz) Muir Glen® organic diced tomatoes, drained

1 can (11 oz) Green Giant® Mexicorn® whole kernel corn with red and green peppers, drained

3 cups frozen potato nuggets (from 32-oz bag)

1) Heat oven to 350°F. In 12-inch skillet, cook turkey over medium heat, stirring frequently, until no longer pink; drain. Stir in chili powder and cumin. Spoon into ungreased 13x9-inch (3-quart) glass baking dish.

2) Gently stir in beans, soup, tomatoes and corn. Place potato nuggets in single layer on top.

3) Bake uncovered 45 to 50 minutes or until bubbly around edges and potatoes are golden brown.

1 SERVING: Calories 420; Total Fat 20g; Sodium 980mg; Dietary Fiber 5g; Protein 21g. EXCHANGES: 2 Starch, 1 Vegetable, 2 Medium-Fat Meat, 2 Fat. CARBOHYDRATE CHOICES: 2-1/2.

Crescent-Topped Pot Roast Pie

PREP TIME: 45 MINUTES (READY IN 1 HOUR 10 MINUTES)
SERVINGS: 4

1 tablespoon oil

1 lb boneless beef top sirloin steak (1 inch thick), cut into thin bite-size strips

2 cups julienne carrots (from 10-oz bag)

2 cups thinly sliced celery (3 to 4 medium stalks)

1 medium onion, halved, thinly sliced

1 jar (12 oz) beef gravy

1 tablespoon Dijon mustard

1 jar (6 oz) Green Giant® sliced mushrooms, drained

1 can (8 oz) Pillsbury® refrigerated crescent dinner rolls

1 tablespoon sesame seed

1) Heat oven to 375°F. Spray 11x7-inch (2-quart) glass baking dish with cooking spray.

2) In 10-inch nonstick skillet, heat oil over medium-high heat. Cook beef in oil 5 to 7 minutes, stirring frequently, until browned. Remove beef; set aside. In same skillet, cook carrots, celery and onion 10 minutes, stirring occasionally, until crisp-tender.

3) Return beef to skillet; stir in gravy, mustard and mushrooms. Cook about 2 minutes or until hot and bubbly. Pour into baking dish.

4) Separate dough into 8 triangles. Arrange triangles over beef mixture, overlapping about ¼ inch to create a braided appearance. Spray triangles with cooking spray; sprinkle with sesame seed.

5) Bake 22 to 24 minutes or until crust is deep golden brown.

1 SERVING: Calories 520; Total Fat 23g; Sodium 1260mg; Dietary Fiber 4g; Protein 39g. EXCHANGES: 1-1/2 Starch, 1/2 Other Carbohydrate, 1-1/2 Vegetable, 4 Lean Meat, 1/2 Medium-Fat Meat, 1-1/2 Fat. CARBOHYDRATE CHOICES: 2-1/2.

tip

Be careful not to overcook the beef strips when browning them for this recipe. Overcooking can make the meat tough.

Seafood Manicotti

PREP TIME: 50 MINUTES (READY IN 1 HOUR 35 MINUTES)
SERVINGS: 4

8 uncooked manicotti pasta shells

1 cup ricotta cheese

1 package (3 oz) cream cheese, softened

4 medium green onions, chopped (¼ cup)

6 oz frozen cooked small shrimp (about 25 shrimp), thawed, tails removed and shrimp cut in half crosswise

1 can (6 oz) crabmeat, drained, flaked

1 ½ cups meatless tomato pasta sauce

½ cup shredded mozzarella cheese (2 oz)

1) Heat oven to 375°F. Cook and drain pasta shells as directed on package, using minimum cook time; rinse with cold water to cool.

2) In medium bowl, mix ricotta cheese and cream cheese. Gently stir in onions, shrimp and crabmeat.

3) Spread ½ cup of the pasta sauce in ungreased 11x7-inch (2-quart) glass baking dish. Fill pasta shells with seafood mixture; place over sauce. Spoon remaining 1 cup pasta sauce over filled shells.

4) Cover tightly with foil; bake 25 to 30 minutes or until bubbly. Uncover; sprinkle with mozzarella cheese. Bake 5 to 8 minutes longer or until cheese is melted. Let stand 5 minutes before serving.

1 SERVING: Calories 460; Total Fat 20g; Sodium 1020mg; Dietary Fiber 3g; Protein 33g. EXCHANGES: 2-1/2 Starch, 1/2 Vegetable, 2 Very Lean Meat, 1-1/2 Lean Meat, 2-1/2 Fat. CARBOHYDRATE CHOICES: 2-1/2.

Stuffed Pasta Shells

PREP TIME: 30 MINUTES (READY IN 1 HOUR 5 MINUTES)
SERVINGS: 4

12 uncooked jumbo pasta shells

1 cup light ricotta cheese

4 oz (half of 8-oz package) fat-free cream cheese, softened

½ cup shredded Italian cheese blend (2 oz)

½ cup frozen cut leaf spinach (from 1-lb bag), thawed, well drained

½ teaspoon garlic salt

1 jar (14 oz) tomato pasta sauce

2 tablespoons shredded Italian cheese blend

1) Heat oven to 350°F. Cook and drain pasta shells as directed on package, using minimum cook time; rinse with cold water to cool.

2) In medium bowl, mix ricotta cheese, cream cheese, ½ cup shredded cheese, spinach and garlic salt. Spread 1 cup of the pasta sauce in ungreased 12x8-inch (2-quart) glass baking dish. Fill each cooked shell with about 2 rounded tablespoonfuls ricotta mixture; place over sauce. Spoon remaining pasta sauce over filled shells; sprinkle with 2 tablespoons shredded cheese.

3) Spray sheet of foil with cooking spray; cover baking dish tightly with foil, sprayed side down. Bake 25 to 35 minutes or until thoroughly heated.

1 SERVING: Calories 420; Total Fat 11g; Sodium 1270mg; Dietary Fiber 4g; Protein 25g. EXCHANGES: 3 Starch, 1/2 Other Carbohydrate, 1/2 Vegetable, 1 Lean Meat, 1/2 Medium-Fat Meat, 1/2 High-Fat Meat. CARBOHYDRATE CHOICES: 3-1/2.

Spinach Pesto Manicotti

PREP TIME: 35 MINUTES (READY IN 1 HOUR 15 MINUTES)
SERVINGS: 6 (2 SHELLS EACH)

12 uncooked manicotti pasta shells

 1 lb extra-lean (at least 90%) ground beef

 1 box (9 oz) Green Giant® frozen chopped spinach, thawed, squeezed to drain

 4 oz mozzarella cheese, diced (about 1 cup)

½ cup basil pesto

 1 egg

 1 jar (26 to 28 oz) tomato pasta sauce

    Shredded mozzarella cheese and chopped fresh parsley

1) Heat oven to 400°F. Spray 13x9-inch (3-quart) glass baking dish with cooking spray. Cook and drain pasta shells as directed on package, using minimum cook time. Rinse with cold water to cool; drain well.

2) Meanwhile, in large bowl, combine beef, spinach, cheese, pesto and egg. If desired, add salt and pepper; mix well. For easier stuffing, place beef mixture in resealable freezer plastic bag; seal bag. Cut about 1-inch hole in bottom corner of bag.

3) Fill each pasta shell by squeezing beef mixture into shell; place in baking dish. Pour pasta sauce over shells.

4) Cover; bake 30 to 40 minutes or until meat thermometer inserted into filling reads 160°F. Sprinkle with shredded cheese and parsley if desired.

1 SERVING: Calories 720; Total Fat 38g; Sodium 1300mg; Dietary Fiber 6g; Protein 33g. EXCHANGES: 2-1/2 Starch, 1 Other Carbohydrate, 1 Vegetable, 3 Very Lean Meat, 1/2 Medium-Fat Meat, 6-1/2 Fat. CARBOHYDRATE CHOICES: 4.

Beef and Spinach Lasagna Roll-Ups

PREP TIME: 35 MINUTES (READY IN 1 HOUR 25 MINUTES)
SERVINGS: 2

½ lb lean (at least 80%) ground beef

1 small onion, chopped (¼ cup)

1 jar (14 oz) tomato pasta sauce

1 egg

¾ cup ricotta cheese

2 tablespoons grated Parmesan cheese

2 teaspoons dried oregano leaves

1¼ cups shredded mozzarella cheese (5 oz)

4 frozen precooked lasagna noodles, thawed

1 cup fresh baby spinach leaves, stems removed

1) Heat oven to 350°F. In 8-inch skillet, cook beef and onion over medium-high heat 5 to 7 minutes, stirring frequently, until beef is thoroughly cooked; drain. Stir in ½ cup of the pasta sauce.

2) Spread 3 tablespoons of the remaining pasta sauce in bottom of ungreased 8-inch square (2-quart) glass baking dish. In medium bowl, beat egg. Add ricotta cheese, Parmesan cheese, oregano and ¾ cup of the mozzarella cheese; mix well.

3) On each lasagna noodle, spread one-fourth each of ricotta mixture, spinach and beef mixture. Starting with short side, gently and loosely roll up noodles; place seam sides down over sauce in baking dish. Top roll-ups with remaining pasta sauce.

4) Cover; bake 30 to 40 minutes or until bubbly and hot. Uncover; sprinkle with remaining ½ cup mozzarella cheese. Bake 2 to 4 minutes longer or until cheese is melted. Let stand 5 minutes before serving.

1 SERVING: Calories 1040; Total Fat 51g; Sodium 1780mg; Dietary Fiber 6g; Protein 64g. EXCHANGES: 3 Starch, 1-1/2 Other Carbohydrate, 2 Vegetable, 1 Lean Meat, 3-1/2 Medium-Fat Meat, 2-1/2 High-Fat Meat, 2 Fat. CARBOHYDRATE CHOICES: 5.

Comforting Classics

These heartwarming dishes provide plenty of comfort during the chilly fall and winter months.

PECAN-COCONUT CRUMBLE YAM
CASSEROLE
PG. 281

PEAR CREAM PIE
PG. 303

CITRUS TURKEY BREAST
PG. 283

SOUTHWEST CORNBREAD, SQUASH
AND SAUSAGE DRESSING
PG. 284

Southwest Cornbread Dressing

PREP TIME: 25 MINUTES (READY IN 2 HOURS)
SERVINGS: 20

CORNBREAD

- 2 pouches (6.5 oz each) cornbread and muffin mix
- $\frac{2}{3}$ cup milk
- $\frac{1}{4}$ cup butter or margarine, melted
- 2 eggs

DRESSING

- 1 lb bulk spicy pork sausage
- 3 tablespoons butter
- 2 large onions, chopped (about 2 cups)
- 1 large red bell pepper, chopped (about 1 cup)
- 1 jalapeño chile, seeded, finely chopped
- 1 $\frac{3}{4}$ cups Progresso® chicken broth
- 1 cup half-and-half
- 2 eggs
- 1 tablespoon ground cumin
- 2 teaspoons ground coriander
- 1 teaspoon salt
- $\frac{1}{4}$ cup chopped fresh cilantro

1) Heat oven to 400°F. Spray 15x10x1-inch pan with cooking spray.

2) In large bowl, stir all cornbread ingredients just until moistened (batter will be lumpy). Spread batter in pan. Bake 10 to 12 minutes or until golden brown. Cool 10 minutes. While still in pan, cut warm cornbread into ½-inch cubes; fluff cubes. Bake 10 minutes; stir. Bake 10 to 15 minutes longer or until golden brown. Reduce oven temperature to 350°F.

3) Meanwhile, in 10-inch skillet, cook sausage over medium heat until no longer pink; remove from skillet. In same skillet, melt butter over medium heat. Cook onions, bell pepper and chile in butter 5 to 6 minutes, stirring occasionally, until onions are softened.

4) In large bowl, mix broth, half-and-half, eggs, cumin, coriander and salt. Stir in cornbread cubes. Add sausage, onion mixture and cilantro; mix well. Spoon into ungreased 13x9-inch (3-quart) baking dish.

5) Cover; bake 45 minutes. Uncover; bake 10 to 15 minutes longer.

1 SERVING: Calories 220; Total Fat 13g; Sodium 590mg; Dietary Fiber 2g; Protein 6g. EXCHANGES: 1-1/2 Starch, 2-1/2 Fat. CARBOHYDRATE CHOICES: 1.

Mashed Sweet Potatoes and Apples

PREP TIME:	20 MINUTES (READY IN 2 HOURS 10 MINUTES)
SERVINGS:	16 (1/2 CUP EACH)

 EASY

Danielle Moore
Fairhope, AK
Celebrate the Season—Thanksgiving Cooking Contest

4 large sweet potatoes (3 ½ to 4 lb)

½ cup butter or margarine, softened

3 medium apples, peeled, chopped (4 cups)

2 teaspoons ground cinnamon or pumpkin pie spice

1 teaspoon sugar

½ teaspoon salt

¼ teaspoon pepper

1) Heat oven to 375°F. Line cookie sheet with foil. Pierce sweet potatoes with fork; place on cookie sheet. Bake 1 hour to 1 hour 15 minutes or until tender when pierced with fork. Let stand 15 minutes or until cool enough to handle.

2) Meanwhile, in 10-inch nonstick skillet, melt 2 tablespoons of the butter over medium heat. Cook apples, cinnamon and sugar in butter 5 to 7 minutes, stirring frequently, until apples are tender.

3) Spray 13x9-inch (3-quart) glass baking dish with cooking spray. Slip off sweet potato skins; place potatoes in large bowl. Add salt, pepper and remaining 6 tablespoons butter; mash until no lumps remain. Add apple mixture; mix well. Spread in baking dish.

4) Cover with foil; bake 25 to 30 minutes or until center is hot.

1 SERVING: Calories 110; Total Fat 6g; Sodium 130mg; Dietary Fiber 2g; Protein 1g. EXCHANGES: 1/2 Other Carbohydrate, 1 Vegetable, 1 Fat. CARBOHYDRATE CHOICES: 1.

Cauliflower and Carrot Gratin

PREP TIME: 25 MINUTES (READY IN 1 HOUR)
SERVINGS: 14 (1/2 CUP EACH)

1 bag (16 oz) ready-to-eat baby-cut carrots

1 head (about 2 ½ lb) Green Giant® fresh cauliflower, cut into florets (6 cups)

6 tablespoons butter

1 medium onion, finely chopped (½ cup)

3 tablespoons all-purpose flour

1 teaspoon salt

1 teaspoon ground mustard

1 ½ cups milk

6 oz (about 8 slices) American cheese, cut into small pieces

½ cup Progresso® panko crispy bread crumbs

1) Heat oven to 350°F. Spray 2 ½-quart casserole with cooking spray.

2) In 5-quart Dutch oven, heat 8 cups water to boiling. Add the carrots and boil uncovered 10 minutes. Add cauliflower; boil 4 minutes longer. Drain; set aside.

3) Meanwhile, in 4-quart saucepan, melt 3 tablespoons of the butter. Cook onion in butter about 4 minutes, stirring occasionally, until softened. Stir in flour, salt and mustard with whisk; cook about 1 minute or until bubbly. Slowly stir in milk. Cook and stir until bubbly and slightly thickened. Remove from heat; stir in cheese until melted. Stir in carrots and cauliflower. Pour into casserole.

4) In small microwavable bowl, microwave remaining 3 tablespoons butter on High 1 minute or until melted; stir in bread crumbs. Sprinkle over vegetable mixture.

5) Bake uncovered 25 to 30 minutes or until bubbly around edges. Let stand 5 minutes before serving.

1 SERVING: Calories 160; Total Fat 10g; Sodium 330mg; Dietary Fiber 2g; Protein 5g. EXCHANGES: 1/2 Starch, 1 Vegetable, 2 Fat. CARBOHYDRATE CHOICES: 1.

Whole Wheat Dressing with Apple Chicken Sausage

PREP TIME: 35 MINUTES (READY IN 1 HOUR 10 MINUTES)
SERVINGS: 14

Trisha Kruse
Eagle, ID
Celebrate the Season—Thanksgiving Cooking Contest

3 ¾ cups cubed day-old whole
    wheat bread

1 ½ cups cubed day-old white bread

1 tablespoon butter or margarine

¾ lb apple chicken sausage or sweet
    Italian turkey sausage, casings
    removed, crumbled

1 ¼ cups chopped celery

1 cup chopped onion

2 cloves garlic, finely chopped

1 to 2 teaspoons dried sage leaves

1 teaspoon dried rosemary leaves,
    crushed

½ teaspoon dried thyme leaves

½ teaspoon salt

¼ teaspoon freshly ground black pepper

1 large apple, chopped (2 cups)

¾ cup sweetened dried cranberries

⅓ cup minced fresh parsley

1 tablespoon soy sauce

¾ to 1 cup Progresso® chicken broth

1) Heat oven to 350°F. Spray 13x9-inch (3-quart) glass baking dish with cooking spray. In large bowl, place bread cubes.

2) In 12-inch nonstick skillet, melt butter over medium-high heat. Cook sausage and celery in butter 7 to 9 minutes, stirring occasionally, until sausage is no longer pink. Add onion, garlic, sage, rosemary, thyme, salt and pepper; cook and stir 2 minutes longer.

3) Pour sausage mixture over bread cubes. Stir in apple, cranberries, parsley and soy sauce. Drizzle with broth; mix lightly. Spoon into baking dish.

4) Cover with foil; bake 20 minutes or until heated through. Uncover; bake 10 to 15 minutes longer or until lightly browned.

1 SERVING: Calories 140; Total Fat 6g; Sodium 500mg; Dietary Fiber 2g; Protein 5g. EXCHANGES: 1/2 Starch, 1/2 Other Carbohydrate, 1/2 Medium-Fat Meat, 1/2 Fat. CARBOHYDRATE CHOICES: 1.

tip

Give limp celery a second chance to season entrees, soups and stews. Cut the ends from the limp stalks, place in a bowl of cold water, then refrigerate for several hours or overnight.

Sweet Corn with Sage

PREP TIME: 25 MINUTES (READY IN 25 MINUTES)
SERVINGS: 8 (1/2 CUP EACH)

 EASY

- 3 tablespoons butter or margarine
- 1 medium onion, finely chopped (½ cup)
- 2 bags (12 oz each) Green Giant® Valley Fresh Steamers™ Niblets® frozen corn
- ¼ cup half-and-half
- 2 tablespoons chopped fresh sage leaves
- ¾ teaspoon salt
- ¼ teaspoon coarse ground black pepper

1) In 10-inch skillet, melt butter over medium heat. Cook onion and corn in butter 10 to 12 minutes, stirring frequently, until onion is tender.

2) Stir in remaining ingredients; reduce heat to low. Simmer uncovered 3 to 5 minutes, stirring occasionally, until flavors are blended.

1 SERVING: Calories 130; Total Fat 6g; Sodium 260mg; Dietary Fiber 2g; Protein 2g. EXCHANGES: 1 Starch, 1/2 Vegetable, 1 Fat. CARBOHYDRATE CHOICES: 1.

Pecan-Coconut Crumble Yam Casserole

PREP TIME:	20 MINUTES (1 HOUR 30 MINUTES)	**e** EASY	Michaela Rosenthal
SERVINGS:	12		Woodland Hills, CA

Celebrate the Season—Thanksgiving Cooking Contest

4 medium yams (about 2 lb)

2 eggs

1 teaspoon vanilla bean paste or vanilla

½ teaspoon salt, if desired

1 can (8 oz) crushed pineapple, well drained

½ cup granulated sugar

¼ cup canned coconut milk (not cream of coconut)

⅔ cup butter or margarine, melted

1 cup flaked coconut

¾ cup packed dark brown sugar

½ cup pecan pieces

⅓ cup all-purpose flour

1) In 4-quart Dutch oven, place yams and enough water to cover. Heat to boiling; reduce heat. Cover and simmer 20 to 25 minutes or until tender when pierced with fork. Drain. When yams are cool enough to handle, slip off the skins.

2) Heat oven to 375°F. Spray 8-inch square (2-quart) glass baking dish with cooking spray.

3) In large bowl, beat eggs, vanilla bean paste and salt until frothy. Add yams; mash until no lumps remain. Add pineapple, granulated sugar, coconut milk and ⅓ cup of the butter; mix well. Spoon into baking dish. In small bowl, mix coconut, brown sugar, pecans, flour and remaining ⅓ cup butter. Sprinkle evenly over casserole.

4) Bake uncovered 30 to 35 minutes or until top is golden brown. Let stand 10 minutes before serving.

1 SERVING: Calories 330; Total Fat 18g; Sodium 120mg; Dietary Fiber 2g; Protein 3g. EXCHANGES: 1/2 Starch, 2 Other Carbohydrate, 1/2 Vegetable, 3-1/2 Fat. CARBOHYDRATE CHOICES: 3.

Mashed Sweet Potatoes with Cinnamon-Brown Sugar Sauce

PREP TIME: 25 MINUTES (1 HOUR 55 MINUTES)
SERVINGS: 8 (1/2 CUP POTATOES AND ABOUT 2 TEASPOONS SAUCE EACH)

3 large sweet potatoes (3 to 3 ½ lb)

¼ cup butter

¼ cup packed brown sugar

2 teaspoons milk

1 teaspoon corn syrup

½ teaspoon ground cinnamon

¼ cup heavy whipping cream, warmed

¾ teaspoon salt

1) Heat oven to 350°F. Pierce sweet potatoes all over with fork; place on cookie sheet with sides. Bake 1 hour 15 minutes to 1 hour 30 minutes or until tender when pierced with fork. Let stand 15 minutes or until cool enough to handle.

2) Meanwhile, in 1-quart saucepan over medium heat, heat butter, brown sugar, milk, corn syrup and cinnamon to boiling, stirring constantly. Boil and stir 1 minute or until slightly thickened. Remove from heat; keep warm.

3) Peel sweet potatoes; place in large bowl. Mash until no lumps remain. Add cream and salt; mash until smooth. Spoon potatoes into large serving bowl. Serve with brown sugar sauce.

1 SERVING: Calories 170; Total Fat 9g; Sodium 290mg; Dietary Fiber 2g; Protein 1g. EXCHANGES: 1-1/2 Starch, 1-1/2 Fat. CARBOHYDRATE CHOICES: 1-1/2.

tip

Orange-fleshed sweet potatoes are often called yams, although true yams are quite different and not readily available in this country.

Citrus Turkey Breast

PREP TIME: 20 MINUTES (READY IN 2 HOURS 30 MINUTES)
SERVINGS: 8

 EASY   LOW FAT

1 bone-in whole turkey breast
(5 to 6 lb), thawed if frozen

1 large lemon

1 tangelo, tangerine or navel orange

1 tablespoon olive oil

1 tablespoon kosher (coarse) salt

½ teaspoon coarse ground black pepper

1) Move oven rack to second to lowest position. Heat oven to 350°F. Using fingers, gently loosen skin covering turkey breast, creating a pocket over each breast.

2) Grate half of the lemon and tangelo to get 1 teaspoon grated peel from each. Slice the remaining halves into very thin slices; set aside. In small bowl, combine grated lemon and tangelo peel, oil, salt and pepper. Slide lemon and tangelo slices between turkey skin and meat, covering entire breast; reserve any remaining slices for garnish.

3) Place turkey, breast side up, on rack in shallow roasting pan. Rub oil mixture over turkey breast. Insert ovenproof meat thermometer so tip is in thickest part of breast and does not touch bone.

4) Roast uncovered 1 hour 30 minutes to 2 hours or until thermometer reads 165°F. Remove the turkey from the oven; cover loosely with foil. Let stand 10 minutes before carving. Garnish with additional fruit slices and fresh herb sprigs.

1 SERVING: Calories 320; Total Fat 4.5g; Sodium 1010mg; Dietary Fiber 0g; Protein 67g. EXCHANGES: 9-1/2 Very Lean Meat. CARBOHYDRATE CHOICES: 0.

Southwest Cornbread, Squash and Sausage Dressing

PREP TIME: 35 MINUTES (READY IN 1 HOUR 30 MINUTES)
SERVINGS: 24

Gloria Bradley
Naperville, IL
Celebrate the Season—Thanksgiving Cooking Contest

1 butternut squash (1 ¼ lb), peeled, seeded and cut into 3/4-inch chunks (4 cups)

1 lb bulk pork sausage

¼ cup butter

1 large onion, chopped (1 cup)

1 medium red bell pepper, chopped (1 cup)

1 jalapeño chile, seeded, finely chopped

2 eggs

1 ½ cups Progresso® chicken broth

1 bag (16 oz) seasoned cornbread stuffing

¾ cup pecan pieces, toasted

⅓ cup chopped fresh cilantro

1 tablespoon chopped fresh sage leaves

1) Heat oven to 350°F. Spray 13x9-inch (3-quart) glass baking dish with cooking spray.

2) In 3-quart saucepan, place squash and enough water to cover. Heat to boiling; reduce heat to medium. Cover; cook 8 to 10 minutes or until almost tender. Drain.

3) In 12-inch nonstick skillet, cook sausage over medium-high heat 8 to 10 minutes, stirring occasionally, until no longer pink; drain. Set sausage aside. Wipe out skillet. In same skillet, melt butter over medium-high heat. Cook onion, bell pepper and chile in butter 5 to 7 minutes, stirring occasionally, until vegetables begin to soften. Remove from heat.

4) In large bowl, beat eggs and broth with whisk. Stir in squash, sausage, vegetable mixture and remaining ingredients. Spoon into baking dish.

5) Cover with foil; bake 45 minutes or until center is hot. Uncover; bake 10 minutes longer or until top is golden brown.

1 SERVING: Calories 110; Total Fat 7g; Sodium 210mg; Dietary Fiber 1g; Protein 3g. EXCHANGES: 1/2 Other Carbohydrate, 1/2 Medium-Fat Meat, 1 Fat. CARBOHYDRATE CHOICES: 1/2.

Sweet Potatoes with Caramel Sauce

PREP TIME: 20 MINUTES (READY IN 2 HOURS)
SERVINGS: 8

 EASY

Gina Colby
Victorville, CA
Celebrate the Season—Thanksgiving Cooking Contest

4 medium sweet potatoes (about 2 lb)

¼ cup butter

1 ½ cups packed brown sugar

¼ cup evaporated milk (from 12-oz can)

1 tablespoon honey

⅓ cup chopped pecans, if desired

1) Heat oven to 375°F. Line cookie sheet with foil. Pierce sweet potatoes with fork; place on cookie sheet. Bake 45 minutes to 1 hour or just until tender when pierced with fork. When cool enough to handle, peel potatoes and cut into ½-inch slices.

2) Reduce oven temperature to 350°F. Grease 11x7-inch (2-quart) glass baking dish with butter or cooking spray. Place sweet potatoes in dish.

3) In 1-quart saucepan, melt butter over medium heat. Stir in brown sugar and evaporated milk until completely incorporated. Cook and stir 2 to 4 minutes or until mixture is smooth and looks like caramel. Stir in honey and pecans. Spoon over sweet potatoes.

4) Cover; bake 30 minutes or until thoroughly heated.

1 SERVING: Calories 280; Total Fat 6g; Sodium 80mg; Dietary Fiber 2g; Protein 1g. EXCHANGES: 3-1/2 Other Carbohydrate, 1/2 Vegetable, 1 Fat. CARBOHYDRATE CHOICES: 3-1/2.

Carrot Soufflé with Pecan Topping

PREP TIME: 25 MINUTES (READY IN 1 HOUR 15 MINUTES)
SERVINGS: 12

Peter Halferty, III
Corpus Christi, TX
Celebrate the Season—Thanksgiving Cooking Contest

1 bag (32 oz) ready-to-eat baby-cut carrots

½ cup unsalted butter or margarine, melted

1 cup granulated sugar

¾ cup all-purpose flour

1 teaspoon salt

4 eggs

1 cup packed light brown sugar

1 cup chopped pecans, toasted

6 tablespoons unsalted butter or margarine, softened

1) Heat oven to 350°F. Grease 11x7-inch (2-quart) glass baking dish with butter or cooking spray.

2) In 3-quart saucepan, place carrots and enough water to cover. Heat to boiling; reduce heat to medium. Cover; cook about 20 minutes or until soft. Drain; cool slightly.

3) In food processor, place carrots, ½ cup butter, the granulated sugar, ¼ cup of the flour, the salt and eggs. Cover; process until pureed. Spoon mixture into baking dish.

4) In medium bowl, mix brown sugar, pecans, remaining ½ cup flour and 6 tablespoons butter until crumbly. Sprinkle evenly over carrot mixture.

5) Bake uncovered 42 to 47 minutes or until center is set.

1 SERVING: Calories 410; Total Fat 22g; Sodium 280mg; Dietary Fiber 3g; Protein 4g. EXCHANGES: 1/2 Starch, 2-1/2 Other Carbohydrate, 1 Vegetable, 4-1/2 Fat. CARBOHYDRATE CHOICES: 3.

Creamy Garlic Mashed Potatoes

PREP TIME: 35 MINUTES (READY IN 35 MINUTES)
SERVINGS: 8

 EASY LOW FAT

8 medium russet or Yukon Gold potatoes (about 3 lb), peeled, cut into quarters

4 large cloves garlic, peeled

½ teaspoon salt

⅛ teaspoon pepper

⅓ cup fat-free (skim) milk, warmed

¼ cup reduced-fat sour cream

1) In 3-quart saucepan, place potatoes, garlic and enough water to cover. Heat to boiling; reduce heat to medium-low. Cover loosely; boil gently 15 to 20 minutes or until potatoes break apart easily when pierced with fork. Drain well.

2) Mash potatoes and garlic until no lumps remain. Add salt, pepper, milk and sour cream; continue mashing until potatoes are smooth.

1 SERVING: Calories 160; Total Fat 1g; Sodium 160mg; Dietary Fiber 3g; Protein 3g. EXCHANGES: 1 Starch, 1-1/2 Other Carbohydrate. CARBOHYDRATE CHOICES: 2.

Cheddar Twisters

KAREN KWAN | BELMONT, CA

 BAKE-OFF® CONTEST 38, 1998

PREP TIME: 10 MINUTES (READY 35 MINUTES)
SERVINGS: 8 ROLLS

 EASY

2 cans (8 oz each) Pillsbury® refrigerated crescent dinner rolls or 2 cans (8 oz each) Pillsbury® Crescent Recipe Creations® refrigerated seamless dough sheet

1 ½ cups finely shredded sharp Cheddar cheese (6 oz)

4 medium green onions, chopped (1/4 cup)

1 egg

1 teaspoon water

2 teaspoons sesame seed

½ teaspoon garlic salt with parsley blend (from 4.8-oz jar)

1) Heat oven to 375°F. Lightly grease large cookie sheet with shortening or cooking spray.

2) If using crescent rolls: Unroll both cans of dough; separate into total of 8 rectangles. Firmly press perforations to seal. If using dough sheets: Unroll both cans of dough; cut into total of 8 rectangles.

3) In small bowl, mix cheese and onions. Spoon slightly less than ¼ cup cheese mixture in 1-inch-wide strip lengthwise down center of each rectangle to within ¼ inch of each end. Fold dough in half lengthwise to form long strip; firmly press edges to seal. Twist strip 4 or 5 times; bring ends together to form ring and pinch to seal. Place on cookie sheet.

4) In another small bowl, beat egg and water until well blended; brush over dough. Sprinkle with sesame seed and garlic salt blend.

5) Bake 15 to 20 minutes or until golden brown. Immediately remove from cookie sheet; cool 5 minutes. Serve warm.

1 ROLL: Calories 310; Total Fat 20g; Sodium 640mg; Dietary Fiber 0g; Protein 10g. EXCHANGES: 1-1/2 Starch, 1/2 High-Fat Meat, 3 Fat. CARBOHYDRATE CHOICES: 1-1/2.

Maple 'n Applesauce Carrots with Candied Pecans

PREP TIME: 20 MINUTES (READY IN 45 MINUTES)
SERVINGS: 12

e EASY

Nikki Wilson
California, MD
Celebrate the Season—Thanksgiving Cooking Contest

1 bag (32 oz) ready-to-eat baby-cut carrots

1 cup applesauce

½ cup real maple syrup

2 teaspoons Dijon mustard

1 teaspoon ground cinnamon

1 tablespoon butter

1 tablespoon sugar

1 cup pecan halves

1) Heat oven to 350°F. Spray 11x7-inch (2-quart) glass baking dish with cooking spray.

2) In 2-quart saucepan, heat 1 inch water to boiling. Add the carrots. Return to boiling; reduce heat. Simmer uncovered 15 to 18 minutes or until crisp-tender.

3) Meanwhile, in 1-quart saucepan, stir applesauce, syrup, mustard and cinnamon. Cook about 10 minutes over medium heat, stirring frequently, until mixture bubbles. Drain carrots; place in baking dish. Pour syrup mixture evenly over carrots.

4) In small skillet, melt butter over low heat. Stir in sugar. Add pecans; turn pecans several times to coat with sugar mixture. Sprinkle over carrots.

5) Bake uncovered 20 to 22 minutes or until hot.

1 SERVING: Calories 150; Total Fat 6g; Sodium 75mg; Dietary Fiber 3g; Protein 1g. EXCHANGES: 1/2 Starch, 1 Other Carbohydrate, 1/2 Vegetable, 1 Fat. CARBOHYDRATE CHOICES: 1-1/2.

Cornbread 'n Bacon Stuffing in Sweet Potato Boats

Barbara Estabrook
Rhinelander, WI
Celebrate the Season—Thanksgiving Cooking Contest

PREP TIME: 45 MINUTES (READY IN 2 HOURS 10 MINUTES)
SERVINGS: 8

4 large sweet potatoes (4 to 4 ½ lb)

2 teaspoons oil

⅓ cup chopped applewood-smoked bacon

¼ cup finely chopped red onion

¼ cup finely chopped celery

1 ½ cups Progresso® chicken broth (from 32-oz carton)

¼ cup unsalted butter, softened

1 box (6 oz) cornbread stuffing mix

¼ cup sweetened dried cranberries

¼ cup coarsely chopped walnuts, toasted

2 tablespoons real maple syrup

Dash ground nutmeg

Additional real maple syrup

1) Heat oven to 400°F. Line cookie sheet with foil; spray foil with cooking spray. Pierce sweet potatoes with fork; rub with oil. Place on cookie sheet. Bake about 45 to 55 minutes or until tender when pierced with fork.

2) Meanwhile, in 12-inch nonstick skillet, cook bacon over medium-high heat until crisp; remove with slotted spoon. Cook onion and celery in bacon drippings over medium-high heat for 1 to 2 minutes, stirring frequently, until softened. Add broth and 2 tablespoons of the butter; heat to boiling. Stir in stuffing mix, bacon, cranberries and 2 tablespoons of the walnuts. Remove from heat; cover until needed.

3) Remove sweet potatoes from oven. Reduce oven temperature to 375°F. When potatoes are cool enough to handle, cut in half lengthwise. Using a melon baller, remove potato flesh, leaving ⅓-inch-thick wall of potato on inside of shell. Set potato shells aside. Place potato flesh in large bowl. Add 2 tablespoons syrup, remaining 2 tablespoons butter and the nutmeg; mash. Spoon about ½ cup stuffing mixture into each potato shell; spoon mashed sweet potato mixture over stuffing, leaving some stuffing exposed around side of shell.

4) Line cookie sheet again with foil; spray foil with cooking spray. Place potato boats on cookie sheet. Bake 15 minutes or until hot. Sprinkle the potatoes with the remaining 2 tablespoons walnuts and drizzle with additional syrup.

1 SERVING: Calories 230; Total Fat 10g; Sodium 300mg; Dietary Fiber 4g; Protein 4g. EXCHANGES: 1/2 Starch, 1 Other Carbohydrate, 1 Vegetable, 2 Fat. CARBOHYDRATE CHOICES: 2.

Tossed Greens 'n Fruit with Sugared Pecans

PREP TIME: 35 MINUTES (READY IN 45 MINUTES)
SERVINGS: 12 (1 CUP EACH)

SUGARED PECANS

1 tablespoon egg white

1 teaspoon water

1 cup pecan halves (about 4 oz)

¼ cup sugar

¼ teaspoon salt

VINAIGRETTE

½ cup vegetable oil

3 tablespoons cider vinegar

2 teaspoons Dijon mustard

1 clove garlic, finely chopped

1 teaspoon salt

¼ teaspoon pepper

SALAD

8 cups chopped romaine lettuce

4 cups fresh baby spinach leaves

1 Braeburn apple, chopped

1) Heat oven to 300°F. Line 15x10x1-inch pan with cooking parchment paper. In medium bowl, beat egg white and water until frothy. Stir in pecans until thoroughly coated. Add sugar and ¼ teaspoon salt; mix well. Spread pecans in single layer in pan.

2) Bake 30 minutes, stirring every 10 minutes. Remove pecans from pan to waxed paper; cool at least 10 minutes. Break apart if necessary.

3) In small bowl, mix all vinaigrette ingredients with whisk. Just before serving, in large bowl, toss salad ingredients with vinaigrette and pecans.

1 SERVING: Calories 200; Total Fat 15g; Sodium 280mg; Dietary Fiber 2g; Protein 1g. EXCHANGES: 1/2 Other Carbohydrate, 1 Vegetable, 3 Fat. CARBOHYDRATE CHOICES: 1.

tip

The recipe for the pecans can easily be doubled. Use the extras as a snack or to serve on top of ice cream or even waffles.

Southwest Turkey

PREP TIME: 20 MINUTES (READY IN 4 HOURS 50 MINUTES)
SERVINGS: 16

 EASY

1   turkey-size oven bag

1   whole turkey (16 to 20 lb), thawed
    if frozen

5   teaspoons chili powder

4   teaspoons kosher (coarse) salt

2   teaspoons ground cumin

2   teaspoons ground coriander

2   teaspoons coarse ground black
    pepper

4   teaspoons grated lime peel
    (from 2 medium limes)

¼   cup vegetable oil

1) Move oven rack to lowest position. Heat oven to 325°F. Prepare oven bag as directed on package.

2) Discard giblets and neck from turkey or reserve for another use. In small bowl, mix remaining ingredients. Rub oil mixture over entire turkey, inside cavity and under skin on breast. If desired, cut up 1 to 2 of the limes and place in cavity.

3) Place turkey in oven bag. Insert ovenproof meat thermometer so tip is in thickest part of inside thigh muscle and does not touch bone.

4) Roast 4 hours to 4 hours 15 minutes or until thermometer reads 165°F and legs move easily when lifted or twisted. Remove turkey from oven; let stand 15 minutes before carving. Reserve drippings if making gravy. Garnish with lime slices and fresh cilantro, if desired.

1 SERVING: Calories 690; Total Fat 37g; Sodium 820mg; Dietary Fiber 0g; Protein 88g. EXCHANGES: 12-1/2 Lean Meat. CARBOHYDRATE CHOICES: 0.

Slow Cooker Brown-Sugared Baby Carrots

PREP TIME: 5 MINUTES (READY IN 4 HOURS 5 MINUTES)
SERVINGS: 10 (1/2 CUP EACH)

 EASY   **lf** LOW FAT

1   bag (32 oz) ready-to-eat baby-cut
    carrots

½   teaspoon salt

½   cup packed brown sugar

2   tablespoons butter, cut into small
    pieces

1   tablespoon chopped fresh parsley

1) Spray 3 ½- to 4-quart slow cooker with
   cooking spray. In slow cooker, place
   carrots; sprinkle with salt, brown sugar
   and butter.

2) Cover; cook on High heat setting 4 to 5
   hours, stirring after 2 hours, or until
   carrots are desired tenderness.

3) Spoon carrots into serving bowl; spoon
   any sauce from slow cooker over
   carrots. Season with additional salt and
   pepper, if desired. Stir before serving.
   Sprinkle with parsley.

1 SERVING: Calories 100; Total Fat 2.5g; Sodium
200mg; Dietary Fiber 2g; Protein 1g. EXCHANGES:
1 Other Carbohydrate, 1 Vegetable, 1/2 Fat.
CARBOHYDRATE CHOICES: 1.

tip

For additional flavor,
cut 1 medium onion
into wedges, then add
to the slow cooker
along with the carrots.

Smokin' Lime 'n Honey Yams

Ken Kumpe
El Dorado, CA
Celebrate the Season—Thanksgiving Cooking Contest

PREP TIME: 35 MINUTES (READY IN 35 MINUTES)
SERVINGS: 10 (1/2 CUP EACH)

4 medium yams (about 2 lb), peeled, diced

2 medium Yukon Gold potatoes, peeled, diced

¼ cup unsalted butter

2 tablespoons honey

1 tablespoon finely chopped chipotle chiles in adobo sauce (from 7-oz can)

1 teaspoon ground cumin

½ teaspoon ground coriander

¼ teaspoon smoked Spanish paprika

Juice of 1 medium lime (about 2 tablespoons)

¼ cup Crema (Mexican-style cream) or sour cream

½ teaspoon salt

⅛ teaspoon ground red pepper (cayenne)

½ cup finely chopped fresh cilantro leaves

1) In 4-quart saucepan, place yams, potatoes and enough water to cover. Heat to boiling; reduce heat. Cover; simmer 10 to 15 minutes or until soft.

2) Meanwhile, in 1-quart saucepan, heat butter, honey, chiles, cumin, coriander and paprika to simmering. Remove from heat; keep warm.

3) Drain yams and potatoes; place in large bowl. Add butter mixture, lime juice, crema, salt and red pepper; mash. Sprinkle with cilantro.

1 SERVING: Calories 150; Total Fat 6g; Sodium 150mg; Dietary Fiber 2g; Protein 1g. EXCHANGES: 1 Other Carbohydrate, 1 Vegetable, 1 Fat. CARBOHYDRATE CHOICES: 1-1/2.

Green Beans with Pearl Onions and Bacon

PREP TIME: 25 MINUTES (READY IN 25 MINUTES)
SERVINGS: 12 (1/2 CUP EACH)

 EASY   LOW FAT

1 lb fresh green beans, trimmed

2 cups frozen pearl onions (from 1-lb bag)

5 slices bacon, chopped

1 tablespoon stone-ground mustard

½ teaspoon kosher (coarse) salt

¼ teaspoon coarse ground black pepper

1) In 3-quart saucepan, heat 4 cups water to boiling. Add beans. Reduce heat to medium. Cover; cook 4 minutes. Add onions. Cover; cook 6 to 8 minutes longer or until beans and onions are desired tenderness.

2) Meanwhile, in 10-inch nonstick skillet, cook bacon over medium heat, stirring occasionally, until crisp. Remove from heat; stir in mustard, salt and pepper. Drain beans and onions; add to bacon mixture in skillet. Cook and stir until coated and hot. Serve immediately.

1 SERVING: Calories 40; Total Fat 1.5g; Sodium 180mg; Dietary Fiber 1g; Protein 2g. EXCHANGES: 1 Vegetable, 1/2 Fat. CARBOHYDRATE CHOICES: 1/2.

tip

To help ease last-minute preparations, trim the green beans and chop the bacon ahead of time.

Cauliflower and Broccoli with Fresh Herb Butter

PREP TIME: 15 MINUTES (READY IN 15 MINUTES)
SERVINGS: 8

e EASY

3 tablespoons butter or margarine, softened

3 tablespoons finely sliced fresh chives

1 ½ teaspoons chopped fresh or ½ teaspoon dried thyme leaves

1 teaspoon grated lemon peel

¼ teaspoon salt

¼ teaspoon pepper

3 cups fresh cauliflower florets (about 1 lb)

3 cups fresh broccoli florets (about 7 oz)

1) In 4-quart saucepan, heat 2 quarts water to boiling over high heat. Meanwhile, in small bowl, stir butter, chives, thyme, lemon peel, salt and pepper until blended; set aside.

2) Add cauliflower to boiling water in saucepan; cook 2 minutes. Add broccoli; cook 2 to 3 minutes longer or until vegetables are crisp-tender. Drain; return to saucepan. Add butter mixture; toss to coat.

1 SERVING: Calories 60; Total Fat 4.5g; Sodium 125mg; Dietary Fiber 2g; Protein 1g. EXCHANGES: 1 Vegetable, 1 Fat. CARBOHYDRATE CHOICES: 0.

Roasted Seasoned Cauliflower

PREP TIME: 15 MINUTES (40 MINUTES)
SERVINGS: 8 (1/2 CUP EACH)

 EASY   LOW FAT

1 head cauliflower (1 ½ lb), divided into large florets (about 6 cups)

4 teaspoons olive or canola oil

1 teaspoon chili powder

1 teaspoon garlic powder

⅛ teaspoon salt

1) Heat oven to 400°F. Line 15x10x1-inch pan with foil; spray with cooking spray. Cut cauliflower florets into ½-inch slices; place in 3-quart bowl.

2) In small bowl, mix remaining ingredients. Pour over cauliflower, tossing to coat cauliflower. Spread in pan.

3) Roast uncovered 20 to 25 minutes, turning after 10 minutes, until cauliflower is tender and slightly brown around edges.

1 SERVING: Calories 35; Total Fat 2.5g; Sodium 55mg; Dietary Fiber 1g; Protein 1g. EXCHANGES: 1/2 Vegetable, 1/2 Fat. CARBOHYDRATE CHOICES: 0.

Squash and Parsnip Gratin

PREP TIME: 30 MINUTES (READY IN 1 HOUR 45 MINUTES)
SERVINGS: 8

1 medium butternut squash (2 ½ lb)

1 lb parsnips (4 medium)

¼ cup butter or margarine

¼ cup all-purpose flour

½ teaspoon salt

¼ teaspoon ground nutmeg

⅛ teaspoon pepper

2 cups milk

1 tablespoon lemon juice

½ cup shredded Asiago or Parmesan cheese

2 cups soft bread crumbs (about 3 slices bread)

3 tablespoons butter or margarine, melted

1) Heat oven to 350°F. Spray 13x9-inch (3-quart) glass baking dish with cooking spray.

2) Peel, halve lengthwise and seed squash; cut crosswise into ¾-inch slices; peel parsnips, halve lengthwise and cut crosswise into ⅛-inch slices. Layer the squash slices in bottom of pan; top with the parsnips.

3) In heavy 2-quart saucepan, melt ¼ cup butter over medium heat. Stir in flour, salt, nutmeg and pepper. Cook and stir 1 minute; remove from heat. Gradually stir in milk. Cook over medium heat 5 to 7 minutes or until thickened and bubbly. Remove from heat; stir in lemon juice and cheese. Pour cheese sauce over squash mixture. Cover with foil.

4) Bake 40 minutes. Meanwhile, mix bread crumbs and 3 tablespoons melted butter. Remove foil. Use spoon to press down on vegetables to moisten evenly; sprinkle with crumb mixture. Bake uncovered 25 to 30 minutes longer or until the vegetables are tender. Let stand 5 minutes before serving.

1 SERVING: Calories 360; Total Fat 16g; Sodium 530mg; Dietary Fiber 5g; Protein 9g. EXCHANGES: 2 Starch, 1 Other Carbohydrate, 1/2 Medium-Fat Meat, 2-1/2 Fat. CARBOHYDRATE CHOICES: 3.

All-Through-the-House Aromatic Roasted Turkey

PREP TIME: 15 MINUTES (READY IN 5 HOURS 15 MINUTES)
SERVINGS: 12

 EASY

Jean Tidwell
Fair Oaks, CA
Celebrate the Season—Thanksgiving Cooking Contest

1 whole turkey (18 lb), thawed if frozen

¼ cup unsalted butter, softened

1 tablespoon garlic salt

1 tablespoon dried oregano leaves

1 tablespoon dried rosemary leaves, crushed

1 ½ teaspoons ground mustard

1 teaspoon ground coriander

½ teaspoon ground red pepper (cayenne)

Salt and pepper to taste

2 tablespoons olive oil

1) Move oven rack to lowest position. Heat oven to 325°F. Discard giblets and neck from turkey or reserve for another use. Using fingers, gently loosen skin covering turkey breast and thighs; spread butter evenly under skin. In small bowl, combine spices. Rub spice mixture over turkey skin. Fold wings across back of turkey so tips are touching.

2) Place turkey, breast side up, on rack in shallow roasting pan. Drizzle oil over turkey. Tuck legs under band of skin at tail, or tie together with heavy string, then tie to tail. Insert ovenproof meat thermometer so tip is in thickest part of inside thigh muscle and does not touch bone. Do not add water to pan.

3) Roast uncovered 2 hours. Cut band of skin or remove string holding legs, to allow the inside of the thighs to cook thoroughly and evenly. Roast 2 hours 15 minutes to 2 hours 45 minutes longer or until thermometer reads 165°F and legs move easily when lifted or twisted (cover loosely with foil if necessary to prevent overbrowning). Remove turkey from oven; let stand 15 minutes before carving.

1 SERVING: Calories 1040; Total Fat 56g; Sodium 580mg; Dietary Fiber 0g; Protein 132g. EXCHANGES: 19 Lean Meat. CARBOHYDRATE CHOICES: 0.

Classic Cranberry Sauce

PREP TIME: 30 MINUTES (READY IN 3 HOURS 30 MINUTES)
SERVINGS: 16 (1/4 CUP EACH)

 EASY LOW FAT

1 bag (12 oz) fresh or frozen
cranberries (3 cups)

2 cups sugar

2 cups water

1) Place cranberries in a strainer; rinse with cool water. Remove any stems or blemished berries.

2) In 3-quart saucepan, heat sugar and water to boiling over medium heat, stirring occasionally. Boil 5 minutes.

3) Stir in cranberries. Heat to boiling over medium heat, stirring occasionally. Boil about 5 minutes, stirring occasionally, until cranberries begin to pop. Spoon into bowl. Cover; refrigerate about 3 hours or until chilled.

1 SERVING: Calories 110; Total Fat 0g; Sodium 0mg; Dietary Fiber 1g; Protein 0g. EXCHANGES: 2 Other Carbohydrate. CARBOHYDRATE CHOICES: 2.

tip

Be sure to cook the cranberries until they pop in order to release the natural pectin which thickens the sauce.

Classic Pan Gravy

PREP TIME:	20 MINUTES (READY IN 20 MINUTES)
SERVINGS:	12 (1/4 CUP EACH)

 e EASY   **lf** LOW FAT

Drippings from roasted turkey

3 cups liquid (turkey juices, canned chicken broth or water)

⅓ cup all-purpose flour

Browning sauce, if desired

¼ teaspoon salt

Dash pepper

1) After removing turkey from roasting pan, pour drippings (turkey juices and fat) into bowl or glass measuring cup, leaving brown bits in pan. Let drippings stand 5 minutes to allow fat to rise. Skim 6 tablespoons fat from top of drippings and return to pan; discard any remaining fat. Add enough broth or water to remaining drippings to measure 3 cups; reserve.

2) Stir flour into fat in pan, using wire whisk. Cook over low heat, stirring constantly and scraping up brown bits, until mixture is smooth and bubbly; remove from heat.

3) Gradually stir in reserved 3 cups drippings. Heat to boiling, stirring constantly. Boil and stir 1 minute or until the gravy thickens. Stir in a few drops of the browning sauce if a darker color is desired. Stir in the salt and pepper.

1 SERVING: Calories 80; Total Fat 7g; Sodium 310mg; Dietary Fiber 0g; Protein 2g. EXCHANGES: 1-1/2 Fat. CARBOHYDRATE CHOICES: 0.

Roasted Harvest Vegetables

PREP TIME: 25 MINUTES (READY IN 1 HOUR 20 MINUTES)
SERVINGS: 8 (3/4 CUP EACH)

4 medium parsnips (about 1 lb), peeled, cut into 1/2-inch slices (3 1/2 cups)

4 medium carrots (about 10 oz), cut into 1-inch pieces (2 cups)

1/4 cup olive or vegetable oil

4 teaspoons chopped fresh or 1 1/2 teaspoons dried thyme leaves

1 teaspoon salt

1/4 teaspoon pepper

2 lb butternut squash, peeled, seeded and cut into 1 1/2-inch chunks (6 1/2 cups)

Fresh thyme sprigs, if desired

1) Heat oven to 425°F. In large bowl, toss parsnips, carrots and half each of the oil, chopped thyme, salt and pepper. In ungreased 15x10x1-inch pan, spread mixture in single layer. Bake 15 minutes.

2) Meanwhile, in same large bowl, toss squash with remaining oil, chopped thyme, salt and pepper. Add to pan; stir to combine vegetables.

3) Bake 35 to 40 minutes longer, turning vegetables twice with pancake turner, until tender. Spoon into serving bowl or on platter; garnish with thyme sprigs.

1 SERVING: Calories 160; Total Fat 7g; Sodium 320mg; Dietary Fiber 4g; Protein 1g. EXCHANGES: 1 Other Carbohydrate, 1 Vegetable, 1-1/2 Fat. CARBOHYDRATE CHOICES: 1-1/2.

tip

If the stem ends of the parsnips are large, cut in half lengthwise, then into 1/2-inch slices to assure doneness.

Cute Turkey Cookies

PREP TIME: 15 MINUTES (READY IN 2 HOURS)
SERVINGS: 8 COOKIES

 EASY

½ cup miniature semisweet chocolate chips

8 fudge-striped shortbread cookies

8 fudge-covered graham crackers

8 miniature chocolate-covered peanut butter cup candies, unwrapped

1 roll (1.7 oz) round chewy caramels in milk chocolate, unwrapped

24 pieces candy corn

1 tube (0.68 oz) Betty Crocker® black decorating gel

1) In small resealable freezer plastic bag, place chocolate chips; seal bag. Microwave on High about 1 minute or until softened. Gently squeeze bag until chocolate is smooth; cut off tiny corner of bag. On work surface, lay shortbread cookies flat, with stripes vertical, in a row. Squeeze bag to pipe a line of melted chocolate across bottom of each cookie, crosswise over fudge stripes. Center longer side of 1 graham cracker on chocolate line; hold until chocolate begins to set. Repeat with remaining cookies and graham crackers. Allow to set up, about 30 minutes.

2) If necessary, reheat chocolate in microwave on High 10 to 30 seconds Gently squeeze bag until chocolate is smooth. Pipe about ½ teaspoon melted chocolate on wider end of 1 peanut butter cup; place over hole on 1 shortbread cookie, resting against graham cracker. Repeat with remaining peanut butter cups.

3) Pipe about ½ teaspoon melted chocolate on bottom of 1 round caramel; place on 1 peanut butter cup (for turkey body). Repeat with remaining round caramels. Allow to set up, about 15 minutes.

4) Turn cookies so graham crackers are flat on work surface and you are looking at the shortbread cookies (turkey feathers). Pipe small amount of chocolate on one side of 1 candy corn piece; center on round caramel and peanut butter cup for beak. Hold in position until chocolate begins to set, 1 to 2 minutes. Repeat with 7 more candy corn pieces.

5) Pipe small amount of chocolate on one side of 1 candy corn piece; place 1 candy corn piece on chocolate, graham crackers against body, on either side for turkey legs. Repeat with remaining candy corn pieces. Using black gel, add eyes on each candy corn beak. Let stand until set, about 1 hour.

1 COOKIE: Calories 190; Total Fat 9g; Sodium 60mg; Dietary Fiber 1g; Protein 1g. EXCHANGES: 2 Other Carbohydrate, 2 Fat. CARBOHYDRATE CHOICES: 2.

Pear Cream Pie

PREP TIME: 1 HOUR 20 MINUTES (5 HOURS 20 MINUTES)
SERVINGS: 8

Bill Blake
Star City, AR
State Fair Pie Competition 2009

CRUST

1 box Pillsbury® refrigerated pie crusts, softened as directed on box

FRUIT FILLING

5 cups sliced peeled fresh pears

¾ cup sugar

¾ teaspoon fruit protector or lemon juice

1 ¼ cups water

CREAM FILLING

3 egg yolks

1 cup sugar

3 tablespoons cornstarch

¼ teaspoon salt

1 ¼ cups milk

¾ cup evaporated milk

1 ½ teaspoons vanilla

¼ cup butter, cut into small pieces

TOPPING

1 cup whipping cream

¼ cup sugar

½ teaspoon vanilla

1) Heat oven to 450°F. Place 1 pie crust in a 9-inch glass pie plate as directed on box for a one-crust baked shell. Bake 9 to 11 minutes or until light brown.

2) To make lattice top, cut second crust into ½-inch-wide strips with pastry cutter. Line large cookie sheet with cooking parchment paper. On cookie sheet, weave strips together to make lattice design; trim to fit top of pie. Bake 7 to 8 minutes or until golden brown.

3) Meanwhile, in large saucepan, place pears, ¾ cup sugar, the fruit protector and water. Cook over medium heat until pears are tender and almost all liquid has evaporated. Cool slightly while cooking cream filling.

4) In medium saucepan, beat egg yolks with whisk or fork. Stir in 1 cup sugar. Add cornstarch and salt; mix well. Stir in 1 ¼ cups milk, the evaporated milk and 1 ½ teaspoons vanilla until blended. Stir in butter. Cook and stir over medium heat until thick and bubbly.

5) Spread fruit filling in cooled, baked shell. Spread cream filling over top. Carefully slide lattice top onto pie. Cool; refrigerate 4 hours or until the filling is set.

6) In chilled small deep bowl, beat all topping ingredients with electric mixer on high speed until stiff peaks form (do not overbeat). Decorate top of pie with whipped cream as desired. Serve with any remaining whipped cream. Store pie covered in refrigerator.

1 SERVING: Calories 690; Total Fat 32g; Sodium 420mg; Dietary Fiber 3g; Protein 5g. EXCHANGES: 2 Starch, 1/2 Fruit, 4 Other Carbohydrate, 6 Fat. CARBOHYDRATE CHOICES: 6.

Pecan-Pumpkin Pie

PREP TIME: 25 MINUTES (READY IN 3 HOURS 15 MINUTES)
SERVINGS: 8

CRUST

- 1 Pillsbury® refrigerated pie crust, softened as directed on box
- 1 teaspoon all-purpose flour

PUMPKIN FILLING

- 1 cup canned pumpkin (not pumpkin pie mix)
- 1 egg, beaten
- ½ cup half-and-half
- ½ cup granulated sugar
- 1½ teaspoons pumpkin pie spice

PECAN FILLING

- ¼ cup light or dark corn syrup
- 2 eggs, beaten
- 2 tablespoons butter or margarine, melted
- ¼ cup packed brown sugar
- ½ teaspoon vanilla
- 1½ cups pecan halves

1) Heat oven to 450°F. Sprinkle both sides of pie crust with ½ teaspoon flour; smooth flour over crust. Place crust in 9-inch glass pie plate. Carefully line pastry with double thickness of foil, gently pressing foil to bottom and side of pastry. Let foil extend over edge to prevent excessive browning.

2) Bake 10 minutes. Carefully remove the foil; bake 3 to 4 minutes longer or until pastry begins to brown and has become set. Reduce oven temperature to 350°F.

3) In medium bowl, beat all pumpkin filling ingredients with whisk until blended. Pour filling into partially baked crust. In another medium bowl, beat all pecan filling ingredients except pecans with whisk until blended. Stir in pecans. Carefully spoon mixture over pumpkin layer.

4) Bake 30 to 35 minutes or until knife inserted 1 inch from edge comes out clean. Cool completely on cooling rack, about 2 hours. Store covered in refrigerator.

1 SERVING: Calories 440; Total Fat 26g; Sodium 190mg; Dietary Fiber 2g; Protein 5g. EXCHANGES: 1-1/2 Starch, 1-1/2 Other Carbohydrate, 5 Fat. CARBOHYDRATE CHOICES: 3.

Sage-Flecked Sweet Potato-Apple Cake
With Caramel-Bacon Crème

PREP TIME: 40 MINUTES (READY IN 3 HOURS 25 MINUTES)
SERVINGS: 16

Janice Elder
Charlotte, NC
Celebrate the Season—Thanksgiving Cooking Contest

2 ½ cups sugar

¼ cup lightly packed fresh sage leaves

3 cups cake flour

2 teaspoons apple pie spice

1 teaspoon baking powder

1 teaspoon baking soda

1 teaspoon salt

¼ teaspoon ground red pepper
(cayenne)

3 eggs

¾ cup canola oil

1 ½ teaspoons vanilla

2 cups diced peeled apples
(about 2 medium)

1 ½ cups mashed sweet potatoes
(from 29-oz can)

1 cup chopped pecans

CARAMEL-BACON CRÈME

½ cup whipping cream

½ cup sour cream

½ cup caramel topping

2 to 3 tablespoons crumbled
crisply cooked bacon

Additional fresh sage leaves
and apple slices, if desired

1) Heat oven to 350°F. Spray 12-cup fluted tube cake pan with baking spray with flour.

2) In food processor, place sugar and sage. Cover; process, using quick on-and-off motions, until well blended (sage should be very small flecks). Set aside. In medium bowl, mix flour, apple pie spice, baking powder, baking soda, salt and red pepper; set aside.

3) In large bowl, beat eggs, oil and vanilla with electric mixer on medium speed. Beat in reserved sugar and flour mixtures (batter will be stiff). Stir in apples, sweet potatoes and pecans just until blended. Spoon batter into pan.

4) Bake 65 to 75 minutes or until toothpick inserted near center comes out clean. Cool 15 minutes. Remove from pan to cooling rack; cool about 1 hour 15 minutes.

5) In medium bowl, beat whipping cream, sour cream and caramel topping with electric mixer on medium speed 1 to 2 minutes or until slightly thickened. Refrigerate until serving time. Stir in bacon just before serving. Top individual cake slices with a dollop of topping; garnish with sage leaves and apple slices.

1 SERVING: Calories 480; Total Fat 21g; Sodium 340mg; Dietary Fiber 2g; Protein 5g. EXCHANGES: 2 Starch, 2-1/2 Other Carbohydrate, 4 Fat. CARBOHYDRATE CHOICES: 4-1/2.

Streusel-Topped Sweet Potato Pie Squares

PREP TIME: 25 MINUTES (READY IN 5 HOURS 30 MINUTES)
SERVINGS: 15

CRUST

1 Pillsbury® refrigerated pie crust, softened as directed on box

FILLING

3 cans (15 oz each) sweet potatoes in syrup, drained, mashed

1 can (14 oz) sweetened condensed milk (not evaporated)

3 eggs, beaten

¾ cup half-and-half

2 teaspoons pumpkin pie spice

½ teaspoon salt

TOPPING

½ cup packed brown sugar

½ cup quick-cooking oats

¼ cup all-purpose flour

½ teaspoon ground cinnamon

¼ cup cold butter or margarine

GARNISH

1 cup heavy whipping cream

2 tablespoons powdered sugar

1) Heat oven to 400°F. Unroll pie crust in ungreased 13x9-inch pan. Press crust in bottom and ¼ inch up sides of pan, cutting to fit; press seams firmly to seal. Do not prick crust. Bake 10 minutes. Remove from oven; immediately press bubbles down with back of wooden spoon.

2) Reduce oven temperature to 350°F. In large bowl, beat all filling ingredients with wire whisk until blended. Pour over partially baked crust.

3) Bake 40 minutes. Meanwhile, in medium bowl, mix brown sugar, oats, flour and cinnamon. Cut in butter, using pastry blender (or pulling 2 table knives through ingredients in opposite directions), until mixture looks like coarse crumbs.

4) Sprinkle streusel over filling. Bake 15 to 20 minutes longer or until knife inserted in center comes out clean (surface may be puffy in spots). Cool completely on cooling rack. Refrigerate at least 2 hours before serving.

5) In chilled medium deep bowl, beat the whipping cream and powdered sugar with electric mixer on high speed until soft peaks form. Cut the dessert into squares; serve with whipped cream. Cover and refrigerate any remaining dessert.

1 SERVING: Calories 400; Total Fat 17g; Sodium 270mg; Dietary Fiber 3g; Protein 6g. EXCHANGES: 3 Other Carbohydrate, 1/2 Milk, 1/2 Vegetable, 2-1/2 Fat. CARBOHYDRATE CHOICES: 3-1/2.

Pumpkin-Chai Cheesecake with Caramel-Rum Sauce

PREP TIME: 35 MINUTES (READY IN 8 HOURS 40 MINUTES)
SERVINGS: 16

CRUST

2 cups crushed teddy bear-shaped cinnamon graham snacks (from 10-oz box)

¼ cup butter or margarine, melted

FILLING

4 packages (8 oz each) cream cheese, softened

1 ½ cups granulated sugar

4 eggs

1 cup canned pumpkin (not pumpkin pie mix)

2 teaspoons pumpkin pie spice

3/4 teaspoon ground cardamom

SPICED CARAMEL-RUM SAUCE

⅓ cup packed brown sugar

⅓ cup light or dark corn syrup

2 tablespoons butter or margarine

⅓ cup whipping cream

1 tablespoon spiced rum or ¼ teaspoon rum extract

GARNISH

Sweetened whipped cream, if desired

1) Heat oven to 300°F. Spray 9-inch springform pan with cooking spray. Wrap foil around pan to catch drips. In small bowl, mix crust ingredients. Press mixture in bottom and 1 inch up side of pan. Bake 8 to 10 minutes or until set. Cool 5 minutes. To minimize cracking, place shallow pan half full of hot water on lower oven rack.

2) In large bowl, beat cream cheese and granulated sugar with electric mixer on medium speed until light and fluffy. Beat in eggs, one at a time, just until blended. Spoon 3 cups of the mixture onto crust; spread evenly. To remaining cream cheese mixture, add pumpkin, pumpkin pie spice and cardamom; mix with wire whisk until smooth. Spoon over mixture in pan.

3) Bake 1 hour 15 minutes to 1 hour 25 minutes or until edge of cheesecake is set at least 2 inches from edge of pan but center of cheesecake still jiggles slightly when moved. Run small metal spatula around edge of pan to loosen cheesecake. Turn oven off; open oven door at least 4 inches. Let cheesecake remain in oven 30 minutes. Cool in pan on cooling rack 30 minutes. Cover loosely; refrigerate at least 6 hours but no longer than 24 hours.

4) In small saucepan, heat brown sugar, corn syrup and 2 tablespoons butter to boiling over medium-low heat, stirring constantly. Boil 5 minutes, stirring occasionally. Stir in whipping cream; heat to boiling. Remove from heat; stir in rum. Cool until warm.

5) Just before serving, run small metal spatula around edge of pan; carefully remove side of pan. Top individual slices with warm sauce and a dollop of whipped cream. Cover and refrigerate any remaining cheesecake.

1 SERVING: Calories 440; Total Fat 28g; Sodium 300mg; Dietary Fiber 1g; Protein 6g. EXCHANGES: 2 Other Carbohydrate, 1 Milk, 4 Fat. CARBOHYDRATE CHOICES: 3.

Cranberry–Raisin Maple Nut Pie

		Donna Buckland
PREP TIME:	25 MINUTES (READY IN 3 HOURS 5 MINUTES)	Billerica, MA
SERVINGS:	8	State Fair Pie Competition 2009

1 box Pillsbury® refrigerated pie crusts, softened as directed on box

⅓ cup packed brown sugar

1 cup chopped walnuts

¾ cup packed brown sugar

½ cup white vanilla baking chips

½ cup real maple syrup

¾ cup half-and-half

3 eggs, slightly beaten

¾ cup sweetened dried cranberries

½ cup golden raisins

1) Heat oven to 425°F. Place 1 pie crust in 9-inch glass pie plate as directed on box for one-crust filled pie.

2) Unroll second crust on work surface. With floured 2 ½- to 3-inch and 1- to 1 ½-inch leaf-shaped cookie cutters, cut 3 leaf shapes of each size from crust; set aside. Cut remaining crust with scissors to resemble crumb topping. In small bowl, mix ⅓ cup brown sugar and ¼ cup of the walnuts; stir in cut-up crust.

3) In 3-quart saucepan, cook ¾ cup brown sugar, the baking chips and syrup over medium heat, stirring constantly, just until chips are melted and mixture is smooth. Stir in half-and-half and eggs until well blended. Stir in cranberries, remaining ¾ cup walnuts and the raisins. Pour mixture into crust-lined plate. Sprinkle with cut-up crust mixture; top with leaf cutouts.

4) Cover crust edge with strips of foil to prevent excessive browning; bake 20 minutes. Remove foil; reduce oven temperature to 350°F. Bake 20 minutes longer. Cool at least 2 hours before serving.

1 SERVING: Calories 700; Total Fat 32g; Sodium 320mg; Dietary Fiber 2g; Protein 8g. EXCHANGES: 2 Starch, 1/2 Fruit, 4 Other Carbohydrate, 6 Fat. CARBOHYDRATE CHOICES: 6-1/2.

Cranberry-Orange Chocolate Meringues

PREP TIME: 30 MINUTES (READY IN 4 HOURS 30 MINUTES)
SERVINGS: 8

Jean Gottfried
Upper Sandusky, OH
Celebrate the Season—Thanksgiving Cooking Contest

MERINGUE SHELLS

- 3 egg whites
- 1 teaspoon vanilla
- ¼ teaspoon cream of tartar
- Dash salt
- 1 cup sugar
- ¼ cup unsweetened Dutch processed baking cocoa

CRANBERRY-ORANGE SAUCE

- 1 bag (12 oz) fresh cranberries (3 cups)
- ½ cup water
- ⅓ cup sugar
- Juice of 1 medium orange (⅓ to ½ cup)
- 1 can (11 oz) mandarin orange segments, drained
- ¾ cup chopped walnuts

FILLING

- 1 package (8 oz) ⅓-less-fat cream cheese (Neufchâtel), softened
- 1 container (6 oz) Yoplait® light orange cream yogurt
- 1 teaspoon grated orange peel

1) Heat oven to 275°F. Line cookie sheet with cooking parchment paper or heavy brown paper.

2) In large bowl, beat egg whites, vanilla, cream of tartar and salt with electric mixer on high speed until foamy. Beat in 1 cup sugar, 1 tablespoon at a time; continue beating until stiff peaks form and mixture is glossy (do not underbeat). Sift cocoa; fold into egg white mixture. Drop meringue by ⅓ cupfuls onto cookie sheet. Shape into 3-inch circles, building up sides with back of spoon.

3) Bake 1 hour. Turn off oven; leave the meringues in the oven with door closed 1 hour. Finish cooling at room temperature, about 2 hours.

4) Meanwhile, in 2-quart saucepan, cook cranberries, water and ⅓ cup sugar over medium heat, stirring frequently, until cranberries pop and sauce begins to thicken. Remove from heat; stir in the orange juice, mandarin oranges and ½ cup of the walnuts. Cool completely, about 30 minutes. Cover; refrigerate until serving time.

5) In small bowl, beat filling ingredients with wire whisk until smooth. Cover; refrigerate until serving time.

6) To serve, spoon 1 teaspoon cranberry-orange sauce in center of each dessert plate. Top with meringue shell. Spoon about 2 tablespoons filling into each shell. Top with about ½ cup cranberry-orange sauce. Sprinkle with remaining ¼ cup walnuts.

1 SERVING: Calories 370; Total Fat 14g; Sodium 150mg; Dietary Fiber 4g; Protein 7g. EXCHANGES: 3 Other Carbohydrate, 1/2 Low-Fat Milk, 1/2 Lean Meat, 2 Fat. CARBOHYDRATE CHOICES: 3-1/2.

Crumbleberry Pear Pie

PREP TIME:	20 MINUTES (READY IN 2 HOURS 25 MINUTES)
SERVINGS:	12

 EASY

CRUST

- 1 Pillsbury® refrigerated pie crust, softened as directed on box

FILLING

- ½ cup butter or margarine
- ½ cup granulated sugar
- 2 eggs
- 1 cup finely ground almonds
- ¼ cup all-purpose flour
- 1 large firm pear or apple, peeled, thinly sliced
- 1 cup fresh or frozen raspberries and/or blueberries, thawed

TOPPING

- ¾ cup all-purpose flour
- ⅓ cup packed brown sugar
- ½ teaspoon almond extract
- ⅓ cup butter or margarine

1) Heat oven to 350°F. Place pie crust in 9-inch glass pie plate as directed on box for one-crust filled pie.

2) In large bowl, beat ½ cup butter and the granulated sugar until light and fluffy. Beat in 1 egg at a time until well blended. Stir in almonds and ¼ cup flour just until evenly moistened. Spread mixture in crust-lined pan. Arrange pear slices on top of filling, overlapping slightly.

3) Bake 20 to 30 minutes or until filling and pears are light golden brown.

4) Meanwhile, in medium bowl, mix ¾ cup flour, the brown sugar and almond extract. Using pastry blender or fork, cut in ⅓ cup butter until mixture resembles coarse crumbs.

5) Sprinkle the raspberries over the pear slices; sprinkle with topping. Bake 18 to 28 minutes or until the topping is golden brown. Serve warm. Store in the refrigerator.

1 SERVING: Calories 370; Total Fat 23g; Sodium 180mg; Dietary Fiber 2g; Protein 4g. EXCHANGES: 1 Starch, 1-1/2 Other Carbohydrate, 4-1/2 Fat. CARBOHYDRATE CHOICES: 2-1/2.

Jeweled Cranberry-Apricot Tart

PREP TIME: 25 MINUTES (2 HOURS 10 MINUTES)
SERVINGS: 12

CRUST

- 1 Pillsbury® refrigerated pie crust, softened as directed on box

FILLING

- 1 package (8 oz) cream cheese, softened
- ⅓ cup sugar
- 2 tablespoons orange-flavored liqueur or orange juice
- 2 eggs

TOPPING

- ½ cup sweetened dried cranberries
- ½ cup chopped dried apricots
- 1 cup cranberry juice cocktail
- ¼ cup seedless raspberry jam
- 1 tablespoon cold water
- 4 teaspoons cornstarch
- ½ teaspoon grated orange peel

1) Heat oven to 450°F. Place pie crust in 10-inch tart pan with removable bottom as directed on box for one-crust filled pie. Press in bottom and up sides of pan. Trim edges if necessary. Do not prick crust. Line crust with heavy-duty foil. Bake 11 minutes. Remove foil; bake 3 to 4 minutes longer or until light golden brown in center and dry in appearance. If crust puffs in center, flatten gently with back of wooden spoon. Reduce oven temperature to 375°F. Cool crust 10 minutes.

2) Meanwhile, in medium bowl, beat cream cheese and sugar with electric mixer on medium speed until light and fluffy. Beat in liqueur and eggs until well blended. Spoon filling into partially baked crust. Bake 15 to 18 minutes or until filling is set. Cool 30 minutes on cooling rack.

3) Meanwhile, in 1-quart saucepan, heat cranberries, apricots and cranberry juice to boiling over high heat, stirring occasionally. Reduce heat to medium-low; simmer 5 minutes, stirring occasionally. Stir in jam; cook 2 minutes. In small bowl, mix water and cornstarch; stir into fruit mixture. Increase heat to medium. Heat to boiling; boil 1 minute, stirring constantly. Remove from heat; stir in orange peel. Cool to room temperature, about 30 minutes.

4) Spread topping over filling. Refrigerate at least 1 hour before serving. Cut into wedges. Cover and refrigerate any remaining dessert.

1 SERVING: Calories 240; Total Fat 11g; Sodium 160mg; Dietary Fiber 0g; Protein 3g. EXCHANGES: 1-1/2 Other Carbohydrate, 1/2 Milk, 1-1/2 Fat. CARBOHYDRATE CHOICES: 2.

CHOCOLATE CHIP-PEANUT BUTTER TORTE
PG. 342

Sweet
Temptations

Indulge your craving for a luscious sweet treat
with one of these irresistibly scrumptious desserts.

CARAMEL APPLE PIE
PG. 334

CHEESECAKE SHOT-GLASS DESSERTS
PG. 335

LIME-GINGER FRUIT CUPS
PG. 336

Chocolate-Cranberry Bread Pudding

PREP TIME: 30 MINUTES (READY IN 1 HOUR 30 MINUTES)
SERVINGS: 12

BREAD PUDDING

- 8 oz day-old French bread, cut into ½-inch cubes (5 to 6 cups)
- 1 cup sweetened dried cranberries
- 4 eggs
- 1 ¼ cups packed brown sugar
- ½ cup unsweetened baking cocoa
- 3 cups half-and-half

SAUCE

- ½ cup granulated sugar
- 2 tablespoons butter
- 1 cup white vanilla baking chips (6 oz)
- 1 cup whipping cream
- 2 tablespoons bourbon or 1 teaspoon vanilla

1) Heat oven to 350°F. Spray 12x8-inch (2-quart) glass baking dish with cooking spray. In baking dish, toss bread cubes and cranberries.

2) In large bowl, beat eggs, brown sugar, cocoa and half-and-half with wire whisk until well blended. Pour over bread mixture; stir gently with large spoon to coat bread with liquid. Let stand 10 minutes; stir.

3) Bake uncovered 45 to 50 minutes or until knife inserted in center comes out clean.

4) In 1-quart saucepan, mix granulated sugar, butter, baking chips and whipping cream. Cook over medium heat 3 to 4 minutes, stirring frequently, until slightly thickened and smooth. Remove from heat; stir in bourbon (sauce will be thin). Serve sauce over warm bread pudding.

1 SERVING: Calories 530; Total Fat 25g; Sodium 220mg; Dietary Fiber 2g; Protein 8g. EXCHANGES: 1 Starch, 3-1/2 Other Carbohydrate, 1/2 Medium-Fat Meat, 4-1/2 Fat. CARBOHYDRATE CHOICES: 4-1/2.

Cranberry Layer Bars

PREP TIME: 15 MINUTES (READY IN 3 HOURS 5 MINUTES)
SERVINGS: 24 BARS

 EASY

1 roll (16.5 oz) Pillsbury® refrigerated sugar cookies

1 can (14 oz) sweetened condensed milk (not evaporated)

2 teaspoons grated orange peel

1 egg

1 cup chopped fresh cranberries

1 cup white vanilla baking chips (6 oz)

1 cup semisweet chocolate chips (6 oz)

1 cup coarsely crushed pretzels (2 oz)

1) Heat oven to 350°F. Spray 13x9-inch pan with cooking spray. Break up cookie dough into pan. With floured fingers, press dough evenly in bottom of pan. Bake 18 to 20 minutes or until puffed and edges are golden brown.

2) In medium bowl, beat the condensed milk, orange peel and egg with whisk until combined. Remove partially baked crust from oven. Spread the milk mixture evenly over the crust; sprinkle evenly with cranberries, chips and pretzels.

3) Bake 25 to 30 minutes longer or until center is set. Cool 1 ½ hours. Refrigerate 30 minutes or until chocolate is set. Cut into 6 rows by 4 rows.

1 BAR: Calories 240; Total Fat 10g; Sodium 140mg; Dietary Fiber 0g; Protein 3g. EXCHANGES: 1 Starch, 1-1/2 Other Carbohydrate, 2 Fat. CARBOHYDRATE CHOICES: 2.

Caramel-Apple-Ginger Crostata

PREP TIME: 20 MINUTES (READY IN 1 HOUR 25 MINUTES)
SERVINGS: 6

 EASY

1 Pillsbury® refrigerated pie crust, softened as directed on box

6 cups thinly sliced peeled apples (about 5 medium)

½ cup packed brown sugar

3 tablespoons all-purpose flour

2 tablespoons finely chopped crystallized ginger

1 teaspoon ground cinnamon

1 tablespoon butter or margarine, cut into small pieces

1 tablespoon granulated sugar

⅓ cup caramel topping

1) Heat oven to 450°F. Line 15x10x1-inch pan with cooking parchment paper. Unroll pie crust in pan.

2) In large bowl, toss the apples, brown sugar, flour, ginger and cinnamon. Spoon the apple mixture onto the center of crust, leaving a 2-inch border (apples will be piled about 4 inches high). Sprinkle butter over the apples. Fold edge of crust over, pleating to fit. Brush crust edge with water; sprinkle with granulated sugar.

3) Loosely cover top and sides with foil; bake 20 minutes. Remove foil; bake 9 to 13 minutes longer or until crust is golden brown and apples are tender. Immediately run a spatula or pancake turner under the crust to loosen. Cool 30 minutes before serving. Cut into wedges; drizzle with caramel topping.

1 SERVING: Calories 380; Total Fat 10g; Sodium 260mg; Dietary Fiber 2g; Protein 2g. EXCHANGES: 1 Starch, 1/2 Fruit, 3 Other Carbohydrate, 2 Fat. CARBOHYDRATE CHOICES: 4-1/2.

tip

Shop for crystallized ginger in the spice aisle or the bulk section of the supermarket.

Easy Apple Cake

PREP TIME: 25 MINUTES (READY IN 1 HOUR 30 MINUTES)
SERVINGS: 8

½ cup butter, softened

1 cup sugar

2 eggs

¼ teaspoon vanilla

1 ¼ cups all-purpose flour

1 teaspoon baking soda

1 teaspoon ground cinnamon

¼ teaspoon salt

1 ½ cups shredded peeled apples
(about 2 medium apples)

½ cup chopped walnuts

1 quart vanilla or cinnamon ice cream

1) Heat oven to 350°F. Spray a 9-inch round cake pan with baking spray with flour.

2) In large bowl, beat the butter and sugar with electric mixer on medium speed until light and fluffy. Beat in eggs, one at a time. Stir in the vanilla, flour, baking soda, cinnamon and salt. Stir in the apples and walnuts. Spoon into pan.

3) Bake 40 to 45 minutes or until toothpick inserted in center of cake comes out clean. Cool 10 minutes. Remove from pan to cooling rack. Cool 10 minutes longer. Serve warm with ice cream.

1 SERVING: Calories 490; Total Fat 25g; Sodium 380mg; Dietary Fiber 2g; Protein 7g. EXCHANGES: 1-1/2 Starch, 2-1/2 Other Carbohydrate, 5 Fat. CARBOHYDRATE CHOICES: 4.

Cardamom Apple Crisp with Caramel Cream

PREP TIME: 20 MINUTES (READY IN 1 HOUR 45 MINUTES)
SERVINGS: 6

 EASY

4 medium tart baking apples, peeled, sliced (4 cups)

⅓ cup plus ⅔ cup packed brown sugar

½ cup all-purpose flour

½ cup quick-cooking oats

½ to ¾ teaspoon ground cardamom

¼ teaspoon ground cinnamon

⅓ cup cold butter or margarine

¼ cup chopped pecans, if desired

1 cup heavy whipping cream

¼ cup caramel topping

1) Heat oven to 375°F. Grease bottom and sides of 8-inch square baking dish with shortening or cooking spray.

2) In medium bowl, toss apples with ⅓ cup of the brown sugar. Spread apples in dish. In another bowl, stir remaining ⅔ cup brown sugar, the flour, oats, cardamom and cinnamon until well mixed. Cut in butter, using pastry blender (or pulling 2 table knives through ingredients in opposite directions), until mixture looks like coarse crumbs. Stir in pecans. Sprinkle over apples.

3) Bake 30 to 40 minutes or until topping is golden brown and apples are tender when pierced with fork. Cool 45 minutes before serving.

4) In chilled large deep bowl, beat whipping cream and caramel topping with electric mixer on high speed until stiff peaks form. Serve caramel cream with warm crisp. Drizzle with additional caramel topping, if desired.

1 SERVING: Calories 490; Total Fat 23g; Sodium 150mg; Dietary Fiber 2g; Protein 3g. EXCHANGES: 1 Starch, 1/2 Fruit, 3 Other Carbohydrate, 4-1/2 Fat. CARBOHYDRATE CHOICES: 4-1/2.

Dulce de Leche Banana Splits

PREP TIME: 15 MINUTES (READY IN 15 MINUTES)
SERVINGS: 4

 EASY

- 1 can (13.4 oz) dulce de leche (caramelized sweetened condensed milk)
- 3 to 4 tablespoons milk
- 2 medium bananas
- 4 small scoops (¼ cup each) vanilla ice cream
- 4 small scoops (¼ cup each) chocolate ice cream
- 1 cup whipped cream topping (from aerosol can)
- ½ cup chopped salted dry-roasted peanuts
- 4 maraschino cherries with stems

1) In small bowl, stir dulce de leche and enough milk with wire whisk to make a smooth, pourable sauce.

2) Cut each banana in half lengthwise and then crosswise. In each of 4 stemmed dessert glasses or bowls, place 2 banana quarters along outer edges. Top each with 1 scoop vanilla ice cream and 1 scoop chocolate ice cream. Spoon dulce de leche mixture evenly over ice cream. Top with whipped cream, peanuts and cherries. Serve immediately.

1 SERVING: Calories 690; Total Fat 25g; Sodium 280mg; Dietary Fiber 4g; Protein 13g. EXCHANGES: 1 Starch, 1/2 Fruit, 5 Other Carbohydrate, 1-1/2 High-Fat Meat, 2-1/2 Fat. CARBOHYDRATE CHOICES: 6-1/2.

Sparkling Cherry Pie

Marianne Carlson
Jefferson, IA
State Fair Pie Competition 2009

PREP TIME: 35 MINUTES (READY IN 3 HOURS 35 MINUTES)
SERVINGS: 8

4 cups fresh or frozen (thawed) pitted sour red cherries

1 ⅓ cups sugar

¼ cup quick-cooking tapioca

1 tablespoon all-purpose flour

Dash salt

¼ teaspoon almond extract

1 box Pillsbury® refrigerated pie crusts, softened as directed on box

1 tablespoon cold butter, cut into small pieces

1 teaspoon milk

1 teaspoon sugar

Vanilla ice cream, if desired

1) Heat oven to 400°F. In large bowl, mix cherries, 1 ⅓ cups sugar, the tapioca, flour, salt and almond extract. Let stand 10 minutes.

2) Meanwhile, make pie crusts as directed on box for two-crust pie using 9-inch glass pie plate. Pour cherry mixture into crust-lined plate; dot with butter. Top with second crust and flute; cut slits in several places. Brush top crust with milk; sprinkle with 1 teaspoon sugar.

3) Bake 20 minutes; cover crust edge with strips of foil to prevent excessive browning. Reduce oven temperature to 350°F; bake 40 minutes longer or until golden brown and bubbly. Cool at least 2 hours before serving. Serve with ice cream.

1 SERVING: Calories 420; Total Fat 14g; Sodium 290mg; Dietary Fiber 1g; Protein. 2g EXCHANGES: 1 Starch, 1 Fruit, 2-1/2 Other Carbohydrate, 2-1/2 Fat. CARBOHYDRATE CHOICES: 5.

tip

Tapioca is a starch made from the root of the cassava plant. It's often used as an ingredient in pie filling to thicken it.

Chewy Chocolate-Peanut Butter Bars

PREP TIME: 15 MINUTES (READY IN 2 HOURS 45 MINUTES)
SERVINGS: 36 BARS

 EASY

1 roll (16.5 oz) Pillsbury® refrigerated sugar cookies

1 can (14 oz) sweetened condensed milk (not evaporated)

1 cup crunchy peanut butter

1 teaspoon vanilla

3 egg yolks

1 bag (12 oz) semisweet chocolate chips (2 cups)

1) Heat oven to 350°F. Spray 13x9-inch pan with cooking spray. Cut cookie dough in half crosswise; cut each section in half lengthwise. With floured fingers, press dough in bottom of pan to form crust. Bake 10 minutes.

2) Meanwhile, in medium bowl, stir condensed milk, peanut butter, vanilla and egg yolks with whisk or spoon until smooth. Remove partially baked crust from oven. Spoon milk mixture over crust; carefully spread. Bake 20 to 25 minutes or until set.

3) Immediately sprinkle with chocolate chips; let stand 3 minutes to soften. Spread chocolate evenly over top. Cool 1 ½ hours or until completely cooled. Refrigerate 30 minutes to set chocolate. Cut into 9 rows by 4 rows.

1 BAR: Calories 190; Total Fat 10g; Sodium 90mg; Dietary Fiber 1g; Protein 3g. EXCHANGES: 1/2 Starch, 1 Other Carbohydrate, 2 Fat. CARBOHYDRATE CHOICES: 1-1/2.

Orange-Chocolate Truffle Bars

DEBBIE HUBER | PETERSBURG, NJ

Pillsbury Bake-Off®   BAKE-OFF® CONTEST 44, 2010

PREP TIME: 25 MINUTES (READY IN 3 HOURS 15 MINUTES)
SERVINGS: 20

BASE

1 cup butter, softened

½ cup powdered sugar

¼ teaspoon salt

1 ¼ cups all-purpose flour

½ cup chopped pecans

TRUFFLE

1 can (14 oz) sweetened condensed milk (not evaporated)

1 bag (12 oz) dark chocolate chips (2 cups)

⅔ cup orange marmalade

TOPPING

1 container (8 oz) mascarpone cheese

1 ⅓ cups granulated sugar

⅔ cup whipping cream

1 tablespoon grated orange peel (from 1 large orange)

1) Heat oven to 350°F. Spray 13x9-inch pan with cooking spray. In medium bowl, beat butter, powdered sugar and salt with electric mixer on medium speed until fluffy. On low speed, gradually beat in flour until dough forms. Stir in pecans. Spread dough in pan. Bake 15 to 20 minutes or until golden brown. Cool completely, about 30 minutes.

2) In medium microwavable bowl, microwave condensed milk and chocolate chips uncovered on High 1 minute; stir. Microwave up to 1 minute longer, stirring until smooth. Stir in marmalade; spread over base. Refrigerate 1 hour or until set. In medium bowl, beat cheese, granulated sugar and whipping cream on medium speed until smooth. Beat on high speed until thickened. Stir in orange peel. Spread over truffle layer. Refrigerate 1 hour or until chilled. Cut into 5 rows by 4 rows. Store covered in refrigerator.

1 SERVING: Calories 430; Total Fat 24g; Sodium 130mg; Dietary Fiber 2g; Protein 4g. EXCHANGES: 1 Starch, 2-1/2 Other Carbohydrate, 4-1/2 Fat. CARBOHYDRATE CHOICES: 3-1/2.

Caramel Monkey Bread

PREP TIME: 25 MINUTES (READY IN 1 HOUR 15 MINUTES)
SERVINGS: 12

 EASY

¾ cup granulated sugar

2 teaspoons ground cinnamon

4 cans (7.5 oz each) Pillsbury® refrigerated buttermilk or country style biscuits

½ cup butter or margarine, melted

¾ cup packed brown sugar

1) Heat oven to 350°F. Grease 12-cup fluted tube cake pan with shortening or cooking spray.

2) In 1-gallon bag, mix granulated sugar and cinnamon. Separate each can of dough into 10 biscuits; cut each biscuit into quarters. Place biscuit pieces in bag; seal bag and shake to coat. Place biscuit pieces in pan. In small bowl, mix butter and brown sugar; pour over biscuit pieces.

3) Bake 40 to 45 minutes or until golden brown. Cool 5 minutes. Place heatproof serving platter upside down over pan; turn platter and pan over. Remove pan. Pull apart to serve; serve warm.

1 SERVING: Calories 350; Total Fat 10g; Sodium 720mg; Dietary Fiber 1g; Protein 4g. EXCHANGES: 2 Starch, 2 Other Carbohydrate, 2 Fat. CARBOHYDRATE CHOICES: 4.

Peach Pie Squares

PREP TIME: 25 MINUTES (READY IN 2 HOURS)
SERVINGS: 9

1 roll (16.5 oz) Pillsbury® refrigerated sugar cookies

½ cup quick-cooking oats

¼ cup packed brown sugar

¼ cup chopped pecans

½ teaspoon ground cinnamon

½ teaspoon ground nutmeg

½ cup granulated sugar

3 tablespoons cornstarch

4 cups sliced peeled ripe peaches (5 to 6 medium) or 4 cups frozen sliced peaches (from two 16-oz bags), thawed

1 tablespoon lemon juice

1) Heat oven to 375°F. Spray 9-inch square baking pan with cooking spray. Break up three-fourths of cookie dough in pan. With floured fingers, press dough evenly in bottom of pan to form crust. Bake 15 to 20 minutes or until golden brown.

2) Meanwhile, in medium bowl, crumble remaining cookie dough. Add oats, brown sugar, pecans, ¼ teaspoon of the cinnamon and ¼ teaspoon of the nutmeg; toss and set aside.

3) In 3-quart saucepan, mix granulated sugar, cornstarch, remaining ¼ teaspoon cinnamon and remaining ¼ teaspoon nutmeg. Stir in peaches and lemon juice until thoroughly coated. Heat to boiling over medium-high heat, stirring constantly. Boil and stir 1 minute.

4) Spoon peach mixture evenly over partially baked crust. Top with oat mixture. Bake 25 to 30 minutes longer or until topping is golden brown and filling is bubbly. Cool 1 hour before serving. Cut into squares.

1 SERVING: Calories 360; Total Fat 12g; Sodium 170mg; Dietary Fiber 2g; Protein 3g. EXCHANGES: 1 Starch, 1/2 Fruit, 2-1/2 Other Carbohydrate, 2-1/2 Fat. CARBOHYDRATE CHOICES: 4.

Strawberry Rhubarb Pie

PREP TIME: 30 MINUTES (READY IN 3 HOURS 20 MINUTES)
SERVINGS: 8

1 box Pillsbury® refrigerated pie crusts, softened as directed on box

2 cups frozen strawberries, thawed, drained and juice reserved

1 cup granulated sugar

2 tablespoons cornstarch

3 cups chopped frozen rhubarb, partially thawed

2 tablespoons cold butter, cut into small pieces

1 egg yolk

1 tablespoon water

3 tablespoons coarse sugar

1) Heat oven to 400°F. Make pie crusts as directed on box for two-crust pie using 9-inch glass pie plate. In large bowl, place reserved strawberry juice. Mix granulated sugar and cornstarch; stir into the strawberry juice with whisk. Stir in strawberries and rhubarb; spoon into crust-lined pie plate. Dot with butter.

2) Cut second crust into ½-inch-wide strips with pastry cutter. Place half of the strips across filling. Weave remaining strips with first strips to form lattice. Trim ends of strips even with edge of bottom crust. Fold trimmed edge of bottom crust over ends of strips, forming a high rim. Seal and flute. Beat egg yolk and water with fork. Brush lattice strips with egg yolk mixture; sprinkle with coarse sugar.

3) Bake 20 minutes. Cover crust edges with foil. Bake 20 to 30 minutes longer or until golden brown. Cool at least 2 hours before serving.

1 SERVING: Calories 550; Total Fat 16g; Sodium 280mg; Dietary Fiber 3g; Protein 2g. EXCHANGES: 1-1/2 Starch, 1 Fruit, 4 Other Carbohydrate, 3 Fat. CARBOHYDRATE CHOICES: 6-1/2.

Mixed Berry-Ginger Cobbler

PREP TIME: 20 MINUTES (READY IN 1 HOUR 10 MINUTES)
SERVINGS: 8

 EASY

FILLING

- 5 cups frozen mixed berries (from two 12-oz bags)
- 1 cup granulated sugar
- 2 teaspoons ground ginger
- 3 tablespoons quick-cooking tapioca
- 2 teaspoons lemon juice

TOPPING

- ¼ cup packed brown sugar
- ¼ cup all-purpose flour
- 2 tablespoons cold unsalted butter
- 1 can (12 oz) Pillsbury® Grands!® Jr. Golden Layers® Butter Tastin'® refrigerated biscuits

  Vanilla ice cream, if desired

1) Heat oven to 350°F. In 3-quart saucepan, stir all filling ingredients. Heat to boiling over medium heat, stirring frequently.

2) Meanwhile, in large bowl, mix brown sugar and flour. Cut in butter with pastry blender or fork until mixture is size of peas. Separate dough into 10 biscuits; cut each into quarters. Add dough pieces to brown sugar-butter mixture; toss to coat.

3) Pour hot filling into ungreased 8-inch square (2-quart) glass baking dish. Sprinkle biscuit pieces over filling. Pour remaining brown sugar-butter mixture over biscuits. Place baking dish on cookie sheet.

4) Bake on middle oven rack 18 to 22 minutes or until top is golden and biscuits are cooked through. Cool at least 20 minutes. Serve warm cobbler in bowls with ice cream if desired.

1 SERVING: Calories 410; Total Fat 13g; Sodium 460mg; Dietary Fiber 2g; Protein 4g. EXCHANGES: 2 Starch, 2-1/2 Other Carbohydrate, 2 Fat. CARBOHYDRATE CHOICES: 4-1/2.

Country Apple-Pear Tart

PREP TIME: 30 MINUTES (READY IN 1 HOUR 40 MINUTES)
SERVINGS: 6

1 Pillsbury® refrigerated pie crust, softened as directed on box

FILLING

2 cups thinly sliced peeled apples

2 cups thinly sliced peeled pears

¾ cup fresh cranberries

⅓ cup granulated sugar

2 tablespoons all-purpose flour

¼ teaspoon ground nutmeg

TOPPING

¼ cup all-purpose flour

¼ cup packed brown sugar

2 tablespoons cold butter

1 teaspoon milk

1 tablespoon granulated sugar

2 tablespoons sliced almonds

1) Heat oven to 425°F. Line cookie sheet with cooking parchment paper. Unroll pie crust on cookie sheet.

2) In large bowl, toss all filling ingredients. Spoon filling evenly onto crust, spreading to within 2 inches of edges. In small bowl, mix ¼ cup flour and the brown sugar. Cut in butter, using pastry blender (or pulling 2 table knives through ingredients in opposite directions), until crumbly. Sprinkle over filling.

3) Fold edge of crust over filling, pleating crust to fit and leaving about 5 to 6 inches in center uncovered. Brush crust with milk; sprinkle with 1 tablespoon granulated sugar.

4) Bake 10 minutes. Reduce oven temperature to 350°F. Sprinkle almonds over filling. Bake 20 to 30 minutes longer or until edges are deep golden brown and fruit is tender.

5) Immediately loosen tart by running pancake turner under crust; place on cooling rack. Cool 30 minutes. Serve warm or cool.

1 SERVING: Calories 220; Total Fat 5g; Sodium 30mg; Dietary Fiber 3g; Protein 1g. EXCHANGES: 1/2 Starch, 1 Fruit, 1-1/2 Other Carbohydrate, 1 Fat. CARBOHYDRATE CHOICES: 3.

Italian Dessert Pizza

PREP TIME: 45 MINUTES (READY IN 1 HOUR 15 MINUTES)
SERVINGS: 16

CRUST

2 cans (8 oz each) Pillsbury® refrigerated crescent rolls

2 teaspoons grated lemon peel (from 1 medium lemon)

3 tablespoons powdered sugar

TOPPING

2 containers (8 oz each) mascarpone cheese, softened

¼ cup powdered sugar

½ teaspoon ground cinnamon

1 lb fresh strawberries, sliced about ¼ inch thick

2 cups seedless green grapes, patted dry, cut in half lengthwise

1 ¼ cups fresh blueberries

⅓ cup sliced almonds, toasted

1) Heat oven to 425°F. Spray 15x10x1-inch pan with cooking spray. Unroll dough into 4 rectangles; place crosswise in pan. Press on bottom and 1 inch up sides of pan; seal perforations. Rub lemon peel over dough. Sprinkle evenly with 3 tablespoons powdered sugar.

2) Bake 8 to 10 minutes or until golden brown. Cool in pan on cooling rack, about 30 minutes.

3) In medium bowl, beat cheese, ¼ cup powdered sugar and the cinnamon with electric mixer on medium speed until smooth. Spread over crust. Arrange fruit on topping in diagonal alternating rows, placing close together. Sprinkle with almonds.

1 SERVING: Calories 286; Total Fat 20g; Sodium 239mg; Dietary Fiber 1g; Protein 3g. EXCHANGES: 1 Starch, 1/2 Other Carbohydrate, 4 Fat. CARBOHYDRATE CHOICES: 1-1/2.

Tiramisu Bites

PREP TIME: 1 HOUR (READY IN 5 HOURS)
SERVINGS: 24

12 slices (¼ inch thick) frozen (thawed) pound cake (from 10-oz package)

¼ cup water

1 ½ teaspoons instant coffee granules or crystals

1 ½ teaspoons rum extract

1 container (8 oz) mascarpone cheese

¼ cup powdered sugar

½ cup whipping cream

½ oz semisweet baking chocolate

24 espresso coffee beans, if desired

1) Place petit four paper cup in each of 24 mini muffin cups. Cut 2 (1 ¼-inch) rounds from each cake slice. Place 1 cake round in bottom of each cup.

2) In small bowl, mix water, coffee granules and ½ teaspoon of the rum extract. Drizzle about ½ teaspoon of the coffee mixture over cake in each muffin cup; set aside.

3) In medium bowl, beat cheese, powdered sugar and remaining 1 teaspoon rum extract with electric mixer on medium speed until creamy. In another medium bowl, beat whipping cream on high speed until soft peaks form. On low speed, beat cheese mixture into whipped cream. Spoon or pipe a rounded tablespoonful of whipped cream mixture into each paper cup, covering cake.

4) Grate semisweet chocolate over each cup. Top each with coffee bean. Refrigerate at least 4 hours to blend flavors. Store covered in refrigerator.

1 SERVING: Calories 260; Total Fat 17g; Sodium 45mg; Dietary Fiber 0g; Protein 3g. EXCHANGES: 1/2 Starch, 1 Other Carbohydrate, 3-1/2 Fat. CARBOHYDRATE CHOICES: 1-1/2.

Strawberry Shortcake Kabobs

PREP TIME:	15 MINUTES (READY IN 25 MINUTES)
SERVINGS:	6

e EASY

6 wooden skewers (8 inch)

12 medium fresh strawberries, stems removed if desired

12 doughnut holes

¼ cup semisweet chocolate chips

2 tablespoons butter or margarine

1) Line cookie sheet with waxed paper. On each skewer, alternately thread 2 strawberries and 2 doughnut holes. Place on cookie sheet.

2) In 1-quart saucepan, melt chocolate chips and butter over low heat, stirring until smooth and well blended. Drizzle chocolate mixture over kabobs. Refrigerate 10 minutes, or up to 4 hours, or until set.

1 SERVING: Calories 200; Total Fat 12g; Sodium 95mg; Dietary Fiber 1g; Protein 2g. EXCHANGES: 1 Starch, 1/2 Other Carbohydrate, 2 Fat. CARBOHYDRATE CHOICES: 1.

Marshmallow Melties

PREP TIME: 15 MINUTES (READY IN 30 MINUTES)
SERVINGS: 24 BARS

 EASY   LOW FAT

3 tablespoons butter or margarine

1 bag (10.5 oz) miniature marshmallows (5 ½ cups)

5 cups Cheerios® cereal

1) Spray bottom and sides of 13x9-inch pan with cooking spray.

2) In large microwavable bowl, microwave butter and marshmallows uncovered on High about 2 minutes, stirring after each minute, until mixture is smooth. With pot holders, remove bowl from microwave.

3) Immediately stir in cereal until evenly coated. Press mixture evenly into pan using buttered back of spoon. Cool at least 10 minutes.

4) With table knife, cut into 6 rows by 4 rows. Store bars in a loosely covered container.

1 BAR: Calories 80; Total Fat 2g; Sodium 60mg; Dietary Fiber 0g; Protein 1g. EXCHANGES: 1/2 Starch, 1/2 Other Carbohydrate, 1/2 Fat. CARBOHYDRATE CHOICES: 1.

tip

For a fun and different flavor, you can substitute Banana Nut Cheerios® for the regular Cheerios® in this recipe.

Lime-Graham Tea Cookies

PREP TIME: 1 HOUR (READY IN 2 HOURS 10 MINUTES)
SERVINGS: 3 DOZEN COOKIES

1 cup butter, softened

1 ½ cups powdered sugar

1 teaspoon vanilla

1 tablespoon frozen (thawed) limeade concentrate

1 tablespoon grated lime peel (from 2 small limes)

1 ¼ cups all-purpose flour

1 cup graham cracker crumbs (about 20 squares)

½ teaspoon salt

¾ cup chopped walnuts

1) In large bowl, beat butter and ½ cup of the powdered sugar with electric mixer on medium speed 3 minutes or until fluffy. Stir in vanilla, limeade concentrate and lime peel. Add flour, graham cracker crumbs and salt; beat on low speed just until incorporated. Fold in the walnuts. Cover; refrigerate 1 hour.

2) Heat oven to 400°F. Shape dough into 36 (1 ¼-inch) balls. On ungreased cookie sheets, place balls 1 inch apart.

3) Bake 8 to 10 minutes or until slight cracks appear and cookies are lightly golden. Remove from cookie sheets to cooling racks; cool 5 minutes. Place remaining 1 cup powdered sugar in shallow dish. Roll warm cookies in powdered sugar; cool. Store tightly covered up to 1 week.

1 SERVING: Calories 110; Total Fat 7g; Sodium 85mg; Dietary Fiber 0g; Protein 1g. EXCHANGES: 1/2 Other Carbohydrate, 1-1/2 Fat. CARBOHYDRATE CHOICES: 1.

Peach Melba Molded Salad

PREP TIME: 20 MINUTES (READY IN 8 HOURS 20 MINUTES)
SERVINGS: 10

 EASY   LOW FAT

1 cup boiling water

1 box (4-serving size) peach-flavored gelatin

¾ cup ginger ale

1 can (15 ¼ oz) peach slices, drained

1 box (10 oz) frozen raspberries in syrup, thawed

Additional ginger ale

1 cup boiling water

1 box (4-serving size) raspberry-flavored gelatin

1) In medium bowl, pour 1 cup boiling water over peach gelatin; stir until gelatin is dissolved. Add ¾ cup ginger ale. Chill until slightly thickened, about 1 hour.

2) Lightly brush 5-cup mold or 1 ½-quart bowl with vegetable oil. Spoon 1-inch layer of peach gelatin into mold. Arrange peach slices over gelatin. Spoon remaining peach gelatin on top. Refrigerate until set but not firm, about 1 hour.

3) In blender or food processor, place raspberries. Cover; blend on low speed 5 to 10 seconds or until smooth. Press through strainer to remove seeds. Add enough additional ginger ale to raspberries to measure ¾ cup.

4) Meanwhile, in medium bowl, pour 1 cup boiling water over raspberry gelatin; stir until gelatin is dissolved. Stir in raspberry mixture; let stand until room temperature, about 20 minutes. Spoon raspberry mixture over peach gelatin layer. Cover and refrigerate at least 6 hours but no longer than 24 hours.

5) To unmold salad, quickly dip the mold, almost to the top, into warm (not hot) water for several seconds. Loosen edge of salad with tip of knife, then tip mold slightly to allow air in and to break vacuum. Rotate mold so all sides are loose. Place serving plate brushed lightly with water upside down on top of mold (the water will let you move gelatin on plate in case it doesn't come out in the center.) Holding both mold and plate firmly, turn mold upside down and shake gently. Carefully lift mold off gelatin. If gelatin doesn't come out, repeat steps. Refrigerate salad until serving. If using decorative bowl, do not unmold; scoop salad from bowl to serve.

1 SERVING: Calories 120; Total Fat 0g; Sodium 80mg; Dietary Fiber 2g; Protein 1g. EXCHANGES: 2 Other Carbohydrate. CARBOHYDRATE CHOICES: 2.

tip

You can substitute 1 cup fresh or frozen (thawed) peach slices for the canned peach slices.

Caramel Apple Pie

PREP TIME: 40 MINUTES (READY IN 3 HOURS 50 MINUTES)
SERVINGS: 8

Judith Waldron
Rossville, IN
State Fair Pie Competition 2009

1 box Pillsbury® refrigerated pie crusts, softened as directed on box

1 cup granulated sugar

1 ¼ cups all-purpose flour

1 teaspoon ground cinnamon

5 cups thinly sliced peeled apples

½ cup caramel apple dip

2 tablespoons milk

½ cup packed brown sugar

½ cup cold butter

Ice cream, if desired

1) Heat oven to 375°F. Place 1 pie crust in 9-inch glass pie plate as directed on box for one-crust filled pie.

2) In large bowl, mix granulated sugar, ¼ cup of the flour and the cinnamon. Add apples; toss to coat. Spoon mixture into crust-lined plate. In small bowl, mix 2 tablespoons of the caramel apple dip and the milk; drizzle over apples.

3) In medium bowl, mix remaining 1 cup flour and the brown sugar. Cut in butter, using pastry blender (or pulling 2 table knives through ingredients in opposite directions), until mixture looks like coarse crumbs. Sprinkle over filling.

4) To make lattice top, cut second crust into ½-inch-wide strips with pastry cutter. Place half of the strips across filling in pie plate. Weave remaining strips with first strips to form lattice. Trim ends of strips even with edge of bottom crust. Fold trimmed edge of bottom crust over ends of strips, forming a high stand-up rim. Seal and flute.

5) Bake 50 to 60 minutes or until golden brown. Cool 10 minutes. Drizzle remaining 6 tablespoons caramel apple dip over pie. Cool at least 2 hours before serving. Serve with ice cream, if desired.

1 SERVING: Calories 630; Total Fat 24g; Sodium 420mg; Dietary Fiber 2g; Protein 4g. EXCHANGES: 2 Starch, 1/2 Fruit, 4 Other Carbohydrate, 4-1/2 Fat. CARBOHYDRATE CHOICES: 6-1/2.

Cheesecake Shot-Glass Desserts

PREP TIME: 30 MINUTES (READY IN 1 HOUR)
SERVINGS: 12

e EASY

2 packages (8 oz each) cream cheese,
  softened

¾ cup sugar

4 teaspoons grated lemon peel

¼ cup graham cracker crumbs

  Fresh blueberries and raspberries

1) In large bowl, beat cream cheese and sugar with electric mixer on medium speed until smooth. Stir in lemon peel.

2) Spoon 2 teaspoons graham cracker crumbs into bottoms of 12 (2-oz) cordial glasses (shot glasses). Top each with 2 tablespoons lemon cream cheese mixture. Sprinkle with 2 teaspoons graham cracker crumbs and another 2 tablespoons lemon cream cheese mixture. Top with berries. Refrigerate at least 30 minutes before serving.

1 SERVING: Calories 210; Total Fat 14g; Sodium 150mg; Dietary Fiber 0g; Protein 2g. EXCHANGES: 1 Starch, 1/2 Other Carbohydrate, 2-1/2 Fat. CARBOHYDRATE CHOICES: 1.

Lime-Ginger Fruit Cups

PREP TIME: 20 MINUTES (READY IN 20 MINUTES)
SERVINGS: 8 (3/4 CUP EACH)

  EASY   LOW FAT

¾ cup sugar

1 tablespoon cornstarch

¾ cup water

1 ½ teaspoons grated lime peel

3 tablespoons fresh lime juice

1 teaspoon grated gingerroot

4 medium oranges, peeled, sectioned

3 medium bananas, sliced

1 cup halved fresh strawberries

1 cup seedless green or red grapes, halved

1) In 1-quart saucepan, mix sugar and cornstarch. Stir in water. Heat to boiling over medium-high heat, stirring constantly. Cook and stir until thickened. Remove from heat. Stir in lime peel, lime juice and gingerroot.

2) In large bowl, gently toss oranges, bananas, strawberries and grapes. Pour lime mixture over fruit; gently toss. Serve immediately, or cover and refrigerate until serving time.

1 SERVING: Calories 180; Total Fat 0g; Sodium 0mg; Dietary Fiber 3g; Protein 1g. EXCHANGES: 1 Fruit, 2 Other Carbohydrate. CARBOHYDRATE CHOICES: 3.

tip

Wrap gingerroot in plastic wrap and refrigerate for up to 1 week. Or place the gingerroot in a small freezer bag and freeze up to 6 months.

Tropical Trifle

PREP TIME: 15 MINUTES (READY IN 50 MINUTES)
SERVINGS: 4 (1 CUP EACH)

e EASY   **lf** LOW FAT

2 cups milk

1 box (4-serving size) vanilla instant pudding and pie filling mix

1 teaspoon grated orange peel

1 round angel food cake (16 oz), cut into 1-inch cubes

2 tablespoons orange-flavored liqueur or orange juice

1 cup cubed fresh pineapple

2 kiwifruit, peeled, cut into ¼-inch slices

1 ripe mango, seed removed, peeled and cut into cubes

2 cups fresh strawberries, cut in half

¼ cup shredded or flaked coconut, toasted

1) In medium bowl, beat milk and pudding mix with wire whisk 2 minutes. Stir in orange peel. Let stand 5 minutes.

2) In 3 ½-quart trifle bowl, place half of cake cubes. Drizzle with 1 tablespoon of the liqueur. Spoon 1 cup of the pudding over cake. Layer with pineapple, kiwifruit and remaining cake cubes. Drizzle with remaining 1 tablespoon liqueur. Spoon remaining pudding over cake. Layer with mango and strawberries. Cover; refrigerate at least 4 hours.

3) Just before serving, sprinkle trifle with toasted coconut. Spoon down to bottom of dish to scoop out servings.

1 SERVING: Calories 270; Total Fat 2g; Sodium 510mg; Dietary Fiber 2g; Protein 5g. EXCHANGES: 1 Starch, 3 Other Carbohydrate. CARBOHYDRATE CHOICES: 4.

Fudgy S'more Bars

PREP TIME: 25 MINUTES (READY IN 1 HOUR 40 MINUTES)
SERVINGS: 32 BARS

1 cup graham cracker crumbs
(15 squares)

¾ cup packed brown sugar

½ cup butter or margarine, softened

½ cup all-purpose flour

½ teaspoon baking soda

4 cups miniature marshmallows

¾ cup candy-coated chocolate candies

¼ cup hot fudge topping, heated

1) Heat oven to 350°F. Grease 13x9-inch pan with shortening.

2) In large bowl, beat crumbs, brown sugar, butter, flour and baking soda with electric mixer on low speed until coarse crumbs form. Press mixture in bottom of pan. Bake 10 to 12 minutes or until golden brown.

3) Remove partially baked crust from oven. Sprinkle marshmallows over crust. Bake 1 to 2 minutes longer or until marshmallows begin to puff.

4) Remove pan from oven. Sprinkle chocolate candies evenly over marshmallows. Drizzle with fudge topping. Cool completely, about 1 hour. Cut into 8 rows by 4 rows.

1 BAR: Calories 120; Total Fat 4.5g; Sodium 75mg; Dietary Fiber 0g; Protein 1g. EXCHANGES: 1/2 Starch, 1 Other Carbohydrate, 1/2 Fat. CARBOHYDRATE CHOICES: 1.

Easter Bird's Nest Cupcakes

PREP TIME: 30 MINUTES (READY IN 1 HOUR 30 MINUTES)
SERVINGS: 12

24 pastel-colored paper baking cups

1 box (1 lb 2.25 oz) milk chocolate cake mix with pudding

1 ¼ cups water

⅓ cup vegetable oil

3 eggs

1 cup milk chocolate creamy ready-to-spread frosting (from 1-lb can)

36 pastel-colored candy-coated chocolate-covered peanut candies

1 bottle (1.75 oz) chocolate decorating decors (⅓ cup)

1) Heat oven to 350°F. Place paper baking cup in each of 24 regular-size muffin cups. Make and bake cake mix as directed on box for cupcakes, using water, oil and eggs; cool completely. Freeze 12 of the cupcakes for a later use.

2) With ½ cup of the frosting, frost remaining 12 cupcakes. Place 3 candies on center of each cupcake for "eggs."

3) In small resealable food-storage plastic bag, place remaining ½ cup frosting; seal bag. Cut small hole in 1 bottom corner of bag; pipe frosting around candies to create ridge on each cupcake.

4) Carefully spoon chocolate decors onto frosting ridge and around candies for "nest."

1 SERVING: Calories 380; Total Fat 16g; Sodium 360mg; Dietary Fiber 0g; Protein 4g. EXCHANGES: 1 Starch, 2-1/2 Other Carbohydrate, 3 Fat. CARBOHYDRATE CHOICES: 4.

Gingered Strawberry Shortcakes

PREP TIME: 10 MINUTES (READY IN 40 MINUTES)
SERVINGS: 4

e EASY   **lf** LOW FAT

3 cups fresh strawberries, sliced

¼ cup sugar

2 tablespoons chopped crystallized ginger

4 individual sponge shortcake cups

½ cup frozen (thawed) whipped topping

1) In medium glass bowl, mix strawberries, sugar and ginger. Let stand 30 minutes to blend flavors, stirring occasionally.

2) To serve, place shortcakes on individual dessert plates. Spoon berries with juices evenly onto each shortcake; top with whipped topping.

1 SERVING: Calories 240; Total Fat 3g; Sodium 15mg; Dietary Fiber 3g; Protein 2g. EXCHANGES: 1/2 Starch, 1 Fruit, 2 Other Carbohydrate, 1/2 Fat. CARBOHYDRATE CHOICES: 3-1/2.

Ginger Apple Crisp

PREP TIME: 15 MINUTES (READY IN 45 MINUTES)
SERVINGS: 6

 EASY

⅓ cup corn flake crumbs

¼ cup firmly packed brown sugar

3 tablespoons all-purpose flour

2 tablespoons crystallized ginger, chopped, or 1 teaspoon ginger

2 tablespoons butter, melted

6 medium apples, peeled, thinly sliced (6 cups)

2 tablespoons sugar

2 teaspoons lemon juice

1 ½ cups nonfat vanilla frozen yogurt or ice milk

1) Heat oven to 400°F. Spray 8-inch square (2-quart) baking dish with nonstick cooking spray.

2) In small bowl, combine corn flake crumbs, brown sugar, flour and ginger; mix well. Stir in butter until well mixed.

3) Place apples in sprayed baking dish. Add sugar and lemon juice; toss to coat. Sprinkle apples with crumb mixture; press gently.

4) Bake at 400°F for 25 to 30 minutes or until apples are tender and mixture is bubbly. Cool slightly. Serve warm with frozen yogurt.

1 SERVING: Calories 280; Total Fat 4g; Sodium 75mg; Dietary Fiber 2g; Protein 3g. EXCHANGES: 1 Starch, 1 Fruit, 2 Other Carbohydrate, 1/2 Fat. CARBOHYDRATE CHOICES: 4.

tip

Firm-fleshed apples are best for baking whole. Some varieties include Empire, Fuji, Golden Delicious, Jonagold, Rome Beauty and Royal Gala.

Chocolate Chip-Peanut Butter Torte

PREP TIME: 30 MINUTES (READY IN 4 HOURS 30 MINUTES)
SERVINGS: 12

1 roll (16.5 oz) Pillsbury® refrigerated chocolate chip cookies

1 package (8 oz) cream cheese, softened

¼ cup sugar

1 egg

1 cup miniature semisweet chocolate chips

1 cup chopped honey-roasted peanuts

1 cup butterscotch chips

¼ cup peanut butter

¼ cup chocolate-flavor syrup

1) Heat oven to 350°F. Break up cookie dough into ungreased 10- or 9-inch springform pan. Press in bottom to form crust. Bake 15 to 18 minutes or until light golden brown. Cool 10 minutes.

2) Meanwhile, in medium bowl, beat cream cheese with electric mixer on medium speed until light and fluffy. Add sugar and egg; beat until well blended. Stir in ½ cup of the chocolate chips and ½ cup of the peanuts. Pour over crust; spread evenly.

3) In medium microwavable bowl, microwave butterscotch chips on High 1 minute, stirring twice, until melted and smooth. Stir in peanut butter until smooth. Drizzle over cream cheese mixture. Sprinkle with remaining ½ cup chocolate chips and ½ cup peanuts.

4) Bake 30 to 40 minutes longer or until edges are set but center is still slightly jiggly. Cool on cooling rack 10 minutes. Run knife around side of pan to loosen; carefully remove side of pan. Cool 1 hour. Refrigerate about 2 hours or until completely cooled.

5) To serve, cut torte into wedges. Drizzle 1 teaspoon chocolate syrup onto each dessert plate. Place wedges over syrup. Store leftovers in refrigerator.

1 SERVING: Calories 560; Total Fat 34g; Sodium 280mg; Dietary Fiber 2g; Protein 8g. EXCHANGES: 1/2 Starch, 3 Other Carbohydrate, 1 High-Fat Meat, 5 Fat. CARBOHYDRATE CHOICES: 4.

Chocolate-Vanilla Layered Bars

PREP TIME: 50 MINUTES (READY IN 2 HOURS 50 MINUTES)
SERVINGS: 16

1 roll (16.5 oz) Pillsbury® refrigerated sugar cookies, broken into large pieces

3 cups milk

2 boxes (4-serving size each) vanilla instant pudding and pie filling mix

1 ¾ cups heavy whipping cream

1 cup semisweet chocolate chips (6 oz)

2 tablespoons powdered sugar

40 vanilla wafers (from 12-oz box)

tip

For a more intense chocolate flavor, use dark chocolate chips instead of semisweet.

1) Heat oven to 350°F. With floured fingers, press cookie dough into bottom of ungreased 13x9-inch pan. Bake 13 to 16 minutes or until golden brown. Cool on cooling rack 10 minutes. In medium bowl, beat milk and pudding mix with whisk 2 minutes. Refrigerate.

2) In small saucepan over medium heat, heat ¾ cup whipping cream to boiling. Remove from heat; stir in chocolate chips until melted. Set aside. In chilled bowl, beat remaining 1 cup whipping cream and powdered sugar with electric mixer on high until stiff peaks form.

3) Spread ½ cup chocolate mixture over crust; freeze 5 to 7 minutes or until set. Spread 1 ½ cups pudding over chocolate layer. Arrange vanilla wafers on top in 5 rows by 8 rows. Spread with ½ cup of the chocolate mixture. Drop whipped cream by spoonfuls on top of chocolate; spread to edges of pan. Top with remaining pudding; spread to edges of pan. Drizzle with remaining chocolate mixture. Cover with foil; chill at least 2 hours. Cut with non-serrated knife dipped in hot water.

1 SERVING: Calories 300; Total Fat 15g; Sodium 280mg; Dietary Fiber 0g; Protein 3g. EXCHANGES: 1 Starch, 1-1/2 Other Carbohydrate, 3 Fat. CARBOHYDRATE CHOICES: 2-1/2.

Alphabetical Index

General Recipe Index

This handy index lists every recipe by food category and/or major ingredient, so you can easily locate recipes to suit your needs.

Grilled Mushroom Swiss Burgers, 132
Home-Style Greek Sandwiches, 215
Italian Meatball Soup, 107
Layered Beefy Mac 'n Cheese, 245
Meatball Primavera, 172
Mexican Manicotti, 262
Mom's Skillet Goulash, 166
On-the-Go Taco Salad, 77
Pizza Skillet Hot Dish, 171
Sloppy Jo-Tater Nugget Hot Dish, 268
Slow-Cooked Lasagna, 236
Spicy Unstuffed Peppers Casserole, 250
Spinach Pesto Manicotti, 272
Three-Cheese Beef Pasta Shells, 264

Ham & Prosciutto

Braciole, 220
Cheesy Ham Breakfast Casserole, 41
Grilled Cheese Italiano, 117
Grilled Ham, Cheddar and Chutney
    Sandwiches, 114
Grilled Ham, Cheese and Apple
    Sandwiches, 122
Ham and Cheese Omelet Bake, 17
Ham and Tomato Quiche, 31
Hearty Ham and Pear Panini, 118
Honey-Dijon Chef's Salad, 77
Meat 'n Pepper Breakfast Kabobs, 14
Muffuletta Egg Bake, 8
Overnight Brunch Egg Bake, 35
Spinach and Ham French Bread Pizza, 156

Lemon & Lime

Citrus Turkey Breast, 283
Cuban Sandwiches with Cilantro-Lime
    Mayonnaise, 223
Key West Ribs, 234
Lemon 'n Herb-Crusted Orzo and Shrimp, 248
Lemon Bread with Apricots, 36
Lime-Ginger Fruit Cups, 336
Lime-Graham Tea Cookies, 332
New England-Style Shrimp Rolls with
    Lemon-Herb Mayonnaise, 141
Raspberry-Lemon Salad, 53
Roast Beef and Bacon Wraps with Spicy
    Chili Lime Mayo, 119
Smokin' Lime 'n Honey Yams, 293
Tuscan Couscous with Lemon Basil
    Dressing, 70

Marshmallows

Fudgy S'more Bars, 338
Marshmallow Melties, 331

Mushrooms

Bacon and Mushroom Stuffed Chicken, 221
Beef-Mushroom Teriyaki Noodles, 180
Grilled Mushroom Swiss Burgers, 132
Portabella Mushroom Burgers, 120
Vegetable Skillet Tetrazzini, 184
Wild About Mushrooms, 241
Wild Rice Stuffing, 225

Nuts & Peanut Butter

Caramel Sticky Buns, 12
Carrot Soufflé with Pecan Topping, 286
Chewy Chocolate-Peanut Butter Bars, 321
Chocolate Chip-Peanut Butter Torte, 342
Cranberry-Raisin Maple Nut Pie, 308
Crowd-Size Coffee Cake, 24
Cute Turkey Cookies, 302
Fruity, Stir-Crazy and Nuts over Suddenly
    Salad, 58
Maple 'n Applesauce Carrots with Candied
    Pecans, 288
Peanut Butter Puddles, 16
Peanut-Chicken Noodle Stir-Fry, 186
Pecan-Chocolate Chip Waffles, 43
Pecan-Coconut Crumble Yam Casserole, 281
Pecan Pancakes with Fudge Syrup, 37
Pecan-Pumpkin Pie, 304
Thai Peanut Ramen, 187
Tossed Greens 'n Fruit with Sugared
    Pecans, 290
Tropical Quinoa Salad, 71

Onions

Caramelized Red Onion-Feta Burgers, 130
Green Beans with Pearl Onions and
    Bacon, 294

Oranges & Tangerines

Citrus Turkey Breast, 283
Cranberry-Orange Chocolate Meringues, 309
Gelatin Pretzel Salad Dressed Up for
    Thanksgiving, 76
Orange-Chocolate Truffle Bars, 322
Orange Pancakes with Raspberry Topping, 42
Orange-Rhubarb Bread, 45
Orange-Spice Carrot Muffins, 34

Pasta

Asiago Cheese-Chick Pea Salad, 55
Asian Beef Noodle Bowls, 165
Bacon-Alfredo Casserole, 256
Bacon 'n Basil Pasta Salad, 66
Bacon-Tomato-Spinach Ravioli Toss, 178
Bacon-Topped Macaroni and Cheese, 229
Basil Pork and Asian Noodles, 194
Beef and Spinach Lasagna Roll-Ups, 273
Beef-Mushroom Teriyaki Noodles, 180
Caesar Tuna "Noodle" Salad, 79
Cajun Pasta with Smoked Sausage, 209
Caprese Sausage Pasta Salad, 48
Cheesy Roll-Ups, 247
Chicken and Pasta Fresca, 158
Chicken and Pastina Soup, 95
Chicken and Sugar Snap Peas Pasta Salad, 71
Chicken-Artichoke Pasta with Herbs, 179
Chicken Pesto Linguine, 192
Chicken with Chipotle Alfredo Sauce, 167
Chinese Chicken Noodle Salad, 68
Cincinnati Chili, 108
Creamy Black and Blue Pasta Salad, 61
Creamy Chicken-Asparagus Pasta, 206
Creamy Chicken Primavera, 181

Creamy Tuna-Broccoli Casserole, 265
Creole Shrimp Pasta, 201
Dilled Shrimp 'n Peas with Linguine, 200
Easy Cheesy Beef and Bow-Ties, 168
Easy Noodles Nicoise, 193
Enchilada Lasagna, 208
Fettuccine with Beef and Peppers, 166
Fettuccine with Two Cheeses, 150
Fiesta Spaghetti, 205
Fruity, Stir-Crazy and Nuts over Suddenly
    Salad, 58
Gazpacho Pasta Salad, 74
Gorgonzola Chicken Salad, 82
Greek-Style Beef and Pasta, 188
Grilled Vegetable Salad, 75
Herbed Veggie-Chicken Fettuccine, 199
Italian Vegetable Soup with White Beans, 93
Layered Beefy Mac 'n Cheese, 245
Lemon 'n Herb-Crusted Orzo and Shrimp, 248
Lickety-Split Alfredo-Style Mac 'n Cheese, 253
Meatball Primavera, 172
Mediterranean Pasta with Shrimp, 196
Mexican Manicotti, 262
Minty Linguine with Grilled Chicken, 195
Mom's Skillet Goulash, 166
Peanut-Chicken Noodle Stir-Fry, 186
Penne with Shrimp and Vegetables, 182
Pizza Pasta, 183
Pizza Skillet Hot Dish, 171
Pork, Broccoli and Noodle Skillet, 174
Ravioli Primavera, 189
Rustic Italian Chicken, 227
Salami-Pesto Fusilli, 190
Sausage and Veggie Spaghetti, 207
Seafood Manicotti, 270
Sesame Chicken Lo Mein, 202
Shortcut Vegetable Lasagna, 254
Shrimp-Vegetable Noodle Stir-Fry, 185
Slow-Cooked Lasagna, 236
Southwest Chicken and Linguine, 198
Southwest Chicken Ranch Pasta Salad, 49
Southwestern Chicken Pasta Salad, 83
Spinach and Bacon Mac 'n Cheese, 197
Spinach Pesto Manicotti, 272
Stuffed Pasta Shells, 271
Suddenly Hot Bacon Salad, 64
Sun-Dried Tomato Chicken Alfredo, 203
Tailgate Pasta Salad, 50
Tex-Mex Macaroni and Cheese, 191
Texas Chili Pasta Bake, 266
Texas-Style Pasta Salad, 80
Thai Peanut Ramen, 187
Thai Shrimp and Mango Pasta Salad, 65
Three-Bean Pasta Salad, 62
Three-Cheese Beef Pasta Shells, 264
Tomato Basil Pasta Salad, 67
Tuna Melt Pot Pie, 259
Turkey Cranberry Bacon Ranch Pasta
    Salad, 51
Turkey Scaloppine with Vegetables, 204
Tuscan Couscous with Lemon Basil
    Dressing, 70
Tuscan Pasta Salad, 81
Two-Bean Minestrone, 89
Vegetable Skillet Tetrazzini, 184

Strawberries

Gingered Strawberry Shortcakes, 340
Smoked Turkey Salad with Strawberries, 63
Strawberry Cheesecake Pancakes, 25
Strawberry-Grapefruit Spinach Toss, 62
Strawberry Rhubarb Pie, 325
Strawberry Shortcake Kabobs, 330

Tomatoes

Bacon-Tomato-Spinach Ravioli Toss, 178
Caprese Sausage Pasta Salad, 48
Creamy Fresh Tomato Soup, 103
Ham and Tomato Quiche, 31
Margherita Pizza, 161
Pesto, Mozzarella and Tomato Panini, 126
Sun-Dried Tomato Chicken Alfredo, 203
Tomato Basil Eggs Alfredo, 9
Tomato Basil Pasta Salad, 67
Turkey-BLT Roll-Ups, 142

Turkey & Turkey Sausage

All-Through-the-House Aromatic Roasted
   Turkey, 298
Breakfast Burgers, 28
California Wraps, 121
Citrus Turkey Breast, 283
Classic Pan Gravy, 300

Family Heroes, 143
Grilled Turkey, Bacon and Swiss
   Sandwiches, 135
Slow Cooker Turkey Breast, 224
Smoked Turkey and Creamy Artichoke
   Sandwiches, 123
Smoked Turkey Salad with Strawberries, 63
Southwest Turkey, 291
Southwestern Spice-Rubbed Turkey
   Thighs, 235
Turkey, Artichoke and Parmesan Panini, 144
Turkey-BLT Roll-Ups, 142
Turkey Scaloppine with Vegetables, 204
Zesty Italian Turkey Burgers, 124

Vegetables

(also see specific kinds)
Asian Pork and Vegetable Stir-Fry, 170
Barbecue Beef and Vegetable Skillet, 173
Cheesy Tuna-Vegetable Chowder, 92
Chicken and Sugar Snap Peas Pasta Salad, 71
Creamy Chicken Primavera, 181
Curried Pumpkin-Vegetable Soup, 96
Dilled Shrimp 'n Peas with Linguine, 200
Eggplant Stew with Polenta, 216
French Vegetable Soup, 106
Garden-Fresh Alfredo Pizza, 154
Gazpacho Pasta Salad, 74

Grilled Vegetable Salad, 75
Herb-Crusted Chicken Ratatouille, 244
Indian-Style Vegetable Casserole, 246
Italian Vegetable Soup with White Beans, 93
Meatball Primavera, 172
Penne with Shrimp and Vegetables, 182
Ravioli Primavera, 189
Roasted Harvest Vegetables, 301
Sausage and Veggie Spaghetti, 207
Shortcut Vegetable Lasagna, 254
Shrimp-Vegetable Noodle Stir-Fry, 185
Squash and Parsnip Gratin, 297
Turkey Scaloppine with Vegetables, 204
Vegetable and Bean Chili, 90
Vegetable Skillet Tetrazzini, 184
Vegetarian Italian Pasta Skillet Dinner, 152
Vegetarian Noodle Soup, 91
Veggie Lovers' Lasagna, 267
Veggie Wraps, 125

Zucchini & Squash

Curried Squash Soup, 94
Southwest Cornbread, Squash and Sausage
   Dressing, 284
Squash and Parsnip Gratin, 297
Winter Squash and Pork Stew, 212